D0898438

Trilingualism in Family, School and Community

BILINGUAL EDUCATION AND BILINGUALISM

Series Editors: Professor Colin Baker, *University of Wales, Bangor, Wales, Great Britain* and Professor Nancy H. Hornberger, *University of Pennsylvania, Philadelphia, USA*

Other Books in the Series
Continua of Biliteracy: An Ecological Framework for Educational Policy, Research, and Practice in Multilingual Settings
   Nancy H. Hornberger (ed.)
Cross-linguistic Influence in Third Language Acquisition
   J. Cenoz, B. Hufeisen and U. Jessner (eds)
English in Europe: The Acquisition of a Third Language
   Jasone Cenoz and Ulrike Jessner (eds)
An Introductory Reader to the Writings of Jim Cummins
   Colin Baker and Nancy Hornberger (eds)
Languages in America: A Pluralist View (2nd Edition)
   Susan J. Dicker
Language, Power and Pedagogy: Bilingual Children in the Crossfire
   Jim Cummins
Language Rights and the Law in the United States: Finding our Voices
   Sandra Del Valle
Language Socialization in Bilingual and Multilingual Societies
   Robert Bayley and Sandra R. Schecter (eds)
Language Use in Interlingual Families: A Japanese-English Sociolinguistic Study
   Masayo Yamamoto
Learners' Experiences of Immersion Education: Case Studies of French and Chinese
   Michèle de Courcy
The Native Speaker: Myth and Reality
   Alan Davies
Power, Prestige and Bilingualism: International Perspectives on Elite Bilingual Education
   Anne-Marie de Mejía
Reflections on Multiliterate Lives
   Diane Belcher and Ulla Connor (eds)
The Sociopolitics of English Language Teaching
   Joan Kelly Hall and William G. Eggington (eds)
World English: A Study of its Development
   Janina Brutt-Griffler

Other Books of Interest
Beyond Bilingualism: Multilingualism and Multilingual Education
   Jasone Cenoz and Fred Genesee (eds)
Beyond Boundaries: Language and Identity in Contemporary Europe
   Paul Gubbins and Mike Holt (eds)
A Dynamic Model of Multilingualism
   Philip Herdina and Ulrike Jessner
English in Africa: After the Cold War
   Alamin M. Mazrui

Please contact us for the latest book information:
Multilingual Matters, Frankfurt Lodge, Clevedon Hall,
Victoria Road, Clevedon, BS21 7HH, England
http://www.multilingual-matters.com

BILINGUAL EDUCATION AND BILINGUALISM 43
Series Editors: Colin Baker and Nancy H. Hornberger

Trilingualism in Family, School and Community

Edited by

Charlotte Hoffmann and Jehannes Ytsma

MULTILINGUAL MATTERS LTD
Clevedon • Buffalo • Toronto • Sydney

Library of Congress Cataloging in Publication Data
Trilingualism in Family, School, and Community/Edited by Charlotte Hoffmann and
Jehannes Ytsma.
Bilingual Education and Bilingualism: 43
Includes bibliographical references and index.
1. Multilingualism. 2. Language policy. I. Hoffmann, Charlotte. II. Ytsma, Jehannes.
III. Series.
P115.T75 2003
306.44'6--dc21   2003008659

British Library Cataloguing in Publication Data
A catalogue entry for this book is available from the British Library.

ISBN 1-85359-693-0 (hbk)
ISBN 1-85359-692-2 (pbk)

Multilingual Matters Ltd
UK: Frankfurt Lodge, Clevedon Hall, Victoria Road, Clevedon BS21 7HH.
USA: UTP, 2250 Military Road, Tonawanda, NY 14150, USA.
Canada: UTP, 5201 Dufferin Street, North York, Ontario M3H 5T8, Canada.
Australia: Footprint Books, PO Box 418, Church Point, NSW 2103, Australia.

Typeset by Florence Production Ltd.
Printed and bound in Great Britain by the Cromwell Press Ltd.

Contents

Introduction

CHARLOTTE HOFFMANN AND JEHANNES YTSMA

Sociolinguistic research into language contact tends to use the term multi-lingualism as a blanket term to refer to a multitude of situations where two or more varieties are in contact with each other. Different linguistic varieties can come together in many different kinds of constellations and they may comprise the standard and non-standard dialects of the same language, or of different languages, and the languages involved may range from local and regional ones to those used for wider or international communication. It is also generally accepted that speakers who live in such multilingual environments need not be multilingual themselves. With the title of this volume we want to draw attention to the fact that the socio-cultural contexts described in virtually all of the contributions to this volume involve three discrete languages and that the speakers who find themselves in these situations can all be referred to as trilingual. This is true, for example, for Russian immigrants in Israel who need to be competent in both Hebrew and English; for young immigrants from the Congo or Vietnam in bilingual Montreal; for adolescent aborigines in Taiwan; and for the inhabitants of a small African country such as Guinea-Bissau, where tribal languages, a Creole used as lingua franca and an official ex-colonial language all have established domains of use.

Such trilingualism results from a variety of political and socio-cultural developments that can be traced from a historical as well as a contemporary perspective. Many of the countries that form the backdrop for the studies described in the following chapters are relatively young, less than 100 years in most cases: Finland, Israel, Taiwan and Guinea-Bissau, with Canada and Belgium a little older. They have in common that right from the beginning different indigenous linguistic groups took part in building the nation, even though some of them may not have enjoyed official linguistic recognition until much later. These countries have also experienced a considerable influx of speakers of other languages through migration

1

and immigration, as has Germany, whose linguistic landscape has been enriched by migrant languages, especially Turkish, Italian and Spanish.

Another contemporary trend contributing to language contact is internationalisation and its concomitant spread of English. Even in many European countries where national languages are backed up by a strong tradition, the position of English is no longer that of a foreign language. Its prominence in an increasing number of public domains ranging from economic life and communication technologies to leisure and pop culture has led to English being used for a variety of functions at a national and international level as well as for transnational communication. This, in turn, has led to greater demands being placed on national education systems to ensure that young Europeans are taught English from an early age. In many instances the acquisition of English is enhanced by learner motivation and positive attitudes on the one hand, and by easy and often attractive access to the language outside the classroom on the other. The fact that very early introduction of English may not be suitable in certain bilingual contexts and that other languages, such as indigenous minority or heritage languages (or indeed a majority language), may be neglected when precious school time is allocated to the early introduction of English rather than to the development of a regional national language does, on occasion, become overlooked.

Trilingualism studies, as opposed to bilingualism studies, have only come to the fore in relatively recent times, accompanied by the claim that they should be accorded special status (Hoffmann, 2001). One of the first publications that quite explicitly went beyond bilingualism contained chapters that treated general and theoretical perspectives and aspects of multilingual education, as well as case studies where such educational models could be found (Cenoz & Genesee, 1998). This has been followed by a growing body of research that responds to the need to identify the specific characteristics that distinguish third language acquisition from second language acquisition and that address questions of a more pedagogic nature (for instance, Cenoz *et al.*, 2001a, 2001b). It is noticeable, however, that studies which approach the subject of trilingualism from an educational, developmental (e.g. Quay, 2001) or psycholinguistic angle (see Cenoz *et al.*, 2001c) far outnumber those that take a sociolinguistic approach. We hope that with this volume we can make a contribution towards redressing the balance.

We have organised the chapters of this volume into three parts. Part 1 opens with a contribution that offers a discussion of multilingual contexts from a general perspective and some conceptual clarification. In contrast, the following chapter describes a number of issues specific to multilingual immigrants in Israel, although it reaches conclusions that are applicable to various multilingual contexts in other parts of the world.

The contributions in this volume focus on two main areas: trilingual language use in the family and wider community, and the formulation and implementation of language policies with regard to education. Thus, some of the questions raised by contributors of chapters included in Part 2 ask whether, and under what circumstances, families foster tri-lingualism – see, for instance, Annick De Houwer's contribution (Chapter 6). Others, such as Patricia Lamarre and Diane Dagenais (Chapter 3) and Hui-chi Lee (Chapter 5), inquire into young people's attitudes towards their languages and the role these play in their lives, and the way they negotiate and construct their identities. The latter also describes the use and function of second and third languages in various domains, as does Gabriele Birken-Silverman (Chapter 4).

Two of the studies presented in Part 3 report on the implementation of language policies dealing with education. Although writing from different perspectives and with regard to completely different socio-cultural and economic contexts, Carol Benson (Chapter 8) and Anat Stavans and Doran Narkiss (Chapter 7) demonstrate how language planning leads to tensions between political ideology and what is practicable and desirable from a pedagogic standpoint when it comes to deciding which languages should be taught to whom, when and how. The other three studies in Part 3 deal with educational considerations regarding trilingual education. The authors focus on Northern and Southern European examples of trilingual education, but they discuss themes of a general scope, such as the optimum age for children to start learning a third language and taking advantage of positive learner motivation, in addition to looking at socio-cultural factors that facilitate the learning of English in European settings.

In the opening chapter Larissa Aronin and Muiris Ó Laoire introduce a new perspective on the study of multilingualism, suggesting the notion of 'multilinguality' as a new research tool. The authors define multilinguality as a personal characteristic, seen as coterminus to multilingualism. At the same time, they stress that multilinguality can be studied in its cultural context, and that by studying and comparing it in a variety of cultural backgrounds it is possible to arrive at a pool of data significant enough for extrapolating its essential features, which can then be transferred to different settings.

Chapter 2 has a rather provocative title: 'Being trilingual or multilingual: is there a price to pay?' No doubt it is a question that has passed through the minds of many, not least those who are multilingual themselves, yet it has so far not elicited answers that go beyond the impressionistic. Elite

Olshtain and Frieda Nissim-Amitai distinguish between multilingualism in a natural environment and multilingualism due to transition. Those born into a multilingual context usually accept the need for multilingualism as a natural phenomenon, whereas speakers who transferred into a multilingual context as a result of immigration have some difficult linguistic choices to make. The language choices and linguistic perceptions made by members of the multilingual Circassian community in Israel illustrate some of the authors' considerations and feelings concerning linguistic gains as well as linguistic cost.

In Chapter 3 Patricia Lamarre and Diane Dagenais report on a comparative study of the language practices of trilingual young people living in Vancouver and Montreal and the way in which they use their language as capital for socialisation in the diverse multilingual contexts in which they find themselves. Their findings show a remarkable diversity of language practices and attitudes among young persons from immigrant backgrounds who acquire three or more languages from their family, community and school environment. They also demonstrate that when it comes to constructing their identities their languages may play a role that ranges considerably in importance.

Chapter 4 also explores the language practices of young people from migrant backgrounds. However, their linguistic setting is quite different from that of Canada, with its official bilingualism and well-established bilingual education programmes involving not only the country's official languages English and French but also a number of heritage languages. Gabriele Birken-Silverman's research was carried out in an inner city German town with a high percentage of residents of migrant origin, especially Turkish and Italian. Her study on language crossing discusses the acquisition of marginal competencies by youngsters of other ethnic origins, as well as Germans, and the quite specific uses they make of their own multilingualism.

Also on the subject of adolescents' use of their languages, Hui-chi Lee in Chapter 5 presents a survey undertaken among young members of Taiwan's different aborigines who are of non-Chinese origin. They are mostly trilingual, being speakers of one tribal language and of two Chinese languages, the official Mandarin and Southern Min. Language competencies and use vary considerably between the three languages, as do their attitudes towards them, in quite intriguing ways. As is the case with so many studies concerning minorities, here, too, there are implications for language maintenance and language education.

In Chapter 6, the findings of Annick De Houwer's survey of trilingual families in Flanders, an officially monolingual region of Belgium, contributes to our understanding of the dynamics of language mainten-ance. Whereas children from such families often do become trilingual, there are considerable variations, and a surprisingly large percentage of children who receive trilingual input do not end up being competent users of those three languages. The study explores four main factors that may contribute towards an explanation of language maintenance within families.

In Chapters 7 and 8 the perspective widens. Now the centre of the atten-tion is not the family and the community, but the state as a whole. Both chapters discuss language planning in education, and both case studies represent multilingual countries that have to accommodate a variety of languages with different national and international status, representing diverse groups of speakers with dissimilar status within the country and contrasting aspirations. Anat Stavans and Doron Narkiss first discuss Israel's language policy in the field of education (Chapter 7). Multilingual and multicultural in composition, it is not surprising that official language planning should encounter linguistic and cultural tensions and inequali-ties. The authors' study is carried out among teachers in the Arab and Jewish sectors in Israel. Its aim is to describe the educational linguistic reality as perceived by teachers and their attitudes toward language teaching and use in the light of the official language policy.

Carol Benson discusses a trilingual education model that was tried on an experimental basis in the small African state of Guinea-Bissau (Chapter 8). The country is characterised by societal trilingualism com-prising a number of indigenous languages, a widely spoken Creole and Portuguese, the ex-colonial language learnt by a small elite. Benson discusses issues of language use in classroom and community, which favoured the use of the Creole over Portuguese, and she reports on the reasons why an experiment that brought educational success had to be abandoned because of the realities of language status and neo-colonialist thinking.

A different sociolinguistic context altogether is the setting of Chapter 9. The Basque Country (Spain) follows a bilingual language policy, and there exist different school models that offer schooling either through Basque or Spanish only or bilingually using both languages as vehicles of instruc-tion. English is the most popular first foreign language taught and in recent years this language has been introduced at ever lower grades. Felix Etxeberria critically examines a development where more and more primary schools work trilingually: the school languages are Basque and Spanish, and English is introduced at the age of four. This trend may yet prove to have unwanted effects as it appears that, although many studies have reported on the successful early introduction of English as a foreign language, these programmes have mainly been carried out in different sociolinguistic environments in which the languages involved were less distant from each other than is the case of the Basque Country.

Chapter 10 is an example of the kind of research into 'the age factor' that has been pursued in the Basque Country and elsewhere, and that has informed educators and language planners. Jasone Cenoz's contribution reports on an empirical study into attitudes towards English and motivation towards the learning of English. The aim was to discover the relative significance that age and length of exposure to English have had on primary and secondary school children in the Basque Country and to consider the educational implications with regard to the introduction of English as a third language in primary schools.

Kaj Sjöholm, in Chapter 11, also writes on the subject of the acquisition of English in a bilingual country, this time Finland. His bilingual subjects (Swedish–Finnish), however, are students at higher grades in secondary schools whose learning of English is greatly enhanced in terms of positive attitudes and accessibility by linguistic input outside the classroom. In Finland, as everywhere else, English plays an important role in youth culture, entertainment and the mass media. The interesting question that emerges in such a situation is whether incidental learning leads to the same kind of proficiency as that which results from formal learning in the classroom, or whether it can be shown that different kinds of proficiencies are involved.

The sociolinguistically-oriented contributions in this volume are all evidence of the inherent complexity of the subject of trilingualism. The authors focus on contextual and educational aspects of trilingualism, on multilingual language use and on language policy. The idea that linguistic and cultural tensions often seem to accompany trilingualism in some form or other is present in most of the chapters. But it is pleasing to see that in three of the contributions which focus on adolescents the young people find new and original ways of acquiring and making use of their languages and of negotiating their identities. As we said at the beginning, trilingualism is a relatively new field of research with many fundamental and practical questions yet to be answered. Such being the case, we note that three chapter titles end with a question mark. It is hoped that this volume provides some first answers as well.

References

Cenoz, J. and Genesee, F. (eds) (1998) *Beyond Bilingualism: Multilingualism and Multilingual Education.* Clevedon: Multilingual Matters.

Cenoz, J., Hufeisen, B. and Jessner, U. (eds) (2001a) Third language acquisition in the school context. *International Journal of Bilingual Education and Bilingualism* 4, special issue.

Cenoz, J., Hufeisen, B. and Jessner, U. (eds) (2001b) *Beyond Second Language Aquisition: Studies in Tri- and Multilingualism.* Tübingen: Stauffenburg.

Cenoz, J., Hufeisen, B. and Jessner, U. (eds) (2001c) *Cross-linguistic Influence in Third Language Acquisition: Psycholinguistic Perspectives.* Clevedon: Multilingual Matters.

Hoffmann, C. (2001) The status of trilingualism in bilingualism studies. In J. Cenoz, B. Hufeisen and U. Jessner (eds) *Beyond Second Language Acquisition: Studies in Tri- and Multilingualism.* Tübingen: Stauffenburg.

Quay, S. (2001) Managing linguistic boundaries in early trilingual development. In J. Cenoz and F. Genesee (eds) *Trends in Bilingual Acquisition.* Amsterdam: John Benjamins.

Part 1: Contexts of Trilingualism

Chapter 1

Exploring Multilingualism in Cultural Contexts: Towards a Notion of Multilinguality

LARISSA ARONIN AND MUIRIS Ó LAOIRE

Multilingualism in a Wider Context of Language/ Society-related Disciplines

In our view, it is necessary to base the study of multilingualism on the notion of identity, given the fact that language constitutes one of the most defining attributes of the individual. Language thus represents and mediates the crucial element of identity. Philosophers constantly place issues of identity in the center of their debates (Doepke, 1996; Garrett, 1998; Swinburne, 1984; Williams, 1989) and the other fields of study are invariably concerned with identity. This widespread and diverse concern largely stems from, and reflects, the contemporary globalization processes (Bauman, 1999; Bendle, 2002). Some of the world's leading sociologists have made identity central to their analyses of globalization (Castells, 1997; Giddens, 1991) as: 'there is a pervasive sense that the acquisition and maintenance of identity has become both vital and problematic under high modernity' (Bendle, 2002: 1). These new problems have arisen as a result of globalization and concomitant societal shifts. Sociology and anthropology, therefore, investigate identity with reference to global processes that have resulted in major shifts in society and speak about cultural, ethnic and national identity (Giampapa, 2001; Olshtain & Horenczyk, 2000; Weinreich, 2000). Studies dedicated to the investigation of changes in identities during immigration focus on identity redefinition (Olshtain & Horenczyk, 2000).

Some of the features which have been cited as part of the postmodern condition can be seen to relate to the issue of identity and language. The growth of interest in sustaining and revitalizing minority (lesser-used) and regional languages in the twentieth century (see, for example, De Bot

(1993), Holm (1993), El Assaiti (1993) and Jones (1995)) could be seen as part of the search for authentic meaning in local identity as a response to feelings of alienation in the Durkheimian sense of rootlessness. This underpins the need to re-examine language acquisition and languages in contact from the perspective of identity.

Researchers concern themselves with identity issues both on societal and individual levels. Edwards (1989), for example, looks into societal problems of identity, while Johnstone (1996) expresses the urgent need for exploring the individual aspect of language use in *The Linguistic Individual*. In the studies involved, identity appears to be a multifaceted composition, with language appearing to be a crucial constituent. Therefore we suggest a new approach to multilingualism, viewing it and singling it out as a category of study in itself within the scope of disciplines related to language and society that have a foundation in identity theory.

Research into multilingualism

Until now, there have been no clear and universally agreed domains in the sub-fields of studies of language and society. Studies in sociolinguistics tend to start with an introduction that attempts to clarify the domain of the discipline and related disciplines: psycholinguistics, sociology of language, ethnology of language etc. (Luckmann, 1975; Mesthrie *et al.*, 2000; Trudgill, 1983; Wardhaugh, 1986; Williams, 1992). Discussions vacillate between the 'socio' and 'language' sides as investigators focus on angles that vary from one to the other. The exact research ground still remains to be defined. We think this difficulty may come from the perspective on multilingualism that is often held. It cannot be defined within the framework of sociolinguistics and sociology of language only. If we take identity studies as a ground for our research, this widens our perspective and highlights a wider scope and the points of view of many disciplines.

Multilingualism, as a field of inquiry, tends to be studied more in the applied linguistics and anthropological linguistics contexts. It has also been studied as an extension of, and as a follow-on from, the research into bilingualism, as Hoffmann (2001a, 2001b) acknowledges. If it has been connected to bilingualism by extension, then *ipso facto* this has been (albeit unwittingly) in the domain of sociolinguistic research. Haugen (1956) referred to multilingualism as 'a kind of multiple bilingualism'. It is the case, nonetheless, that it has to date received more attention from those researching second language acquisition and psycholinguists than from sociolinguists.

Studying languages in contact, however, necessarily involves an inter-disciplinary overlap for the applied linguist or sociolinguist (see Table 1.1). It is interesting to delineate the way in which research has unfolded over time. At the beginning of the twentieth century the concern was firstly with generalities, with the focus on general topics of philosophy and philosophy of language (Bloch and Trager, 1942; Chomsky, 1957; Sapir, 1921, 1947; Saussure, 1916; Whorf, 1956) (see Table 1.1, box [1]). Gradually, the focus of research shifted 'vertically' to the realm of individual language

Table 1.1 Disciplines and fields of study connected with language and society

Society	[1] (Uni)lingualism	[3] Bilingualism	[5] Multilingualism

	philosophy
	anthropology
	linguistics
	cognition
	education
	language teaching
		sociology
		sociolinguistics
		demography
		politics
		geography
		immigration
		language policy
		language
		  planning
			sociology
			sociolinguistics
			demography
			politics
			geography
			immigration
			language policy
			language
			  planning

	Identity	Identity	Identity
Individual	[2] (Uni)linguality	[4] Bilinguality	[6] Multilinguality

	psychology
	communication
	linguistics
	education
	language
	learning/
	  acquisition
		psycholinguistics
		neurophysiology
		psychology
		communication
		social identity
		cultural identity
		acculturation
		immigration
		language
		learning/
		  acquisition
			psycholinguistics
			neurophysiology
			psychology
			communication
			social identity
			cultural identity
			acculturation
			immigration
			language attrition
			language
			learning/
			  acquisition

behavior (see Table 1.1, box [2]). The topics of research thus included the psychology of language learning, behaviorism etc. When the social perspective and human sciences gained currency, bilingualism started being investigated (Cummins, 1981; Fishman, 1976; Gal, 1979; Genesee, 1983; Romaine, 1995) (see Table 1.1, box [3]).

Significantly, 'bilinguality' – located in the domain of psycholinguistic research – stressed the merit of studying the bilingual mind, allowing research on the cognitive relationship that takes place between two given languages in contact in a bilingual situation (Hamers & Blanc, 1983) and thus opening a discussion of the advantages and disadvantages of bilingualism for the individual (see Table 1.1, box [4]). The last few decades have witnessed a focus on multilingualism (Cenoz & Genesee, 1998; Cenoz *et al.*, 2001; Cenoz & Jessner, 2000; Skuttnab-Kangas, 1981) (see Table 1.1, box [5]) as a corollary of which we see a need to begin investigating the notion of multilinguality (see Table 1.1, box [6]).

Table 1.1 presents the sociolinguistic phenomena in 'horizontal' (boxes [1], [3], [5] or [2], [4], [6]) and 'vertical' (boxes [1] and [2] or [3] and [4] or [5] and [6]) directions. Thus, if we look at the table 'horizontally' and compare the columns, we'll see that each column introduces different, but increasing, levels of complexity, e.g. monolingualism – bilingualism – multilingualism. Not only is each phenomenon quantitatively 'bigger' and more complex, but it is also qualitatively different and not just an aggregate. With every new language added, the phenomena become more complex. Bilingualism becomes multidimensional, for example, as the ties between 'society' and 'language' are understood to be manifold and multidirectional. New representations and constructs, such as this, call for a readjustment to existing disciplines, including the admission of more domains of knowledge into the existing research to re-explain ever-changing (parallel to world change) phenomena. The most recent theoretical research even maintains that 'research on linguistics should be centered on the multilingual speaker as a norm, not on the monolingual individual' (Herdina & Jessner, 2002: 1).

Perhaps this essential interconnectedness of the disciplines and fields of study is the reason for the difficulty in arriving at a definition of the notion of bilingualism and multilingualism in the first place. Since multilingualism is multidimensional, it seems that the definition likewise must be multidimensional. Skuttnab-Kangas (1981) listed the definitions based on competence, function and attitudes, which correspond to the principal domains of various disciplines: linguistics, linguasociology and linguapsychology. These coalesce when looking at multilingualism as the linguistic identity of a person.

The 'horizontal' dichotomies

(1)-(3): (Uni)lingualism versus bilingualism

Lyon (1996: 3) states that one of the reasons for the paucity into research into bilingual language acquisition so far is that there has been no single body of work that encompasses this particular research field. Much of the work on monolingual language acquisition has been useful, but issues relating to bilingual acquisition must involve a study of the social bilingual context; hence, there has been interest in sociolinguistics, language policy, language planning etc. leading to an 'eclectic', interdisciplinary approach to the research field of bilingualism.

(3)-(5): Bilingualism versus multilingualism

There are, it seems, no more doubts about the qualitative differences of multilingualism as opposed to bilingualism (Herdina & Jessner, 2000b; Hoffmann, 2001a, 2001b). Multilingualism appears to be more complex than bilingualism, with qualitative rather than quantitative difference being the departure point. In recent years, the linguistic research focused on the 'horizontal' (see Table 1.1) dichotomy bilingualism/ multilingualism.

With emerging studies on specific aspects of multilingualism yielding new data, new concepts are being posited to account for some of the facts and phenomena detected. Earlier and more recent studies in multilingualism endeavor to develop theoretical concepts to explain multilingual processes (Cenoz, 2000; Cenoz & Genesee, 1998; Cenoz & Jessner, 2000; Cenoz & Valencia, 1994; Grosjean, 1985; Ringbom, 1987; Swain *et al.*, 1990).

Bilingualism/bilinguality dichotomy

As early as 1981, Hamers differentiated between bilingualism and bilinguality. Bilinguality was posited as the psychological state of an individual who has access to more than one linguistic code as a means of social communication; the degree of access will vary along a number of dimensions which are psychological, cognitive, psycholinguistic, social psychological, sociological, sociolinguistic, sociocultural and linguistic (Hamers, 1981). The concept of bilingualism, on the other hand, includes that of bilinguality (or individual bilingualism), but refers equally to the state of a linguistic community in which two languages are in contact, with the result that two codes can be used in the same interaction and that a number of individuals are bilingual (societal bilingualism). As with other conceptualizations of 'lingualism' and 'glossia', societal bilingualism is premised on the existence of a relatively fixed intranational set of macro-ecologies. Hoffmann also points to the changes brought about here by the effects of immigration and in-migration societies. She writes:

> Nevertheless, a move from the macro-level of analysis of the societal presence of English in European countries to a micro-analysis of its presence shows that beyond these ecologies it is the single speaker, with his or her potential for using English societally with other single speakers in multifarious emerging and shifting micro-contexts, who forms the locus for the popular use and spread of English as a lingua franca today. In sum, EFL constitutes an aspect of both societal and individual bilingualism, its potential ubiquity in Europe forcing a serious reconsideration of the intertwining of both. (Hoffmann, 2000: 31)

Thus, the corpus of thesaurus and notions is being formed in bilingualism and, in part to some extent, in tri/multilingualism.

The Aim and Scope of the Study

The aim of the current study is to introduce a new perspective on multilingualism, as well as to clarify some of the basic notions and terms of multilingualism and their interrelationships in order to refine the research tools and, consequently, gain a deeper understanding into multilingualism and multilingual acquisition. As 'multilinguality' has not, as of yet, been singled out as a distinct phenomenon and has not been studied as an entity worthy of investigation in itself, we propose the term and the notion of multilinguality as being coterminous or dichotomous to multilingualism.

Multilingualism and Multilinguality

Multilingualism as defined by Cenoz and Genesee refers to 'the process of acquiring several non-native languages and the final result of this process' (1998: 2). Researchers endeavoring to explain the dynamics of multilingualism have focused on different aspects, for example geographical distribution and sociological issues (Edwards, 1994; Hoffmann, 1999). While multilingualism, like bilingualism, refers itself to the situation, multilinguality refers more to inner constructs of a single speaker. In this study we adapt the model presented by Cenoz (2000: 39), which distinguishes the process of multilingualism from its product, by adding one further aspect to the equation, i.e. the 'individual aspect'.

GENERAL	◄────────►		INDIVIDUAL
Product	*Process*		
Multilingual acquisition	Multilingualism	+	*Multilinguality*
Third language acquisition	Trilingualism	+	*Trilinguality*
Fourth language acquisition	Quadrilingualism	+	*Quadrilinguality*

Source: Adapted from Cenoz, 2000: 39

Researchers have already referred to the individual aspect of multilingualism. Cook (1995: 94–6) argues, for instance, that multilinguals, who possess multilingual competence, 'have a different state of mind'. For him, the notion of multicompetence is connected with mind and knowledge. Kesckés and Papp (2000a, 2000b) argue that what makes a speaker multicompetent is the common underlying conceptual base, rather than the existence of two grammars in the mind, and have postulated a multilingual language processing device which consists of two or more constantly available interacting systems. While the processes used in L3 and L4 (Fouser, 2001) may be similar to those used in L2 acquisition (Cenoz, 2001: 8), as Clyne (1997) points out the factor of the additional languages being acquired complicates the process. Hoffmann (1999) argues that trilingual language competence contains linguistic aspects from the three language systems, as well as the ability to function in trilingual contexts (decisions on code choice and code switching). Cenoz and Genesee use the term 'individual multilingualism' (1998: 17) in the sense of being the individual's acquisition of multilingual competence, stating that 'multilingual competence in individuals can be understood as the capacity to use several languages appropriately and effectively for communication in oral or written language', but they caution as to the applicability of this definition. Herdina and Jessner, advocating a holistic view on the language phenomena, refer to the complex psycholinguistic system to be found in a multilingual (2000b: 84).

Thus, researchers have already noted the complex nature of an individual aspect of multilingualism, pointing to the presence of individual or personal characteristics, the presence of language competence and the capacity to use the languages effectively. Thus, multilinguality is the inherent, intrinsic characteristic of the multilingual. We define it as an individual's store of languages at any level of proficiency, including partial competence and incomplete fluency, as well as metalinguistic

GENERAL	←————————→		INDIVIDUAL
Product	*Process*		
Multilingual acquisition	Multilingualism	+	*Multilinguality*
Third language acquisition	Trilingualism	+	*Trilinguality*
Fourth language acquisition	Quadrilingualism	+	*Quadrilinguality*

Source: Adapted from Cenoz, 2000: 39

Researchers have already referred to the individual aspect of multilingualism. Cook (1995: 94–6) argues, for instance, that multilinguals, who possess multilingual competence, 'have a different state of mind'. For him, the notion of multicompetence is connected with mind and knowledge. Kesckés and Papp (2000a, 2000b) argue that what makes a speaker multicompetent is the common underlying conceptual base, rather than the existence of two grammars in the mind, and have postulated a multilingual language processing device which consists of two or more constantly available interacting systems. While the processes used in L3 and L4 (Fouser, 2001) may be similar to those used in L2 acquisition (Cenoz, 2001: 8), as Clyne (1997) points out the factor of the additional languages being acquired complicates the process. Hoffmann (1999) argues that trilingual language competence contains linguistic aspects from the three language systems, as well as the ability to function in trilingual contexts (decisions on code choice and code switching). Cenoz and Genesee use the term 'individual multilingualism' (1998: 17) in the sense of being the individual's acquisition of multilingual competence, stating that 'multilingual competence in individuals can be understood as the capacity to use several languages appropriately and effectively for communication in oral or written language', but they caution as to the applicability of this definition. Herdina and Jessner, advocating a holistic view on the language phenomena, refer to the complex psycholinguistic system to be found in a multilingual (2000b: 84).

Thus, researchers have already noted the complex nature of an individual aspect of multilingualism, pointing to the presence of individual or personal characteristics, the presence of language competence and the capacity to use the languages effectively. Thus, multilinguality is the inherent, intrinsic characteristic of the multilingual. We define it as an individual's store of languages at any level of proficiency, including partial competence and incomplete fluency, as well as metalinguistic awareness, learning strategies and opinions, preferences and passive or active knowledge on languages, language use and language learning/ acquisition.

Multilinguality and 'individual multilingualism'

Here, it seems appropriate to distinguish between 'tri-multilinguality' and 'individual tri-multilingualism', and explain why do we need a new notion – multilinguality, or linguistic identity – when the term 'individual tri-multilingualism' is already frequently used. Multilinguality is far from being strictly language-related. It is intertwined with many, if not all the aspects of identity – for example emotions, attitudes, preferences, anxiety, cognitive aspect, personality type, social ties and influences and reference groups. Multilinguality, in our view, is a notion which is more connected to personality and intrapersonal dynamics, while 'individual trilingualism' places more emphasis on the language systems and language codes in use by an individual in a 'languages in contact' situation, thus concerning itself more with a descriptive universalistic notion of a state of languages in contact. Multilinguality, therefore, is also about abilities and resources, while individual multilingualism is referred to only as the process and the result of third language acquisition. These notions are different. They are part of the multilingualism thesaurus. Multilinguality corresponds with 'communicator' in social and physiological environments and thus includes idiosyncrasies, peculiarities of communicators, legacies, embedded assumptions and individual disabilities such as dyslexia, as well as society, communication and sociology. Individual multilingualism, on the other hand, concerns the 'speaker', linguistics and language.

Multilinguality is also about linguistic and cognitive behavior, career choices and social stratification choices and opportunities, language and milieu, and educational/upbringing awareness, as well as the range of accompanying and pervading emotions, affective states, attitudinal preferences and, subsequent to this, social, family and career activities and lifestyles. Also, (bi)lingualism is premised on the existence of two or more linguistic codes, i.e. languages distinguished according to their linguistic form or substance, while (di)glossia is premised on the existence of two or more linguistic varieties, i.e. languages distinguished according to their (socio)linguistic function. In other words, the emphasis of this notion is on diversity, while the emphasis of 'multilinguality' is on the impenetrability, complexity and unity of the phenomena.

Each individual possesses his/her own multilinguality, which depends on a set or sets of languages (or constellations, as Hoffmann (2001a: 20) puts it), levels of mastery of each language etc. Multilinguality, therefore, constitutes an individual subset of the universality of multilingualism, while still reflecting the essential characteristics of multilingualism. Multilinguality also includes cognitive and linguistic abilities, potential to gain knowledge, self-image as a language-learner, preferences and the tangible impact of the cultural context.

Every multilingual individual possesses a real concrete multilinguality of his or her own. At the same time, groups of people and populations who live in the same environment, e.g. groups of immigrants, may have typical sets of languages in use that are common for (the majority of) this population. For example, for Russian immigrants to Israel the most essential languages for their survival in the host society would be Russian (L1), Hebrew – the official language of the country they have come to live in, and English – the language of academic studies, promotion and prestige in Israel, and also the language that may substitute for the yet imperfect command of Hebrew. We call such constellations **Dominant Language Constellations (DLCs)**. Apart from the DLC, one individual member of the community may also have knowledge of other languages, for example Ukrainian, Belorussian, or any other language of the former Soviet Republic that an immigrant may have come from. A person may also know German or French as a foreign language studied at school, Yiddish as a legacy language spoken by grandparents etc.

Multilinguality allows us to research the cognitive relationship that takes place between given languages in contact in subjects in a trilingual (or bilingual) situation, facilitating contact and interactions in trilingualism. If we need to use this data we will have to make the concept of trilinguality operative.

The biotic model of multilinguality stresses its individual character and entity, incorporating various aspects, not only the language one. We propose, therefore, to describe multilinguality in terms of a biotic system, wherein sets of languages operate and function together as a single entity. In the _Webster's New Encyclopedic Dictionary_ the word 'biotic' is explained as follows: 'adj. of or relating to life, esp. composed or caused by living things'. 'A biotic potential' is described there as 'the inherent capacity of an organism or species to reproduce and survive' (1994: 98). Publications on ecolinguistics have already used this metaphor of ecology (e.g. Herdina & Jessner, 2000a). Our use of the term 'biotic system' is consonant with the term 'eco' in describing the ecological phenomenon intrinsic to the nature cycle, thus emphasizing the essential dynamics of growth, change, fluctuation, input, absorption and decay, while stressing the complexity of multilingualism. Language learning and use in a multi-lingual person implicates a wide range of modifications occurring and interacting simultaneously through the mix of languages L1, L2, L3 etc: acquired in various stages, which constitute a kind of ecosystem or bio-system.

An understanding of individual multilingualism or multilinguality in terms of a biotic system may invoke any, or all, of the following nine char-acteristics, at any one point or stage of acquisition, including 'instructed acquisition':

Complexity

Being itself a construct within identity and used for the study of real phenomena of acquisition and use of many languages, a biotic model of multilinguality consists of a number of constituents. Among them are the dominant language constellation and peripheral languages, as well as various skills 'serving' these languages, i.e. reading and writing skills, and free command of the DLC languages. People may, in effect, passively possess a limited knowledge of several languages, i.e. some words and expressions from unstudied languages, or the ability to comprehend without the ability to write etc. Multilinguality also com-prises metalinguistic awareness, which is indispensable for the system being discussed. The very definition of multilinguality displays its complexity, including in it a wide range of competencies, learning strategies, opinions, preferences, language use, functions and language acquisition, as well as potential, self-image as a learner and the picture of whatever or whoever facilitates the language learning, to name just some of the constituents.

Interrelatedness

The parts of the system interact with one another in various patterns.

Interrelations, exchanges and contacts occur on all levels and are both minor and major. Research literature is full of reports on this matter, such as instances of using suffixes and words of one language in the other, or the production of speech with constant or intermittent switching between two or more languages, confusing usage of cognates or near cognates, using the form knowledge of one language when studying another and so on. The mixture and interrelatedness and the unity (of several languages, not separate systems for every language) are reflected in a fact that was noted by the researchers: it is hard to define strictly which language is L1 or L2 for any given multilingual individual. In this context, indeed, it is hard, of course, to define the difference between L2 and L3 or L3 and L4 (Aronin & Toubkin, 2001: 116; Cenoz & Jessner, 2000). As Cenoz and Jessner state: 'When a third language is acquired, however, the chronological order in which the three languages have been learnt does not necessarily correspond to the frequency of use by, or level of competence in the trilingual speaker' (2000: 3). In the course of life languages are activated and used at different times and interchange constantly, as also referred to in the dynamic model of multilingualism (Herdina and Jessner, 2002).

Fluctuation

The passage of time effects changes in the level of mastery of every language involved in the system. Various items of the system are subjected to fluctuation: languages, identity of the multilingual and culture of the multilingual. Some languages are less often activated at some particular times than others, some more so, with some languages being studied or brushed up on, while some could be said to be put on a back burner. The set of languages that a multilingual individual possesses may vary, new languages may appear and the level of mastery in the already existing languages may change more often than in the used and better-maintained languages. The languages, skills and knowledge from various language systems overlap, fluctuate and interchange. With passing time and changing circumstances the knowledge, frequency of use and the status of the languages may change accordingly. Not only language and knowledge fluctuate, but also and primarily the personality of the multilingual – the essence of the multilinguality fluctuates and changes depending on the changes in his or her life. An important finding of Maines is that 'the migration of "selves" (or identities) usually follows different timetables than those of their corresponding "bodies"' (1978). Horenczyk similarly claims that 'selves arrive "later" than bodies' and that ' "selves" tend to migrate not only "more slowly" but also in a more complex trajectory than their containing "bodies" and that unlike physical transitions changes in ethnic and cultural identity are usually not abrupt' (2000: 14) – this has significant implications for studying multi-linguality. Horenczyk also says:

> Unlike physical transitions changes in ethnic and cultural identity are usually not abrupt: during all phases of the intercultural migration process, newcomers must continually reorganize the delicate structure of their various sub-identities – those related to their membership

in the new host society and those involving their attachment to the values of their former culture. Stretching the metaphor a little more, we would say that while bodies can occupy only one place in space at a time, selves can (and often do) split and reside both in the new and in the old locations, the old location being gradually replaced by the minority/immigrant culture within the majority host society. (2000: 14)

Another example of fluctuation is the emotional changes accompanying the process of acquiring a new language while moving from a mono- or bilingual state to a multilingual one (Aronin, 2002). In their turn, emotional changes trigger actions, which in their turn lead to further constant alterations, modifications and fluctuations. Even the perception of the mother tongue may shift from one language to another (Aronin, 2002). Yet another example of fluctuations in the shifts and changes within the multilingual identity is the development of the cognitive potential of multilinguals.

Variation and inconsistency

A bilingual or multilingual individual may have a perfect command of one or two languages, a limited mastery of some, and a passing knowledge of even more. Some languages in the linguistic repertoire may remain unused and inactivated and thus are simply suspended in memory.

Multifunctionality

This single system performs multiple functions characteristic of any language. These include oral and written communication for a range of purposes, giving and receiving information, thinking and reflecting, understanding, studying, composing, entertaining, performing, persuading, lecturing, sharing, showing attitude emotion and repairing communication etc. Language functions also refer to negotiation of one's identity in typical and new cultural environments (Ben-Rafael, 1994; Pavlenko, 2001), conceptualizing emotions and expressing oneself through emotion discourse (Pavlenko, 2002; Wierzbicka, 1999). Even language anxiety in L2 and L3 language learners described by Dewaele (Dewaele, 2002; Dewaele & Pavlenko, 2002) performs a specific function within the construct of multilinguality. In the ecosystem of a multilingual these functions are divided as to necessity and frequency of use between the languages involved. The functions described are not only purely linguistic functions, but also extensions of the forms of socially essential functions.

Inequality of function

One language may be used for communication with friends, another for business communication and yet another for work; even the function of reading may be divided into many parts. For example, a Russian-speaking trilingual may read up on a given topic in Hebrew and in English as part of his or her studies and may consult reading material on the same topic in Russian in order to gain a deeper understanding of it. In the same cultural context, a person may read general political topics in Hebrew newspapers, while resorting to Russian newspapers to become acquainted with advertisements, 'sell–buy' items and community news in Russian. Reading in Irish in Ireland, unlike reading in English, may in fact be a way of remaining in contact with the wider but dispersed language community.

Self-balance

The phenomenon of language attrition can be seen to perform the function of self-balancing in the biotic system of multilingualism. Examples of skills deterioration and skills development in general complete the system, so that all the functions of a language are covered. Skills developed in one aspect tend to deteriorate in the other, unless they are consciously and deliberately maintained. As one student succinctly put it: 'When I learned a little bit more Hebrew it sometimes became rather difficult for me to express some idea in Russian [native language]. I would easier express them in Hebrew.' Self-balance of the whole system – not only languages, but also self-image – is always on the move. Skutnabb-Kangas (1981) describes the path of immigrants from monolingualism to bilingualism and to monolingualism in the majority language. The move is determined socially. Learning the prestigious language is maintaining one's status balance. Switching or using the words of L2 in L3 – or vice versa – is also a kind of balance, and there is no need for two words if everyone understands one in one language. Balance is exercised in many aspects, for example by balancing the situation in the choice or deployment of language from the constellation, or again by balancing in the learning context, e.g. asking for known words in class.

Self-extension

At the same time, there is a marked tendency with multilinguals to extend their knowledge, skills and skill-application. This is often explained in terms of common sense. There tends to be increased motivation when one knows more. Research on motivation and cognition of bilinguals (Bialystok, 1991; Sharwood Smith, 1991) and to a lesser extent in the case of trilinguals (Fouser, 2001; Thomas, 1988) shows the tendencies of multiple language speakers to extend and multiply skills and knowledge. Multilinguals tend to extend their knowledge of a new language (e.g. register) by using aspects and items from another, as well as by applying language knowledge to extend to other language domains. Not only languages extend. The social status of a multilingual speaker may equally be extended by the ability to converse with people from differing socio-economic groupings.

Non-replication
The examples already referred to illustrate the inequality of function. Every language performs its function, however small, and the set functions do not overlap. All the attributes discussed above are interrelated and intertwined. Thus, multilinguality as an ecological model possesses inextricability and interdependability. Practical implications for such an understanding include pedagogical ones for learners and teachers, syllabus reorientation and design of course materials. The crucial point is that neither learner, nor teacher, nor educator can disregard any language in the linguistic repertoire of a multilingual, because doing so would serve to unset the essential balance of the ecosystem.

Multilinguality in cultural contexts

Multilinguality does not exist on its own – it is shaped by the sociolinguistic settings in which a multilingual individual lives. Cenoz writes in this regard: 'In multilingual acquisition the context of acquisition is likely to present more complex patterns, because of the number of language acquisition situations involved' (2000: 41). The sociolinguistic environment or cultural context, therefore, plays a decisive role in the structure and 'specifications' of multilinguality. Consider, for example, multilinguality with the focus exclusively for the present on the native language. Russian is the native language for many people in Russia, in the states of the former USSR (i.e. Lithuania, Estonia, Latvia, etc.), in the USA and in Israel. The language – Russian – is the same for all the populations, being the mother tongue or native language of all the populations mentioned. But the real 'performance' of this language – its status, functions, situations of use, time of use and 'quality' of use – are noticeably different. In Russia, the Russian language dominates in the multilinguality; it is an official language and is used in all spheres of life. The other, possibly well-mastered languages, are left with minimum functions to perform, although they may enjoy high status. In the former republics of the USSR, the Russian language has lost its official status, acquired new political overtones and reduced its use considerably to communication in the home and community communication (Leontiev, 1995). On the other hand, Russian in Israel is a language of with fellow repatriates. It is also the language in which to survive, being used in cafeterias, newspapers, television programs, services and schools, with notices and advertising on the streets and in official places (Spolsky & Shohamy, 1999).

Therefore, it is essential to study multilinguality in different cultural contexts. From this perspective, the prospects for subsequent investigations and directions for future research are clear. Given that multilinguals are qualitatively different from monolinguals and even bilinguals, it may be legitimate to assume that teaching the very same set of languages, in two distinctly different cultural contexts, would yield different results. It may further be assumed, in all probability, that teaching/learning multilinguals in similar cultural contexts but with different or slightly different DLCs may have much in common. All the aforementioned make investigation into the multilingualism/multilinguality dichotomy in cultural context a pressing necessity.

Singling out the notion of multilingualism and its interpretation in terms of an ecological unity paves the way for new explorations in multilingual and third language acquisition contexts.

Conclusion

The study endeavored to put forward a holistic perspective on multilinguality, by extending the remit of the disciplines and fields of study pertaining to multilingual acquisition and by drawing on the construct of identity. Looking at the study and use of new languages from the perspective of identity allows for a more complicated view of the speaking individual, and a more detailed insight into what the personality undergoes in the circumstances of global shifts.

Given the ever-growing and ever-expanding research into multilingualism, the need for compiling a thesaurus of multilingualism is apparent. We propose to single out the notion and the term 'multilinguality', viewed as being coterminous with multilingualism. Multilinguality constitutes an individual subset of universality, while reflecting the essential characteristics of multilingualism. We have defined multilinguality as a personal characteristic that can be described as an individual's store of languages, including partial competence and metalinguistic awareness. Multilinguality may also be called the linguistic identity of the multilingual. For the purposes of refining the theoretical understanding of multilingualism, we propose the biotic model of multilinguality. Multilinguality as a biotic model possesses inextricability and inter-dependability. Practical implications for such an understanding include pedagogical ones for learners and teachers, such as syllabus reorientation and design of course materials. The crucial point is that neither learner, nor teacher, nor educator can disregard any language in the linguistic repertoire of a multilingual, because doing so would serve to unset the essential balance of the ecosystem.

Multilinguality exists and can be studied in its cultural context(s). The term Dominant Language Constellation is proposed here to denote the typical set of languages used in daily interactions by varying population groups and sub-groups. The practical implications, as well as the need for further research, lie in discovering typical kinds of multilinguality in order to provide consequent positive changes in language use and language learning and teaching for multilinguals, as well as to isolate advantageous conditions for developing pedagogical practice and materials.

References

Aronin, L. (2002) Multilinguality and emotions: Trilingual students' emotions towards themselves and languages in the period of identity transition. Paper presented at the Second University of Vigo International Symposium on Bilingualism, Vigo, Spain, October.

Aronin, L. and Toubkin, L. (2001) An English immersion programme for native Russian speakers. In Siv Björklund (ed.) *Language as a Tool. Immersion Research and Practices* (pp. 114–26). Vaasa: University of Vaasa.

Bauman, Z. (1999) *Globalization: The Human Consequences.* Cambridge: Polity Press.

Ben-Rafael, E. (1994) *Language, Identity and Social Division: The Case of Israel.* Oxford: Clarendon Press.

Bendle, M. (2002) The crisis of 'identity' in high modernity. *The British Journal of Sociology* 53 (1), 1–18.

Bialystok, E. (1991) *Language Processing in Bilingual Children.* Cambridge: Cambridge University Press.

Bloch, B. and Trager, G.L. (1942) *Outline of Linguistic Analysis.* Baltimore: Linguistic Society of America/Waverly Press.

Castells, M. (1997) *The Power of Identity.* Oxford: Basil Blackwell.

Cenoz, J. and Genesee, F. (eds) (1998) *Beyond Bilingualism: Multilingualism and Multilingual Education.* Clevedon: Multilingual Matters.

Cenoz, J., Hufeisen, B. and Jessner, U. (eds) (2001) *Looking Beyond Second Language Acquisition: Studies in Tri and Multilingualism.* Tübingen: Stauffenburg Verlag.

Cenoz, J. and Jessner, U. (eds) (2000) *English in Europe: The Acquisition of a Third Language.* Clevedon: Multilingual Matters.

Cenoz, J. and Valencia, J.F. (1994) Additive trilingualism: Evidence from the Basque Country. *Applied Psycholinguistics* 15, 195–207.

Chomsky, N. (1957) *Syntactic Structures.* The Hague: Mouton.

Clyne, M. (1997) Some of the things trilinguals do. *The International Journal of Bilingualism* 1, 95–116.

Cook, V. (1995) Multi-competence and the learning of many languages. *Language, Culture and Curriculum* 8 (2), 93–8.

Cummins, J. (1981) *Bilingualism and Minority Language Children.* Ontario: Ontario Institute for Studies in Education.

De Bot, K. (ed.) (1993) *Case Studies in Minority Languages. AILA Review* 10.

Dewaele, J.M. (2002) Psychological and sociodemographic correlates of communicative anxiety in L2 and L3 production. *The International Journal of Bilingualism* 6 (1), 23–38.

Dewaele, J.M. and Pavlenko, A. (2002) Emotion vocabulary in interlanguage. *Language Learning*, 52 (2), 265–324.

Doepke, F. (1996) *The Kinds of Things: A Theory of Personal Identity Based on Transcendental Argument.* Illinois: Carus Publishing Company.

Edwards, J. (1989) *Language, Society and Identity.* Oxford: Basil Blackwell.

Edwards, J. (1994) *Multilingualism.* London: Routledge.

El Assaiti, A. (1993) Berber in Morocco and Algeria: Revival or decay. In K. de Bot (ed.) *Case Studies in Minority Languages. AILA Review* 10, 88–109.

Fishman, J. (ed.) (1976) *Bilingual Education: An International Sociological Perspective.* Rowley, MA: Newbury House.

Fouser, R. (2001) Too close for comfort? Sociolinguistic transfer from Japanese into Korean as an L≥3. In J. Cenoz, B. Hufeisen and U. Jessner (eds) *Looking Beyond Second Language Acquisition: Studies in Tri and Multilingualism* (pp. 149–69). Tübingen: Stauffenburg Verlag.

Gal, S. (1979) *Language Shift: Social Determinants of Linguistic Change in Bilingual Austria.* New York: Academic Press.

Garrett, B. (1998) *Personal Identity and Self-consciousness.* London: Routledge.

Genesee, F. (1983) Bilingual education of majority-language children: The immersion experiments in review. *Applied Pyscholinguistics* 4, 1–6.

Giampapa, F. (2001) Hyphenated identities: Italian–Canadian youth and the negotiation of ethnic identities in Toronto. *The International Journal of Bilingualism* 5 (3), 279–315.

Giddens, A. (1991) *Modernity and Self-Identity.* Cambridge: Polity Press.

Grosjean, F. (1985) The bilingual as a competent but specific speaker–hearer. Journal of Multilingual and Multicultural Development 6, 467–77.

Gubbins, P. and Holt, M. (eds) (2002) *Beyond Boundaries: Language and Identity in Contemporary Europe.* Clevedon: Multilingual Matters.

Gumperz, J.J. (1982) *Language and Social Identity.* Cambridge: Cambridge University Press.

Hamers, J.F. (1981) Psychological approaches to the development of bilinguality. In H. Baetens Beardsmore (ed.) *Elements of Bilingual Theory.* Brussels: Vrije Universiteit.

Hamers, J.F. and Blanc, M. (1983) *Bilingualité et bilingualisme.* Brussels: Mardaga.

Haugen, E. (1956) *Bilingualism in the Americas.* Alabama: Alabama Dialect Society.

Haugen, E. (1972) *The Ecology of Language.* Stanford: Stanford University Press.

Herdina, P. and Jessner, U. (2000a) Multilingualism as an ecological system: The case for language maintenance. In B. Kettemann and H. Penz (eds) *ECOnstruction, Language, Nature and Society: The Ecolinguistic Project Revisited. Essays in Honour of Alwin Fill.* Tübingen: Stauffenburg Verlag.

Herdina, P. and Jessner, U. (2000b) The dynamics of third language acquisition. In J. Cenoz and U. Jessner (eds) *English in Europe: The Acquisition of a Third Language* (pp. 84–98). Clevedon: Multilingual Matters.

Herdina, P. and Jessner, U. (2002) *A Dynamic Model of Multilingualism: Perspectives of Change in Psycholinguistics.* Clevedon: Multilingual Matters.

Hoffmann, C. (1999) Trilingual competence: Linguistic and cognitive issues. *Applied Linguistic Studies in Central Europe* 3, 16–26.

Hoffmann, C. (2000) The spread of English and the growth of multilingualism with English in Europe. In J. Cenoz and U. Jessner (eds) *English in Europe: The Acquisition of a Third Language* (pp. 1–21). Clevedon: Multilingual Matters.

Hoffmann. C. (2001a) The status of trilingualism in bilingualism studies. In J. Cenoz, B. Hufeisen and U. Jessner (eds) *Looking Beyond Second Language Acquisition: Studies in Tri and Multilingualism* (pp. 13–25). Tübingen: Stauffenburg Verlag.

Hoffmann, C. (2001b) Towards a description of trilingual competence. *The International Journal of Bilingualism* 5 (1), 1–17.

Holm, E. (1993) Language values and practices of students in the Faroe islands: A survey report. In K. de Bot (ed.) *Case Studies in Minority Languages. AILA Review* 10.

Horenczyk, G. (2000) Conflicted identities: Acculturation, attitudes and immigrants' construction of their social worlds. In E. Olshtain and G. Horenczyk (eds) *Language, Identity and Immigration* (pp. 13–30). Jerusalem: Magnes Press.

Johnstone, B. (1996) *The Linguistic Individual: Self-expression in Language and Linguistics.* Oxford: Oxford University Press.

Jones, M. (1995) Euro-citizenship 2000: A historic role for the lesser-used language communities. In E. Ní Dheá, M. Ní Neachtain and A. Ó Dubhghaill (eds) *The Lesser Used Languages and Teacher Education: Towards the Promotion of the European Dimension* (pp. 161–4). Limerick: Clouts Mhuire gan Smál.

Keskés, I. and Papp, T. (2000a) Metaphorical competence in trilingual language production. In J. Cenoz and U. Jessner (eds) *English in Europe: The Acquisition of a Third Language* (pp. 99–120). Clevedon: Multilingual Matters.

Keskés, I. and Papp, T. (2000b) *Foreign Language and Mother Tongue.* Hillsdale, NJ: Lawrence Erlbaum.

Leontiev, A.A. (1995) Multilingualism for all: Russians? In T. Skutnabb-Kangas (ed.) *Multilingualism for All* (pp. 199–213). Lisse: Swets and Zeitlinger.

Luckmann, T. (1975) *The Sociology of Language.* Indianapolis: PRESS.

Lyon, J. (1996) *Becoming Bilingual: Language Acquisition in a Bilingual Community.* Clevedon: Multilingual Matters.

Maines, D.R. (1978) Bodies and selves: Notes on a fundamental dilemma in demography. *Studies in Symbolic Interaction* 1, 241–65.

Mesthrie, R., Swann, J., Deumert, A. and Leap, W. (2000) *Introducing Sociolinguistics.* Philadelphia: John Benjamins.

Olshtain, E. and Horenczyk, G. (eds) (2000) *Language, Identity and Immigration.* Jerusalem: Magnes Press.

Pavlenko, A. (2001) 'In the world of tradition, I was unimagined': Negotiation of identities in cross-cultural autobiographies. *The International Journal of Bilingualism* 5 (3), 317–44.

Pavlenko, A. (2002) Bilingualism and emotions. *Multilingua* 21 (1), 45–78.

Ringbom, H. (1987) *The Role of the First Language in Foreign Language Learning.* Clevedon: Multilingual Matters.

Romaine, S. (1995*) Bilingualism.* Oxford: Basil Blackwell.

Sapir, E. (1921) *Language.* New York: Harcourt Brace.

Sapir, E. (1947) *Selected Writings in Language, Culture and Personality.* Berkeley: University of California Press.

Saussure, F. de (1916) *Cours de linguistique générale.* Paris: Payot. (English translation (1959) *Course in General Linguistics.* New York: McGraw.)

Sharwood-Smith, M. (1991) Language modules and bilingual processing. In E. Bialystok (ed.) *Language Processing in Bilingual Children* (pp. 10–24). Cambridge: Cambridge University Press.

Skutnabb-Kangas, T. (1981) *Bilingualism or Not: The Education of Minorities.* Clevedon: Multilingual Matters.

Spolsky, B. and Shohamy, E. (1999) *The Languages of Israel: Policy, Ideology and Practice.* Clevedon: Multilingual Matters.

Swain, M., Lapkin, S., Rowen, N. and Hart, D. (1990) The role of mother tongue literacy in third language learning. *Language, Culture and Curriculum* 3, 65–81.

Swinburne, R. (1984) *Personal Identity: The Dualist Theory.* In S. Shoemaker and R. Swinburne *Personal Identity* (pp. 1–66). Oxford: Basil Blackwell.

Thomas, J. (1988) The role played by metalinguistic awareness in second and third language learning. *Journal of Multilingual and Multicultural Development* 9, 235–46.

Trudgill, P. (1983) *Sociolinguistics: An Introduction to Language and Society.* Harmondsworth: Penguin Books.

Wardhaugh, R. (1986) *An Introduction to Sociolinguistics.* Oxford: Basil Blackwell.

Webster's New Encyclopedic Dictionary (1994) Cologne: Könemann.

Weinreich, P. (2000) Ethnic identity and 'acculturation': Ethnic stereotyping and identification, self-esteem and identity diffusion in a multicultural context. In E. Olshtain and G. Horenczyk (eds) *Language, Identity and Immigration* (pp. 31–63). Jerusalem: Magnes Press.

Whorf, B.L. (1956) *Language, Thought and Reality: Selected Writings.* Edited by J.B. Carroll. Cambridge, MA: MIT Press and New York: Wiley.

Wierzbicka, A. (1999) *Emotions Across Languages and Cultures: Diversity and Universals.* Cambridge: Cambridge University Press.

Williams, C.J.F. (1989) *What Is Identity?* Oxford: Clarendon Press.

Williams, G. (1992) *Sociolinguistics: A Sociological Critique.* London: Routledge.

Chapter 2
Being Trilingual or Multilingual: Is There a Price to Pay?

ELITE OLSHTAIN AND FRIEDA NISSIM-AMITAI

Introduction

For many of us, living in a monolingual context might be so natural that we develop a very special appreciation for anyone who knows more than one language. A bilingual, trilingual or multilingual person seems to be an unusual phenomenon. Yet, Spolsky claims that 'Monolingual speech communities are rare and monolingual countries are even rarer' (1998: 51) so that, in fact, in the modern world all of us encounter multi-lingual situations. In the present contribution we would like to focus on monolingual versus plurilingual perceptions that are based on the social and linguistic context within which these perceptions develop. Many researchers have previously addressed the complexities of trilingual education (e.g. Cenoz, Hufeisen & Jessner, 2001; Ytsma, 2001) and the linguistic and pedagogic factors which impact on such education. The present chapter is concerned, primarily, with the multilingual context within which trilingualism is likely to develop.

For the initial step in the discussion we might distinguish between a context of natural multilingualism, as opposed to a situation where multi-lingualism is one of the outcomes of group or individual transition. In the first case a person is born into an existing multilingual situation, such as South Africa, Nepal, India or any other such context. In South Africa, for instance, a child might be born into a situation where the mother speaks one African language (such as Xhosa), the father may speak another African language (such as Sotho) and the dominant school language might be a third African language (such as Zulu). In addition to the domi-nant school language this child will soon learn English as the local and universal LWC (language of wider communication) and use all four languages to various degrees and in various situations. This child will soon recognize the multilingual situation as normal and acceptable, and will develop to be naturally multilingual. In this context, personal multi-lingualism is typical of most members of the community or, in Hamers and Blanc's (1989) terminology, a multilingual community is made up of individuals who develop multilinguality. A small community in Israel, made up of speakers of Circassian, will serve as a case study for our subsequent discussion of natural multilingualism.

When personal multilinguality is the result of transition (the new context creates a multilingual situation for the newcomer), personal and group perceptions are quite different from the ones found in natural multilingualism. Transition can result from migration of a group (small or large) moving from one country to another and therefore leaving behind the culture, language and social context of the original homeland, while trying to integrate into a new and different society. Such a transition may be intended as permanent or temporary (immigrants as opposed to guest workers). In either case, the adults in such a group will probably remain proficient in their first language while gradually acquiring the new language or languages, to various levels of proficiency, depending on situational factors and personal preferences.

Transition resulting from temporary migration, such as in the case of foreign workers, is strongly affected by the intended length of stay in the new context. Learning the new language, under such circumstances, is usually limited to survival skills.

Transition may also result from political changes that affect the language situation, creating contexts of multilingualism, but this is beyond the scope of the present contribution. Furthermore, this contribution will not address the situation where personal trilingualism or multilingualism is a result of formal schooling.

Natural multilingualism and transition multilingualism

The two contexts of multilingualism discussed here present somewhat different perceptions of monolingualism and plurilingualism. We shall discuss, in this respect, perceptions of language proficiency, perceptions of identity and perceptions of language dominance, focusing on how they might lead to preferences of language choice.

Perceptions of language proficiency

How do people in the two contexts perceive the concept of language proficiency? A person born into a monolingual community, whose mother tongue happens to coincide with the dominant language in the community, tends to perceive the desired language proficiency in that language as being 'close to perfect'. This means that knowledge of the language should reach a high level of literacy in both the oral and the written modes. The educated native speaker is perceived as having mastered the language linguistically and socio-culturally and has a native-like command in basic oral communication, as well as in the whole gamut of language literacy contexts, compatible with his or her education. Consequently, such a speaker poses a perceived monolingual standard of language proficiency.

The perceived monolingual standard of language proficiency is very powerful in cases where the migrant moves from one monolingual community to another. There is a strong feeling of having achieved the desired level of language proficiency in the first language and now, when one has to acquire the second or third language, the first one might be endangered. Issues of first language maintenance become central in such communities.

A different perception of language proficiency is most likely to develop in the context of natural multilingualism, as in the case of South Africa or India. Since each speaker uses two or three different languages in daily encounters, the need for mastering each language may not be the same. One language might be used only within the family and the close environment, another may be used especially at work and a third for educational and professional purposes. This situation leads speakers to think of the knowledge required in each language as suited to the actual patterns of language use. We would like to refer to this as the multilingual perception of proficiency.

Perceptions of identity

Language is a salient dimension of ethnic identity and, as such, plays an important role in intergroup relations when languages and cultures are in contact. This is usually the situation in the natural multilingual context, which we have established earlier. Language is not only a symbol of identity but also the main instrument upholding or promoting the groups' ethnic identities. Furthermore, language may play an important role in the power relations holding between the different ethnic groups. Most social scientists today would agree (Hamers & Blanc, 1989: 156) that the key concept is the subjective definition of ethnic groups. Only those dimensions which members themselves perceive as significant are defining characteristics of the group. When language is the defining characteristic of an ethnic group, it is necessary to understand and speak it in order to belong to the group, or at least in order to be recognized as belonging to the group. Such an ethnic language, if it is not endagered by external factors, will become a natural characteristic of the group.

Questions of identity also play a very important role in the context of multilingualism due to transition or change. Migration often serves as a catalyst for acculturation of both the group and the individuals making up the group, which results from the interface between immigrants and hosts in the new milieu. Acculturation has been viewed by some as a 'state', but more recently as a dynamic 'process', implying change over time of beliefs, emotions, behaviors and identities, particularly in work done by Berry (1997), Liebkind (in press) and others. Berry (1997) argues that a complex pattern of continuity and change characterizes the migrant's transition to a new cultural context. Migrants must confront two important issues – the degree to which the original cultural heritage and identity should be maintained, and the desired degree of intercultural contact with dominant group members. According to Berry (1997) and others, assimilation takes place when the migrant group or individual adopts the majority culture while relinquishing former ethnic affiliations; integration, on the other hand, leads to adoption of components from both minority and majority cultures serving as a good basis for bilingualism or trilingualism in the migrant community, as well as bilinguality and tri-linguality among its members (Hamers & Blanc, 1989). This approach allows members to maintain two or three languages while also promoting two or three different identities. The melting pot ideology, which was common in most immigration countries at the beginning of the twentieth century, would not have encouraged such development. The melting pot approach often led to marginalization in which the migrant community rejected both cultures and was left in a semilingual situation, not reaching linguistic literacy in any language and giving up, to a certain extent, their original identity without really gaining a new one. Marginalization was often accompanied by separation, which was characterized by retention of a strong allegiance to the minority culture and identity and rejection of the host community, minimizing social mobility within the new culture. Berry (1997) shows in his work that integration orientation with its bi-lingual or trilingual goal is the most adaptive mode even in 'melting pot'-type societies, as happened to various immigrant groups in Germany, such as the Turkish community (Schmitz, 1992). La Framboise, Coleman and Gerton (1993), however, propose an alternative model, which posits that the most adaptive individuals are those who learn to alternate their cultural behavior to suit situational demands, by preserving their cultural heritage on the one hand, while adapting to mainstream society on the other. In some sense, such a model leads to a multilingual perception of language use, which is more typical of the natural multilingual situation. Whichever model we prefer, it is obvious that language and identity are closely connected for immigrant communities on their road to integrating into a new society and culture. The main point here is that not only is the linguistic situation in transition but also the perceived identity of the speakers. It is this process of transition that is a major force affecting the immigrant's perceptions and attitudes.

There is a general consensus in the literature regarding the inextricable relationship which holds between language and identity. Nevertheless, the nature and direction of this relationship is far from being clear, according to Shohamy (1999). Whether construed as a cause or consequence of identity, language is commonly believed to be one of the most important indicators of ethnic affiliation. Dittmar *et al.* (1998) suggest that the investigation of identity may provide a better insight into language choice, since in any given interaction individuals will choose to represent themselves in the language that will best enhance their social identity.

Perceptions of language dominance

The individual's choice to become trilingual or multilingual, and the preferences reserved for one or two of the languages above the others, is closely related to perceptions of language dominance and language status. It is usually obvious which culture is the dominant one in a particular environment. A dominant culture, which consists of values, norms, beliefs and images, and which serves as the central political power in creating societal integration, is represented by a language that has dominant status. This is the language of the legal system, of statehood, of communication, of education and of the media, and social mobility depends greatly on how well we master the dominant language. Sociologists often refer to such knowledge as linguistic capital. Speakers whose native language is different from the dominant language will often invest time and effort to ensure native-like proficiency in both basic communication and literacy, in order to avoid social marginality and move into the mainstream of society, irrespective of how they may feel about the dominant culture.

In the context of natural multilingualism the individual places high value on literacy and schooling in the perceived dominant language, unless, due to political and social conflicts, another language is temporarily or permanently preferred. In the case of South Africa (Mbude, 2001), a special Language in Education policy was established in 1997 so that learners may study both their home language and English as instruction languages at school. However, the lack of teaching materials, trained teachers and other resources cannot provide an equal opportunity for all African languages. It is English, therefore, which is recognized as the important language for learning and for social mobility.

The subsequent description of the Circassian community in Israel will serve as a framework in which to discuss the various features of multi-lingualism in a concrete and distinct case. Linguistic perceptions and language choices made by the members of the community illustrate some of the considerations and feelings concerning linguistic gains as well as linguistic cost.

The Case of the Circassian Community

The Circassian speakers living in Israel function within a typically natural multilingual context. This is a small community which has lived in Israel for over 100 years and has maintained its language and culture of heritage. They came to this part of the world from the Caucasus region, speaking their Abkhaz-Adyghe language (Bram, 1999). They were brought here by the Turks at the time of the Ottoman Empire as a loyal Moslem community. Today one might say that they function in the following manner: they speak Circassian as their mother tongue and home language, they acquire Arabic at a very early age as the language of religion and of communication with the immediate environment and as the main language of instruction in school, and they acquire Hebrew as their second school language and the language of the state in which they live. They learn English as a foreign language to serve as their LWC.

The data collected for this study are based on interviews and questionnaires administered in the northern community of Rehaniya. Data collection took place between the end of 2001 and the summer of 2002. In phase one of the data collection we administered a questionnaire to 36 eighth graders (the total population of 14-year-olds in the Rehaniya community at the time). They were selected as the group which had experienced the study of the four languages in school and which continues to use the four languages in the normal course of events. The questionnaires focused on issues of language attitudes, personal preferences, identity and self-evaluation of language proficiency. A similar questionnaire was administered to 12 adults, 10 of whom are teachers in the school system. They were selected as informants with respect to policy and practice within the Israeli school system. In the second phase of this study 20 students and 4 teachers, who had participated in the first phase, were interviewed in depth, relating to the issues raised in the questionnaires.

Perceptions of language proficiency in the Circassian community

With respect to perceptions of language proficiency we asked all informants: 'How many languages do you know?' The answer was consistently: 'Four: Circassian, Hebrew, Arabic and English.' When asked how well they knew each language, the answer was always given in very definite terms: 'We know each of the four languages according to the way we need to use it.'

The level of mastery and the skill of use in the four languages is not the same for our Circassian informants, but they all share a perceived multilingual proficiency, which is quite different from the perceived monolingual standard. Thus, the Circassian member of the community living in Israel speaks Circassian for basic communication at home and within the immediate community, speaks, reads and writes Arabic to suit his religious and larger community needs, speaks, reads and writes Hebrew to fit his school needs and the needs of the larger society, as well as the needs for social and professional mobility in the larger society, and knows English as an LWC and a language required for mobility, higher education or professionalism. Such a person does not have a monolingual standard for each of the four languages, but rather a perceived multilingual standard, which is defined by societal needs.

The multilingual standard is so acceptable to these people that, when asked how well they know Circassian, they give it the highest-level rating on a scale, yet may not even know how to count to 10 in this language. It turns out that they tend to count in Arabic or Hebrew, even before they learn these languages, and everybody finds counting in Circassian very difficult, probably because of its complex phonological system. Furthermore, they do not learn how to read and write Circassian until they reach the sixth grade. This is, altogether, a rather recent development – there was no writing system used among the members of this community until the 1950s when the literary language and the Cyrillic script were introduced in the community. It took quite a few years to develop knowledge of it among the members of the community and, since 1971, it is taught in school starting in sixth grade. Now, there is regular contact with the Circassian community in the Caucasus and both media and printed matter are available. Books, textbooks and other printed materials are brought in from the home country.

The personal perception of youngsters and adults in this community is such that they master the Circassian language just well enough to use it as their home and family language, and that is as perfect as it needs to be in terms of language proficiency. In other words, they feel very comfortable in this language in terms of daily conversations within the family, storytelling and various other cultural and ethnic activities. In fact, these multilingual youngsters equate knowledge of a language with speaking. When asked: 'What does it mean to know a language and, specifically, what does it mean to know Circassian, Arabic, Hebrew or English?', the answer is consistently: 'speaking'. There seems to be special emphasis on the communicative function of language and they tend to emphasize communicative ability regardless of linguistic proficiency.

Perceptions of identity and language dominance in the Circassian community

Ethnic communities differ in their commitment to the home culture and heritage and in their eagerness to maintain close ties with the old country. Some communities prefer to disconnect from the old country and become integrated into the new society. In order to understand which factors may promote or impede the maintenance of an ethnic minority language, Giles, Bourhis and Taylor (1977) developed the concept of perceived ethnolinguistic vitality. This concept has been extended and applied to a variety of contexts and found useful in understanding the development of group and individual perceptions of language status and institutional power (Kraemer *et al.*, 1994; Ytsma *et al.*, 1994).

The concept of perceived ethnolinguistic vitality also takes into account individual members' cognitive representations of the social conditions under which they live and mediates their intergroup behavior. This concept provides a theoretical and empirical starting point for bridging the conceptual gap between sociological and social psychological approaches to inter-ethnolinguistic group relations. Groups who perceive that they have high enthnolinguistic vitality tend to use their own language more frequently and in a wider range of domains than those who have a low perceived vitality.

In our case study of the Circassian community in Israel we focused on three factors which are related to the concept of ethnolinguistic vitality: language status, political influence of the group and social status of the group, as perceived by the members of the community. Using a written questionnaire,[1] we concentrated on perceived language status as declared by the informants (Figure 2.1); on the perceived political influence of some major groups, including the Circassians (Figure 2.2); and on perceived social status of the group (Figure 2.3), when compared to other relevant ethnic groups.

Perception of language status in society

Figure 2.1 shows a very realistic perception of the status of the Circassian language among the various languages spoken in Israel – it is viewed as relatively insignificant. Hebrew is more powerful than other languages since it is the language of the majority and the dominant language, while Russian and Arabic are the major minority languages and English functions as an LWC.

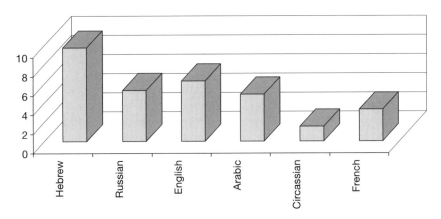

Figure 2.1 What, in your opinion, is the social status of the following languages?

Perceived political influence of major groups

We focused on perceptions of political power as assigned to various ethnic groups within Israeli society. Figure 2.2 presents the perceptions of political power: Jews (the majority in Israel), Arabs (about 20%), new immigrants (over 20%), the Druz community, which is a powerful group within the Arab population, and Circassians. The results indicate again a very realistic perception of political influence with the Circassians being the weakest group (also by far the smallest group).

Perceived social status of major groups

Finally, to provide an additional factor within the perceived ethnolinguistic vitality, we asked about the perceived social status of the groups mentioned. This time, as shown in Figure 2.3, the results are quite surprising: the new immigrants are viewed as having a rather high social

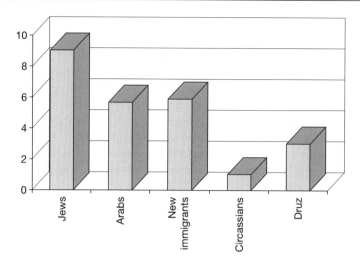

Figure 2.2 How strong is the political influence of each of these groups?

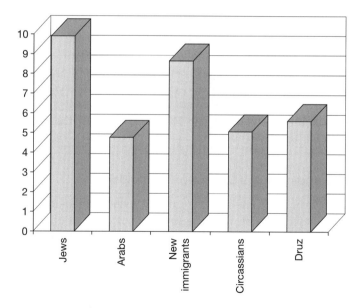

Figure 2.3 What, in your opinion, is the social status of each of these groups in Israel?

status, almost as high as the majority, with the Druz, as well as the Circassians, having a slightly higher status than the Arabs.

There is no doubt that some of the perceived social status is based on the fact that the Druz and the Circassians serve in the army while Arabs do not. In Israel, serving in the army is one way to belong to the mainstream of society. The Druz community is larger in number than the Circassian community but both groups perceive themselves as taking an important position in the army. However, the interesting finding in this figure is the fact that the Circassians perceive of themselves as having, relatively, a much higher social status than their size and impact on the Israeli society could justify (Figure 2.3). There is no doubt that such perceptions contribute to the concept of identity and to the maintenance of heritage, and provide the community with some self-esteem.

Our case study of the Circassian community in Israel exhibits the importance of language as a defining feature of ethnic identity. When we interviewed teenagers and asked them how they would like to be identified by other people (if they left their small community and traveled to a large city), they all responded by making it clear that 'Circassian' is their choice. This is their perceived and declared identity. When we continued to ask whether they would mind being identified as Arabs or Jews, most of them said that it is very important for them to be identified as Circassian and only about 20% said that they wouldn't mind if they were thought of as Jews or Arabs. In the unique context of the Circassian community, being a Moslem like the Arabs, a contributing citizen like the Jews and a Circassian by ethnicity, can be easily accepted. It is a clear manifestation of a triple identity with a strong indication for their ethnic identity. Most importantly, they perceive the situation of multilingualism and multi-identity as permanent.

Language choice in the Circassian community

In our study of the Circassian community we found that teenagers have made their choice of Hebrew as the language of wider communication in the larger community, recognizing it as the preferred dominant language. Although they speak Circassian at home, start school in first grade in Arabic as the medium of instruction and take Hebrew as a third language starting in second grade, they view Hebrew as the most important language since 'this is the language of the country and this is the language of the Hebrews'. The adults will also explain that the most important language for them is Hebrew, since they need it for higher education, for social mobility and for professional purposes. Additionally, they all watch television and listen to the radio in Hebrew.

In our attempt to get to the active choices made by teenagers we employed a number of indirect questions relating to the use of Hebrew. When we asked them what they found difficult in each of the four languages they said: 'Writing is very difficult in Circassian, speaking in English, literacy in Arabic, but Hebrew is very easy.' They consistently reported having no difficulty in Hebrew. When asked in what language they would write a letter to a friend or a member of the family they chose Hebrew. This sounded strange, since they use Arabic as the language of instruction in school and Hebrew only as an additional language. Yet, the answers were consistent across the board, and all the respondents explained that it was easier for them to write Hebrew. When asked what they would do in Arabic only, most of them indicated religion and prayers as the major area for Arabic use.

We used a 'can-do' self-evaluation questionnaire, which has five scales for each language skill (speaking, listening, reading and writing) represented by five different statements regarding that skill. The results presented in Figure 2.4, relate to the four languages that the subjects speak.

Language proficiency: speaking

When we look at self-evaluation regarding speaking (see Figure 2.4), we see that Hebrew and Circassian compete for the highest position in all task types, while English is limited, since it is only a school subject, and Arabic is slightly lower than the first two languages.

Language proficiency: reading

The same type of self-evaluation regarding reading is presented in Figure 2.5. The data presented further strengthen the position of Hebrew and Circassian and places Arabic in a slightly lower position. The Circassian population living in the small community in the north of Israel exhibits an interesting set of patterns of language use, which is compatible with their ability to function in each of these languages and with their ethnolinguistic perceptions of the different groups and languages spoken in the country: Circassian at home, Arabic at school and the neighboring villages, Hebrew at school and within the larger society, and English at school.

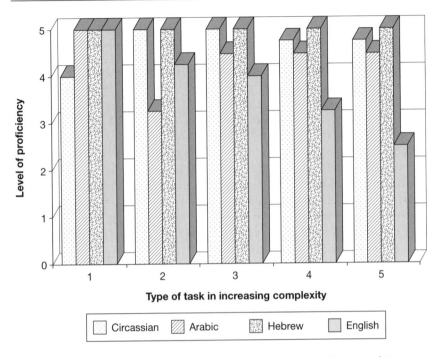

Figure 2.4 Self-evaluation in the four languages regarding speaking-based tasks

Comparing Language Choice in the Two Multilingual Types of Contexts

When comparing the two contexts in terms of perceptions of multilingualism, we find that immigrants, who came from monolingual contexts, tend to maintain their monolingual standard of proficiency. This means that they are somewhat frustrated by the fact that being trilingual in the new community (speakers of Russian in Israel acquire Hebrew as the local language and English as the LWC) may result in attrition of their first language and only limited knowledge of the new languages. This often leads them to say: 'Today I don't have a good dominant language – I lost the old and I haven't acquired the new one(s).' This is obviously the result of their perceived monolingual standard of proficiency, since they aspire to develop perfect kowledge in each language. A person with a multilingual perception would simply say: 'I read literature in Russian, I speak Hebrew for basic communication and I read English professionally, and that is just fine.'

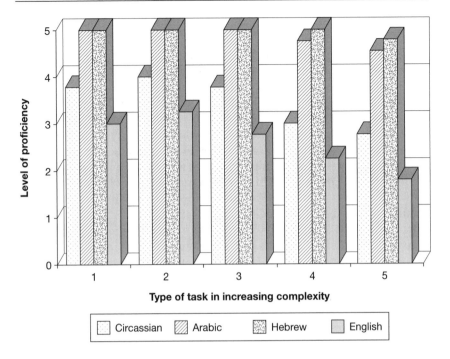

Figure 2.5 Self-evaluation in the four languages regarding reading-based tasks

In our case of the Circassian community in Israel, two languages compete for the position of dominance, Arabic and Hebrew. For youngsters who are still in school the preferences may depend on which of the two languages is a more powerful medium of instruction. However, once these youngsters reach the level of higher education the preference for literacy becomes more pronounced in Hebrew, since this is the language of instruction and professional or academic interaction. Furthermore, English may gain considerable importance in comparison to the other languages, since it is both a universal LWC and an important vehicle for accessing professional and scientific literature. Thus, the perceptions of ethnolinguistic vitality as exhibited in Figures 2.1, 2.2 and 2.3 account, at least partially, for the patterns of language use that develop in this community.

Furthering proficiency in any one of the languages a person knows is basically perceived as linguistic and social gain, and the question of price only comes up when a person realizes that he or she may have to put more effort into developing literacy in the dominant language, at the expense of one or more of the other languages. Thus, the Circassian youngster, having learned to read and write Circassian in the sixth grade of the elementary school, may say: 'I would love to become literate in my mother tongue but right now it is more important for me to excel in Hebrew and English. Later in life when I have time, I will work at improving my reading and writing in Circassian.' On the other hand, adult intellectuals and professionals in the community expressed their regrets for not having achieved higher levels of literacy in Hebrew. It seems that, sometimes, multilinguals feel that they have a price to pay for maintaining the use of different languages and not becoming fully proficient in the dominant language. Professionals in the Circassian community expressed this feeling of cost and benefit.

In the context of natural trilingualism or multilingualism, the individual makes choices with respect to a dominant language among three or four, depending on perceptions of societal dominance, personal aspirations and attitudes towards the different languages. This choice of dominance might be very closely related to schooling. If one of the languages is the major language for the advancement of literacy, this is the language that might become the dominant one for all the individuals within the school system. English in the South African school system may play such a role.

Individual dominance can, however, become obvious much earlier than that. An interesting case is described by Hoffmann and Widdicombe (1999). The study presents a case of a four and a half-year-old trilingual in French, English and Italian, who grew up bilingually at home with English and Italian and went to nursery in French, the language of wider communication in the community. On the basis of the type of code-switching and code-mixing employed by this child, the investigators could identify the tendency towards viewing French as the dominant language, even at such an early age.

In the context of multilingualism as a result of transition or change, perceptions of language dominance are greatly affected by one's first language in comparison to the new language. Russian scientists immigrating to Israel or the US will be confronted with slightly different situations: the immigrant in the US has no problem accepting English as the dominant language of the new community and as a universal LWC which is required for academic international exchange. In Israel, on the other hand, although Hebrew might be the obvious local dominant language, English is still the academic LWC and therefore the immigrant's decision might be to develop Hebrew for basic communication and survival purposes, but to promote literacy in English. We see here an important distinction that has to be made between linguistic ability to communicate in basic interaction and schooled, literate use of the language. If the immigrant holds a monolingual standard perception of proficiency he or she might feel unhappy with this state of affairs, having not gained full mastery of either language.

Multilingual Language Use: Code-mixing and Code-switching

Language choice is defined as convergent when interactants attempt to decrease the social distance between themselves and out-group members as their interlocutors, and it is defined as divergent when interactants try to increase social distance between themselves and their interlocutors. In our case study the Circassian subjects reported a very strong convergent orientation as being part of their basic perception of trilingualism or multilingualism. 'We speak Circassian to another member of the family or the community, we speak Arabic to people from the neighboring villages and we speak Hebrew to all the Hebrew speakers. We want them to know that we can speak in their language.' Convergence and divergence can be expressed through language choice or through features of code-mixing and code-switching.

Being a trilingual or a multilingual speaker allows one to participate in a variety of encounters with other multilinguals. Some of the languages might be shared by the interlocutors. This situation is quite conducive to code-switching and code-mixing. In our work we have adopted a definition of code-switching for when the speaker switches from one language to the other for utterances that contain at least one clause, while we use code-mixing for incorporation of 'guest' expressions within the 'host' language, which happens to be used for the communicative event. The multilingual speaker can make choices with respect to code-switching and code-mixing as part of the convergent or divergent preferences. Grosjean (2001), in his discussion of bilingual and trilingual language modes, focuses on the various types of activation of the base language chosen for the interaction and of the other languages available to the interlocutors. Thus a speaker of Hebrew, Arabic and English interacting with a speaker of Arabic and English may choose either Arabic or English to activate as the base language, while the alternative language is used for code-switching. Various factors may affect such choices and the degree of activation, such as: language proficiency, situation, content, language mixing habits and attitudes, degree of formality etc. Dewaele (2001) further explored the language mode continuum and found formal versus informal situations as being crucial in positioning the speaker along the continuum.

In our work we found that, in the natural multilingual context, some content areas are more prone to code-mixing, such as: cultural interactions and events, topics requiring specialized lexical items, religious events, professional jargon etc. Thus, for our Circassian population we find some of the following code-mixing tendencies: when Circassian functions as the base language, Arabic is used in code-mixing and switching mostly in cultural religious and shopping activities, while Hebrew is used for professional and higher education topics. When the base language is Hebrew, English is often used for code-mixing. In general, code-mixing and code-switching are normal occurrences.

The phenomenon of code-mixing and code-switching is just as common among trilinguals or multilinguals in the context resulting from transition. In the very early stages of language acquisition, learners are often unable to use code-mixing effectively, since their proficiency in the target language is so limited. We found this to be the case with Russian-speaking subjects (Olshtain & Kotik, 2000), similarly to De Angelis' and Selinker's study (2001). Newcomers, when interacting with speakers of the target language, will start mixing expressions and lexical items from their first language when they perceive them as being of a universal nature. For speakers of European languages such a perception of an international or universal stock of lexical items often relates to what they perceive as Latin roots. When interacting with other newcomers, the production of mixed utterances can either indicate weaker competence in the target language (Dewaele, 2001) or an initiation of the process of first language attrition. In general, the intergenerational code-switching continuum described by Backus (1999) can be recognized in our work as well, with the first generation using a more limited amount of the target language with considerable code-switching and mixing of the first language, the intermediate generation increasing the use of the target language, and the second generation using mostly the target language with some switching and mixing of the first language, which has become the home language for them. Consequently, we find that in the multilingual situation resulting from transition one can recognize a gradual shift from the first language to the new language or languages across generations. This is a non-stable pattern that undergoes transition over time. This is in clear contrast to the natural multilingual context, where code-mixing and code-switching are normal features of being a multilingual.

Concluding Remarks

Language choice and preferences for code-switching and code-mixing are processes that are affected by perceptions of desired language proficiency and perceptions of identity, in both the natural multilingual context and in multilingualism resulting from transition. We have seen that the natural context leads to a dynamic concept of language use with embedded adaptability to interaction in various situations. Such adaptability allows the multilingual speaker to perceive language proficiency as dynamic and as suited to practical needs, and personal identity as having a multi-faceted nature. Accordingly, language choice and the degree of code-switching and code-mixing will be conditioned first and foremost by the interlocutor in the communicative situation, since multilingual speakers tend to adjust their patterns of language use to the addressee (convergence). In the natural multilingual context these concepts exhibit relative stability over time.

In a multilingual context resulting from transition, the processes tend to change over time and generations. Acculturation attitudes and perceptions of the host society's ideologies have a strong impact on the immigrants' first generation preferences for first language maintenance, which might be minimal in the case of assimilation and rather strong in the case of separation (Horenczyk, 2000). The intermediate generation (who arrived as young adults) and the second generation usually tend to move towards social and cultural integration into the new society and their patterns of language use change over time, moving towards bilingualism (Olshtain & Kotik, 2000). The most important feature of this context is change over time.

Figure 2.6 shows how multilingual speakers are affected by perceptions of proficiency and identity in both types of multilingual contexts, with a more stable pattern in the natural environment and a more transient pattern in the other environment.

Very often national and political policies dictate language choices to ethnic groups that speak a language different from the dominant language via subtractive or additive bilingualism or trilingualism. Cummins (2001a), in his discussion of how 'bilingual children end up in the cross fire of policy makers', pinpoints the need to look at the real issues of multilingualism. We tend to agree with his basic position but we would like to emphasize the fact that the question 'Is there a price to pay?' has two perspectives.

On the one hand, the multilingual perception is open, liberal and easy to live with, since it allows for viewing mastery in a language as

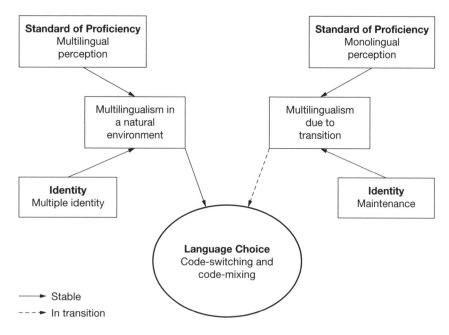

Figure 2.6 Language choice in the two multilingual contexts

compatible with social and cultural needs of the individual. Such a view encourages language learning and language choices, placing high value on the communicative function of language. This is a perspective which focuses on the fact that not only isn't there a price to pay for multilingualism, but in fact there are obvious gains and advantages. Multilinguality is perceived as enriching and expanding one's linguistic repertoire (Zentella, 1997).

On the other hand, one needs to be concerned with social, economic and educational mobility within society. It is therefore important that the dominant language or the important language in any society be made accessible to all multilingual speakers. Policy should ensure that any member of the society has the opportunity and availability to develop a level of proficiency in the dominant language that will secure him or her the needed mobility. Lack of mastery is likely to block opportunities. Cummins (2001b) emphasizes the need to create instructional conditions for academic language learning in the languages which are required for successful functioning within school and later within society. The ability to use the language in oral and written modes enables speakers to express their identities and their intelligence and knowledge in powerful ways, opening a path to social and economic mobility. It is only the child or speaker, who has not been given the opportunity to develop mastery in the dominant language, who may pay a high price for multilingualism.

There is no doubt that today's world is moving from monolingual, bilingual and trilingual contexts to more and more multilingual contexts. Scholars and policy makers need to promote a multilingual context in which nobody pays a heavy price and all have access to social mobility and linguistic choices and preferences.

Note

1. We used two additional languages in the questionnaire: Russian, which is spoken natively by over 20% of the population in Israel, and French, which is another European language studied in schools.

References

Backus, A. (1999) The intergenerational codeswitching continuum in an immigrant community. In G. Extra and L.Verhoeven (eds) *Bilingualism and Migration: Studies on Language Acquisition* (pp. 261–79). Berlin: Mouton de Gruyter.

Berry, J.W. (1997) Immigration, acculturation and adaptation. *Applied Psychology: An International Review* 46 (1), 5–68.

Bram, C. (1999) Circassian reimmigration to the Caucasus. In S. Weil (ed.) *Roots and Routes: Ethnicity and Migration in Global Perspective* (pp. 205–22). Jerusalem: Magnes Press.

Cenoz, J., Hufeisen, B. and Jessner, U. (eds) (2001) *Cross-linguistic Influence in Third Language Acquisition: Psycholinguistic Perspectives.* Clevedon: Multilingual Matters.

Cummins, J. (2001a) Empowerment through biliteracy. In C. Baker and N.H. Hornberger (eds) *An Introductory Reader to the Writings of Jim Cummins* (pp. 258–84). Clevedon: Multilingual Matters.

Cummins, J. (2001b) Instructional conditions for trilingual development. *International Journal of Bilingual Education and Bilingualism* 4 (1), 61–75.

De Angelis, G. and Selinker, L. (2001) Interlanguage transfer and competing linguistic systems in the multilingual mind. In J. Cenoz, B. Hufeisen and U. Jessner (eds) *Cross-linguistic Influence in Third Language Acquisition: Psycholinguistic Perspectives* (pp. 42–58). Clevedon: Multilingual Matters.

Dewaele, L.M. (2001) Activation or inhibition? The interaction of L1, L2 and L3 on the language mode continuum. In J. Cenoz, B. Hufeisen and U. Jessner (eds) *Cross-linguistic Influence in Third Language Acquisition: Psycholinguistic Perspectives* (pp. 69–89). Clevedon: Multilingual Matters.

Dittmar, N., Spolsky, B. and Walters, J. (1998) Language and identity in immigrant language acquisition and use: A framework for integrating sociological, psychological and linguistic data. In V. Regan (ed.) *Contemporary Approaches to*

Second Language Acquisition in Social Context (pp. 124–36). Dublin: University College Dublin Press.

Giles, H., Bourhis, R.Y. and Taylor, D.M. (1977) Towards a theory of language in ethnic relations. In H. Giles (ed.) *Language, Ethnicity and Intergroup Relations.* New York: Academic Press.

Grosjean, F. (2001) The bilingual language modes. In J.L. Nicol (ed.) *One Mind, Two Languages: Bilingual Language Processing* (pp. 2–22). Oxford: Blackwell Publishers.

Hamers, J.F. and Blanc, M.H.A. (1989) *Bilinguality and Bilingualism.* Cambridge: Cambridge University Press.

Hoffmann, C. and Widdicombe, S. (1999) Code-switching and language dominance in a trilingual child. Proceedings of the 8th EUROSLA Conference in Paris. *AILE (Acquisition et interaction en langue étrangère)* 1, special issue, *The Bilingual Person*, 51–61.

Horenczyk, G. (2000) Conflicted identities: Acculturation attitudes and immigrants' construction of their social worlds. In E. Olshtain and G. Horenczyk (eds) *Language, Identity and Immigration* (pp. 13–30). Jerusalem: Magnes Press.

Kraemer, R., Olshtain, E. and Badier, S. (1994) Ethnolinguistic vitality, attitudes, and networks of linguistic contact: The case of the Israeli Arab minority. *International Journal of the Sociology of Language* 108, 79–95.

La Framboise, T., Coleman, H.L.K. and Gerton, J. (1993) Psychological impact of biculturalism: Evidence and theory. *Psychological Bulletin* 114 (3), 395–412.

Liebkind, K. (in press) Acculturation. In R. Brown and S. Gaertner (eds) *Intergroup Processes.* Blackwell Handbook of Social Psychology 4. Oxford: Blackwell Publishers.

Mbude, Z. (2001) Trilingualism in South Africa and the Dual-medium Education Program. Paper presented at the 2nd International Conference on Third Language Acquisition and Trilingualism Conference in Leeuwarden, The Netherlands.

Olshtain, E. and Kotik, B. (2000) The development of bilingualism in an immigrant community. In E. Olshtain and G. Horenczyk (eds) *Language, Identity and Immigration* (pp. 201–17). Jerusalem: Magnes Press.

Schmitz, P. (1992) Acculturation styles and health. In S. Iwawaki, Y. Kashima and K. Leung (eds) *Innovations in Cross-cultural Psychology.* Amsterdam: Swets and Zeitlinger.

Shohamy, E. (1999) Language and identity of Jews in Israel and the diaspora. In D. Zisenwine and D. Schers (eds) *Present and Future: Jewish Culture Identity and Language* (pp. 79–94). Tel-Aviv: School of Education.

Spolsky, B. (1998) *Sociolinguistics.* Oxford: Oxford University Press.

Ytsma, J., Viladot, M.A. and Giles, H. (1994) Ethnolinguistic vitality and ethnic identity: Some Catalan and Frisian data. *International Journal of Sociology of Language* 108, 63–78.

Ytsma, J. (2001) Towards a typology of trilingual primary education. *International Journal of Bilingual Education and Bilingualism* 4 (1), 11–22.

Zentella, A.C. (1997) *Growing Up Bilingual.* Oxford: Blackwell Publishers.

Part 2: Multilingual Language Use

Chapter 3

Language Practices of Trilingual Youth in Two Canadian Cities

PATRICIA LAMARRE AND DIANE DAGENAIS

Introduction

Over the past few decades, with dramatic increases in immigration to Canada from an increasingly broad range of countries, the language backgrounds of youth in Canadian cities have become much more diversified (Marmen & Corbeil, 1999). Depending on where they settle, the children of immigrants learn English or French, i.e. one of Canada's two official languages. They also receive instruction in the other official language through second language programs offered in the school. For many immigrant and second-generation youth, these languages are added to repertoires that already include one or more languages acquired at home, and in some cases, learned through prior schooling in their countries of origin and residence. In the past, research has examined bilingualism among immigrant and second-generation youth. As Cenoz and Genesee (1998) indicate, it is only recently that multilingualism has become a focus of study and drawn more attention.

We examine here the phenomenon of multilingualism in Canada in relation to demolinguistic and policy contexts. Using the term multilingual to refer to speakers of three or more languages, we describe how multilingual youth perceive languages as linguistic capital and attribute value to languages in relation to particular linguistic markets, locally, nationally and internationally. Finally, we consider how these youth describe multilingualism in reference to their identity.

Our discussion draws on the results of a comparative study of the language experiences of multilingual youth residing in Montreal and Vancouver. These two cities were chosen as research sites because they represent quite different contexts of language socialization in Canada.

More specifically, in Montreal, Quebec, most immigrant students are schooled in French and receive second language instruction in English until the end of secondary school. French–English bilingualism is an asset for youth in this city when they enter the labour market, where it is often a prerequisite for employment. In contrast, in Vancouver, British Columbia, on the Canadian West Coast, the dominant language of schooling is English and second language instruction is provided in French up until secondary school. English dominates the labour market in Vancouver and competence in other languages is also an asset, but is not required for most jobs.

Our work is informed by theoretical discussions of language socialization (Schieffelin & Ochs, 1986) that examine the inextricable relationship between language practices, social context and institutions such as schools and families. In our analysis, we draw on Bourdieu's (1977, 1982) notions of field, habitus and linguistic capital and Norton's (2000) discussion of investment in language learning. We argue that the youths in our study view multilingualism as a resource and invest in learning multiple languages as a means of accessing various linguistic markets. Referring to recent work on the transnational perspective adopted by immigrants and migrants (Meintel, 1993; Mitchell, 2001), we also consider Heller's (2000) discussion of globalization and the value attributed to languages. Citing Deprez (1994) and Woolard (1985), we suggest that language serves to construct identity and secure group solidarity for multilingual youth.

We begin by elaborating on the above theoretical perspective to explain how it informs our analysis. We then situate the two research sites, Montreal and Vancouver, in terms of their geographic location and the demographics of official bilingualism and multilingualism in Canada. Differences and similarities in the linguistic markets (Bourdieu, 1982) and policy frameworks of these two cities are then highlighted to illustrate how the language practices and educational trajectories of multilingual youth are affected by contextual factors. Following this, we outline the methodology of our comparative study and discuss some of the themes emerging from our analysis which include: (1) multilingualism as resource, (2) language status and competition, (3) the symbolic value of languages and (4) multilingual identity. We call for a recognition of the insight youth have into linguistic markets and their ability to attribute value to the languages in their repertoires locally, nationally and internationally. We conclude by considering the implications of this research for educational practice and language policy.

Theoretical Framework

Recent research in applied linguistics and language education has built on Schieffelin's and Ochs' (1986) definition of language socialization that describes language learning as a process whereby youngsters adopt the social norms and shared meanings of their language groups. Central to this perspective is the interconnection between language, learning, social practices, values, interpersonal relationships and cultural institutions.

More recently, researchers studying the social aspects of language learning have drawn on Bourdieu's (1982, 1983) social reproduction theory, which attributes a central place to language in the competitive dynamics of society. Bourdieu's constructs of habitus, field, language capital and linguistic markets allow us to interpret how individuals interact within intersecting social spaces and provide conceptual tools for analysing the role of language within these interactions. Essentially, Bourdieu argues that individuals acquire a habitus – a system of dispositions, practices and representations, mostly learned at home – that enables them to move with greater or lesser ease through different fields of competition (Bourdieu, 1983; Bourdieu & Wacquant, 1992). In Bourdieu's writing, fields are described as structured social spaces characterized by discourse and social activity. According to this definition, institutions such as school, family and the workplace can be considered as fields. Describing language as capital, Bourdieu (1977, 1982) proposes that language is convertible to economic, social and symbolic capital within particular fields.

Expanding on Bourdieu's theory, Carrington and Luke (1997) propose that the habitus is not only constructed at home, but also through a life-long process of language socialization. As well, Lamarre and Rossell Paredes (2003) add to this discussion by suggesting that different sites play specific roles in the language socialization process as youth move through various friendship networks and from school to the labour market.

Norton (2000) applies Bourdieu's theory to language learning, suggesting that learners invest in additional languages in order to acquire greater symbolic and material resources that enrich their capital. In other words, they imagine that this investment will yield 'a return that will give them access to hitherto unattainable resources' (Norton, 2000: 10). Dagenais (2001) applies this concept of investment to an analysis of the reasons why immigrant families opt to promote the development of child multilingualism and attribute value to it in reference to national and international market forces.

Although Bourdieu (1977) recognizes the symbolic value and importance of language, he has focused on how language allows dominant
social groups to maintain their position and has not tried to account for
people's interest in acquiring or maintaining minority languages that
have little economic value in local markets. To address this issue, we refer
to Deprez (1994) and Woolard (1985) who have examined how people
attribute symbolic value to minority languages. Deprez, for instance, has
shown in her research with immigrant families living in Paris, France,
that they invest in maintaining a minority language, regardless of its lack
of economic importance, because it ensures familial and affective ties with
language communities locally and in the country of origin. Similarly, in
cities like Montreal and Vancouver, maintaining a heritage/minority
language provides membership in minority language communities. In
this sense, symbolic value is attributed to a heritage/minority language
within particular, community-delimited, linguistic markets.

Furthermore, as Heller (2000) proposes, with increasing trends toward
globalization, international market forces are redefining the value of
languages, as well as the workings of local marketplaces. Heller argues
that these phenomena must be considered in any contemporary analysis
of learners' language practices and representations. Along similar lines,
Meintel (1993) and Mitchell (2001) have argued that a number of immigrants and second generation youth look beyond the borders of a
particular nation state, such as Canada, to adopt a transnational perspective as their frame of reference. This means that maintenance of a
heritage/minority language might be perceived as valuable capital within
one's local language community as well as within a larger transnational
community. For example, by maintaining Spanish, youth may claim
membership not only in the Latino communities of Montreal or
Vancouver, but also in language communities in their country of origin
and other Spanish-speaking nations. The emergence of a transnational
perspective in immigrant and second generation youth challenges
researchers and educators to reconsider the parameters of linguistic
markets and the reasons why learners invest in language and education.

Clearly, it appears that a broader, more dynamic view of language
socialization is needed to account for overlapping fields of practice and
linguistic markets in multiple sites such as the home, educational institutions, informal friendship networks and the workplace. Such a
perspective would provide more helpful theoretical tools for understanding the complex phenomenon of multilingualism in modern
societies. We adopt this theoretical stance to consider, in the next sections,

how language practices and identity are shaped in multilingual youth living in two different urban linguistic markets.

The Geography and Demographics of Language Knowledge in Montreal and Vancouver

Though Canada became an officially bilingual country in 1969, it is by no means uniformly so. When the actual importance of English and French is considered, Canada can be divided into three linguistic zones: a dominantly English-speaking area; a primarily French-speaking one; and a bilingual belt where the two languages co-exist (Joy, 1972, 1992). Within the Canadian population, 83% speak either French or English as a first language, while 17% of residents from a wide range of linguistic origins declare a non-official language as 'first language spoken and still understood'.

Only 17% of the total Canadian population speak both official languages (Marmen and Corbeil, 1999) and the majority of bilinguals live in Canada's 'bilingual belt', which includes parts of Quebec, Ontario and New Brunswick. The greatest concentration of bilinguals is found in Quebec, the only province where the majority is French-speaking, but where the importance of English within the labor market is apparent.

Multilingualism in Canada follows the same trend and is nine times higher in Quebec than in other provinces, specifically 46.8% for Quebec as compared to 5.4% for the rest of Canada (Marmen & Corbeil, 1999). Focusing on the two metropolitan census areas of this study, 44% of Montrealers who speak a non-official language are trilingual, declaring knowledge of both English and French; whereas in Vancouver, only 4% of the population answer to this description. These statistics draw attention to the distinct sociolinguistic and sociopolitical contexts of Montreal and Vancouver and their different linguistic markets.

In terms of language dynamics, both cities have undergone dramatic changes in the last few decades. In Quebec, since the late 1960s, considerable effort has gone into improving the status of French. In Montreal, economic and social incentives to communicate in French have increased significantly in a very short period (Bourhis, 2001; Levine, 1990). Despite the growing need for French in the city, English retains its status as the dominant language for economic and social transactions within North America, and Montreal remains the Canadian city where English–French bilingualism is most common.

The linguistic market of Vancouver has changed as well in the last few decades, due both to the Federal government's efforts, since the 1960s, to promote official bilingualism and, more recently, to an influx of immigrants from Asia and elsewhere. Consequently, Asian languages are second to English in importance in social and economic exchanges in Vancouver and French has a de facto status of minority language in social interactions, despite its *de jure* status as an official language of the Federal government, equal to English. Thus, French competence has some limited potential as linguistic capital, most notably for positions within Federal institutions. Nevertheless, as the statistics indicate, official bilingualism does not have the same value in Vancouver as in Montreal.

Considering educational contexts more specifically, we draw attention to the fact that, since 1982, constitutional guarantees protect the rights of official language minorities to schooling in their language everywhere in Canada. Essentially, this means that all provincial governments are obliged to provide a dual school system based on language of instruction. Rights to instruction in an official minority language are hereditary and are acquired through parental claim to this type of schooling. Beyond respecting this constitutional right, provinces have complete jurisdiction over how schooling is organized within their territories. What this means is that immigrant families are able to use the school system to acquire English–French bilingualism in different ways, depending on their heritage and place of residence in the country. In Vancouver, most immigrant youth are enrolled in English language schools and some in French Immersion programs that provide instruction both in French and English. Others may qualify, under the constitution, to enroll in Vancouver's French language schools if they or their parents were educated in French prior to arrival in the province. Thus, those children who maintain their family languages and enroll in French schools or French immersion programs can use the school system to become multilingual, while living in a city where English dominates the public space (Dagenais & Berron, 2001; Dagenais & Day, 1999).

In Montreal, the situation is quite different and immigrants do not have the same opportunities to use the school system to become multilingual. In 1977, in an effort to reverse the trend of immigrant anglicization, Quebec adopted a language charter known as Bill 101, which made French schools the only option available to new immigrants to the province. This provoked a dramatic and rapid change in enrolment trends and, today, over 90% of the immigrant population is enrolled in French schools, as compared to only 11% in 1971 (Ministère de l'Éducation du Québec, 1997). According to the terms of Quebec's language charter and the Canadian Constitution, English language schools in Quebec are available only to students with a hereditary right to official minority schooling. Moreover,

Quebec's Education Act places restrictions on the amount of time allocated to English instruction in French schools. As intended, this eliminates the possibility of a bilingual program in French schools. These restrictions are not imposed on Quebec's English language schools, however, where bilingual and French immersion programs have flourished at the request of English-speaking parents, particularly as the need for French competence has increased in the province.

In summary, most families in Montreal cannot use the public school system as a strategy to acquire bilingualism or multilingualism. Interestingly, this does not seem to have affected the growth of bilingualism or multilingualism in the province, which statistics reveal to be higher than in any other province and steadily increasing (Marmen and Corbeil, 1999). Nevertheless, language policies play an important role in determining the value of languages and shaping language knowledge within the local linguistic markets of Montreal and Vancouver. Since Ottawa and Quebec adopted language policies aimed at improving the status of French, statistics show that knowledge of this language has increased across the country. Educational policies also determine the educational opportunities available to immigrants and impact on their efforts to build a linguistic repertoire. However, it seems that bilingualism and multilingualism are more influenced by market forces than by educational opportunities, as is evident in the case of Montreal.

The Comparative Study

This study adopts a qualitative form of educational inquiry (LeCompte *et al.*, 1993) and, specifically, a dual case study approach. We conducted semi-structured individual interviews in Montreal and Vancouver with 22 youths who also provided information on their backgrounds through a closed questionnaire.

Interviews explored students' daily language practices in and out of school, their representations of multilingualism and the languages in their repertoire. To gain insight into their identity construction, which we view as complex and multidimensional (Leung, Harris & Rampton, 1997), some interview questions explored their representations of self as multilingual. Each audiotaped interview took place on school grounds and lasted from 60 to 90 minutes. The background information questionnaire took about 20 minutes to administer individually prior to the interview. The qualitative data analysis program NUD*IST was used for storage, coding and analysis procedures.

The following initial questions guided the research:

(1) What are the language practices of multilingual youth of immigrant families living in Montreal and Vancouver?
   (a) How did they acquire the languages in their repertoire?
   (b) How do they use these languages in everyday situations?
(2) How do students perceive language as capital and how do they describe their languages in relation to linguistic markets?
   (a) What value do they attribute to multilingualism and to the specific languages in their repertoire?
   (b) What are the benefits/drawbacks of multilingualism for them as individuals (in their city, province, country, parents' country of origin, internationally)?
(3) How do they identify themselves?
   (a) What is their language affiliation?
   (b) How do they represent themselves as multilinguals?

In Vancouver, 12 high school students between ages 16 and 18 participated in the interviews. They were enrolled in the senior secondary grades of a Francophone program in the provincial Francophone School District of British Columbia (*Le Conseil scolaire francophone de la Colombie-Britannique*). In this program, all subjects in the curriculum are taught in French, except for English as a second language instruction, which is introduced at grade 4. Spanish as an additional language is also offered as an optional subject.

The Francophone school is housed in the building of an English school within a large urban school district in Vancouver. Both schools have a high concentration of students from diverse linguistic and ethnic backgrounds. The English stream of the school offers several other programs, including a French Immersion program. Although the Francophone program is administered separately, students and staff from both schools intermingle in the halls and in extra-curricular activities. In our visits to the school, we heard several languages spoken among students, including French, but English dominated social interactions in public spaces in and around the building.

In Montreal, the students were all between 18 and 20 years old. They were enrolled in an English language college (*Cégep*) situated in a northern suburb of Montreal[1]. A French language college is within walking distance, but there is little, if any, contact between students from the two institutions. A high proportion of first and second generation Canadians live in the neighbourhood, but it also has an important number of French speakers of French Canadian ancestry. The student population of the English college is highly multicultural and multilingual and a significant number of students are French speaking. On our visits to the college, we observed students from many different cultural and linguistic backgrounds mingling in the halls and cafeterias. English clearly dominated these interactions, but many other languages were used as well, including French.

The Vancouver and Montreal students come from a broad diversity of language origins as is evident in Table 3.1, presenting background information on the participants.

Table 3.1 Background information on the participants

Site	*Number*	*Gender*		*Languages*
		Male	*Female*	
Vancouver	12	3	9	Arabic, Persian, Turkish, Lingala, Portuguese, Spanish, Vietnamese, Cantonese, Mandarin, Cambodian, French, English
Montreal	10	6	4	Arabic, Portuguese, Spanish, Vietnamese, Cantonese, Fanti, Italian, Punjabi, Tagalog, French, English

Discussion of Emerging Themes

In the following section, we discuss four themes that emerged from our analysis of the interview transcripts. The first theme, multilingualism as a resource, refers to students' perception that their multilingual repertoire enriches them, providing them with an advantage over others. The second theme, language status, suggests that students recognize how context defines the relationship between language, power and social status. The third theme, the symbolic value of languages, underscores that languages are valued not only economically but also for their role in constructing social networks and identity. The final theme, multilingual identity, reveals the complexity of identity construction among the students in our study.

Multilingualism as a Resource

In both cities, the young people we interviewed describe language as a resource that gives them access to a greater body of knowledge and larger social circles. Several claim that knowledge of multiple languages and cultures enables them to have a better understanding of others. They state that multilingualism provides them with an advantage over unilinguals. One student even explains that she feels badly for the latter because they assume to know everything even though they understand only one language.

Excerpt 1
Il y a toujours des avantages à parler le plus de langues possibles. Les personnes que tu rencontres dans la rue, les différentes coutumes que tu peux apprendre, les différentes choses . . . même la télévision bien sûr et les voyages.

There are always advantages to speaking as many languages as possible. The people that you meet in the street, the different customs that you can learn, the different things . . . even television of course and travelling. (Vinh, Vancouver)

Excerpt 2
. . . ils pensent qu'ils savent tout, que c'est le plus important. Mais y a des choses que . . . en apprenant, en partageant d'autres langues, c'est plus facile d'apprendre l'anglais, de comprendre les autres langues quoi. Et puis eh, je pense que ça m'aide bien quoi.

. . . they think they know everything, that it's the most important. But there are things that . . . in learning, in sharing other languages, it's easier to learn English, to understand other languages what. And so ah, I think that it helps me a lot what. (Sahar, Vancouver)

Excerpt 3
Some people who, they only know French and nothing else. And I'm sad, you know. It's kind of sad because they can't . . . I think it's a great treasure, like, to have many (languages). *Je me sens mal pour les gens qui parlent juste l'anglais ou le français.*

I feel badly for people who speak only English or French. (Sandra, Montreal)

Thus, in keeping with Norton's (2000) research, investment in language learning is associated with an enrichment of social and cultural capital. These multilingual youth clearly believe that their investment has enabled them to acquire more resources and greater advantages than unilinguals. In Montreal, where linguistic cleavage between the English-speaking and French-speaking communities has a long history, we found that students talk about their multilingualism as a type of passport that allows them to cross traditional linguistic boundaries and move in different networks. For example, they move easily between friendship networks where different languages dominate social interactions.

Language Status and Competition

Most of the students interviewed in Montreal and Vancouver were born outside of Canada. For many, early language socialization in their country of origin took place in situations of diglossia where the language of the home was different from the language of schooling. On arriving in Canada, they already had a complex linguistic repertoire, a heightened sense of the different value of languages and knowledge of the relationship of language to power and social status. In both cities, interviews revealed that participants are keenly sensitive to differences in linguistic markets and aware that a language considered valuable in one market might not be of much value in another. Some students attribute the least value to their own heritage/minority language, particularly in cases where this language is not considered to be international. The interviews suggest that students judge the value of each language in their repertoire with respect to different markets.

Excerpt 4
(Languages) are all important in different situations . . . in different places . . . so I don't know if one is more important than the others. It's depending on the circumstances. French is important because I live here. If I didn't live here, I don't know if I would have learned French. But because I live here, it's important. (Sandra, Montreal)

Excerpt 5
Intervieweure: *Alors, comment te sens-tu envers . . . le cambodgien, puis le dialecte chinois . . . ?*
Tche-Reth: *Je m'en fous.*
Intervieweure: *Tu t'en fous? Mais penses-tu que ce sont des langues utiles?*

Tche-Reth: Ben non, on vit au Canada présentement. Mais si on retourne au Cambodge, ce serait utile . . . c'est juste, il y a pas vraiment beaucoup de personnes cambodgiennes au Canada.

Intervieweure: L'anglais est-il important pour toi?

Tche-Reth: Oui, très important parce que c'est la langue officielle du Canada . . . et le français aussi . . . c'est aussi la langue officielle du Canada, donc, l'anglais et le français c'est pour ça, c'est important pour moi . . . c'est juste comme ça.

Interviewer: So, how do you feel about . . . Cambodian and the Chinese dialect?

Tche-Reth: I couldn't care less.

Interviewer: You couldn't care less? But do you think they are useful languages?

Tche-Reth: Well no, we live in Canada presently. But if we were to return to Cambodia, it would be useful . . . it's just, there really aren't many Cambodian people in Canada.

Interviewer: . . . Is English important to you?

Tche-Reth: Yes, very important because it's Canada's official language, so English and French, that's why, it's important to me . . . that's how it is. (Tche-Reth, Vancouver)

The interviews also revealed that multilingual youth can deconstruct what is meant by the importance of a language. As illustrated in the following excerpt, they distinguish between the practical utility of a language and its symbolic relationship to identity:

Excerpt 6

Intervieweure: Si tu avais à mettre sur une échelle l'importance des langues, parmi les trois que tu connais, la première serait?

Raniah: La première que je mettrais?

Intervieweure: Oui, la plus importante.

Raniah: La plus importante ou la plus utile, c'est différent. . . . La plus importante pour moi c'est arabe, français, anglais. La plus utile, c'est anglais, français, arabe.

Interviewer: If you had to put languages in order of importance, of the three you know, the first would be?

Raniah: What I think would be first?

Interviewer: Yes, the most important.

Raniah: The most important or the most useful? It's different. . . . The most important for me are Arabic, French, English. The most useful, it's English, French, Arabic. (Raniah, Vancouver)

A striking finding was that all the Montreal participants consider French to be the most important language within the local context, and yet they view English–French bilingualism as the most valuable capital to acquire and as securing the most advantages. English is accorded the most importance on the international market, as are languages that are spoken in many countries, such as Spanish. Internationally, French is perceived as important, but not as important as Spanish. The importance accorded to French in Montreal, however, reflects a major shift in attitudes over the last decades and reveals to what degree efforts to change the status of French in Quebec have been successful.

Excerpt 7
To be able to work in Montreal, you have to be able to know the two languages. First, I think you need to learn French. And then to learn some English. In Montreal, it's not as important as French. (Jo, Montreal)

Competition between the French and English, situated in a national history of inter-group conflict and political polarization between speakers of these official language communities, is reflected in the participants' discourse. Interestingly, these tensions are more evident in what the youth in Vancouver had to say.

Excerpt 8
Mais les anglophones, ils ont une manière de nous exclure du groupe de l'école . . . mais je trouve qu'ils sont un peu jaloux parce que nous on a l'avantage de parler notre langue . . . donc quand ils voient de français ils commencent à dire des choses comme 'You people are weird'. . . . Mais ils blaguent, mais je me dis que si eux ils avaient l'avantage de parler le français comme nous on le parle, ils seraient contents, ils feraient 'ouais, je parle une autre langue'.

Well, anglophones, they have a way of excluding us from the group at school . . . but I think they are a bit jealous because we have the advantage of speaking our language . . . so when they see French, they start to say things like 'You people are weird'. . . . But they're joking, but I say to myself that if they had the advantage of speaking French like we do, they would be happy, they would say 'ya, I speak another language'. (Maria, Vancouver)

Perhaps this reflects the fact that the Vancouver students share their school space with an English high school and are outnumbered by English students within the building. Even though it has housed a Francophone program for years, the building is owned by the English school board and has a long history as an English high school.

Conversely, students enrolled in an English language institution in Montreal, who live in the very heart of historic linguistic tensions in Canada, have a very different attitude to the use of French within the institutional setting. Although students claim to use English all the time and insist that the school is an English place, they also agree that using French in an English college is not offensive, since English–French bilingualism is taken for granted among their age group. As one said, 'everyone can understand what you are saying'.

Recalling Bourdieu's (1982) discussion of language markets, it becomes clear that these multilinguals understand the competitive, dynamic and unequal status of different linguistic capital. Also, they can deconstruct their linguistic repertoires and accord value to specific languages within particular settings. Students are also conscious of their ability to move more easily from one field to another by drawing on different aspects of their linguistic repertoires.

Youth living in Vancouver invest in multilingualism, believing that it provides them with advantages over unilinguals. The investment of Montreal youth is less clear. Even though all the Montreal participants refer to having more than one language as advantageous and some see themselves as active agents – as having an active role – in developing their multilingualism, much like their Vancouver counterparts, others, in contrast, describe multilingualism more in terms of a consequence of immigrating to a city where two languages are required for economic mobility. They seem to view multilingualism as inevitable, as something that is imposed externally rather than strategically sought after.

For example, on the once hand, Sandra explains how her parents are committed to having their children learn Portuguese and look for every opportunity to improve their children's written and oral skills. She also emphasizes how her parents carefully planned her integration into a French language school and later enrolled her in an intensive English program offered within the same school. All through Sandra's childhood, her parents insisted that learning languages is an opportunity and that multilingualism will bring rewards throughout life. In this family, language learning is definitely treated as an investment. On the other hand, Jo, another Montrealer, seems somewhat less engaged about acquiring a multilingual repertoire. He describes growing up in Ghana, speaking one language at home and learning English at school. He explains how he arrived in Montreal at the age of 15 and 'was put' into a special French-as-a-second-language program for immigrants. He recounts that he was then 'moved' into a regular program in a French language school. At the college level, when he was finally able to exercise his own choice about schooling, he decided on an English language institution. While this enables him to perform well academically, he recognizes that he must improve his French if he wants to stay in Quebec. He also knows that he has to improve his English, which he perceives as the dominant language worldwide. Jo reports no discussion at home about the value of multilingualism and does not appear to have been proactive in acquiring his multilingual repertoire.

The Symbolic Value of Languages

Though all the multilinguals in our research attribute important economic value to English in local, national and international markets, some, like Sahar from Vancouver, indicate that they do not necessarily feel a close attachment to this language and express stronger affiliation with their family language, regardless of its status and economic value.

Excerpt 9
. . . Ma famille parle en persan quoi et je parle en persan. Et puis si j'irai visiter en Iran, il faut que je parle le persan. Et même si ça serait pas utile, c'est nécessaire pour moi, même si pas pour la vie, mais pour moi-même, pour me sentir bien parce que c'est ma langue. . . . Euh, l'anglais c'est plus ou moins la dernière langue que j'ai appris et c'est juste là quoi. Ça va pas se perdre, c'est partout dans le monde où on le parle. . . . Alors, bon il faut que je le parle pour pouvoir communiquer un jour partout . . . mais c'est pas important pour moi.

My family speaks in Persian like and I speak in Persian. And if I were to go visit Iran, I have to speak Persian. And even if it weren't useful, it's necessary for me, even if not for life, but for myself, to feel good because it's my language. . . . Ah, English, it's more or less the last language I learned and it's just there like. It won't get lost, it's spoken everywhere in the world. . . . So, well I have to speak it to be able to communicate one day everywhere . . . but it's not important to me. (Sahar, Vancouver)

Excerpt 10
Ca sert à communiquer avec la famille, et c'est ça, la langue je trouve que c'est un outil très important pour pouvoir comprendre une culture et pouvoir faire des alliances avec, de où tu viens, des choses comme ça.

It serves to communicate with the family and that's it, language I think is a very important tool to be able to understand a culture and be able to make alliances with, where you come from, things like that. (Sohila, Vancouver)

Excerpt 11
Dans l'avenir, je pense que le français, l'anglais, je vais les prendre pour mon travail, parce que je vais . . . travailler avec des gens, des patients, avec des clients peut-être si jamais je suis pas médecin, docteur ou infirmière. Et lingala je pense que je vais juste l'utiliser avec ma famille, mes parents.

In the future, I think that English, French, I will take them for work, because I will . . . work with people, patients, with clients maybe if ever I become a doctor or nurse. And Lingala I think that I will just use it with my family, my parents. (Aminata, Vancouver)

These multilinguals view the family language in terms of securing ties and alliances with their language communities. They report that speaking their family language is often a requirement for acceptance by the family language community. These excerpts lend further support to the work of Deprez (1994), Woolard (1985) and others, who highlight the symbolic value people attribute to minority languages and their attachment to them, regardless of their economic value. For the multilingual youth in our research, affiliation with these languages serves to solidify group membership and orients identity construction.

Multilingual Identity

Generally speaking, the young people we interviewed express a positive representation of themselves as multilinguals.

Excerpt 12
Intervieweure: Comment te sens-tu le fait d'être multilingue, comment tu te sens?
Zita: Ah, c'est le fun.
Intervieweure: Oui, pourquoi?
Zita: Parce que je sais pas, j'ai l'impression d'être mieux instruite que certains (rires). C'est vrai, souvent je me sens un peu supérieur parce que je comprends plusieurs langues et . . . ouais. Et mes amis disent: 'Oh my God, you speak like four langages.' Je trouve ça vraiment comme . . . c'est bien.

Interviewer: How do you feel about being multilingual, how do you feel?
Zita: Ah, it's fun.
Interviewer: Yes, why?
Zita: Because I don't know, I have the impression that I am more educated than others (laughter). It's true, often I feel a little superior

because I understand many languages and . . . ya. And my friends say: 'Oh my God, you speak like four languages.' I find that really like . . . it's nice. (Zita, Montreal)

Yet, the following excerpts show how they perceive their identity as complex, even contradictory and ambiguous.

Excerpt 13
You are one person spread four ways, as opposed to one person that's concentrated in one direction. . . . I think I am like an empty space. I don't know . . . I don't call myself Italian. I don't say I'm Spanish, 'cause I'm both and I realize . . . I have some characteristics of one and of the other. And of the English culture, since I've grown up . . . and with the French people and everything. I' m just like one big clay. I'm like you see blue clay and red clay and white clay, you know. I'm just one big ball of clay. No identity to it, not yet at least. They haven't characterized us yet. Maybe put us a name or something. Well, I guess in having many different identities . . . you produce . . . you come out as one identity. (Daniel, Montreal)

Excerpt 14
I'm a multilingual person. I'm a multiculturalist. I just feel okay, I learned the languages and I know a little bit about the cultures, that's all I mean. It's not like I know only about Indian culture. I know about other people's cultures. (Meena, Montreal)

Moreover, as the discussion with one Vancouver student reveals, identity is articulated in terms of a transnational frame of reference.

Excerpt 15
J'appartiens à tout le monde. C'est sûr que je suis née au Congo et j'appartiens au Congo d'abord, mais moi-même en tant que personne, je considère que j'appartiens au monde, une citoyenne du monde.

I belong to the whole world. Sure I was born in the Congo first, but me, my self, as a person, I consider that I belong to the world, a citizen of the world. (Frock, Vancouver)

Such a transnational perspective, as Mitchell (2001) suggests, allows immigrants to look beyond citizenship in one particular country. It serves to construct a personal identity that is broader than the boundaries of nationality, ethnicity or language. The multilingual youth in our study describe their identity as multiple, like their linguistic repertoires, which can be drawn upon differently according to context. They strategically appropriate a particular identity in certain situations, thereby securing group solidarity and affiliation, according to their best interests.

For some multilingual youth, however, it appears that an identity has been attributed to them because of their physical attributes. This identity is more narrowly defined in terms of specific national, ethnic and linguistic affiliation.

Excerpt 16
Si ils me demandent mon identité c'est mélangé entre iranien et canadien, parce que quand je dis Canadien, je pense à français, anglais, parce que pour moi c'est quoi être Canadien. Et l'iranien, c'est parce que c'est où je suis née, puis c'est moi, c'est mon physique, c'est mon apparence.

If they ask me my identity it's mixed between Iranian and Canadian, because when I say Canadian, I think of French, English, because, for me, that's what Canadian is. And Iranian, it's because that's where I was born, and it's me, it's my physique, my appearance. (Sohila, Vancouver)

Excerpt 17
Tche-Reth: *Mais, chaque fois que je dis ça à quelqu'un que je suis canadien et ils me croient pas, donc, c'est, je, je dis juste que je suis cambodgien, c'est tout.*
Intervieweure: *. . . . ils te croient pas quand tu dis que tu es canadien?*
Tche-Reth: *Non, il faut leur expliquer, ah oui, mes parents sont venus ici et puis après je suis né ici.*
Intervieweure: *Les gens pensent toujours que tu es né au Cambodge?*
Tche-Reth: *Ben en Chine, j'ai l'air plus d'un chinois que d'un cambodgien.*
Intervieweure: *Comment tu te sens quand ils te disent ça?*
Tche-Reth: *Je m'en fous vraiment, c'est vraiment pas important pour moi . . . c'est juste parce que si je dis je suis cambodgien, j'ai rien à expliquer. . . . C'est beaucoup plus facile! Ça sauve beaucoup de salive!*

Tche-Reth: But, each time I say this to someone that I am Canadian and they don't believe me, so, it's, I, I just say that I am Cambodian, that's all.
Interviewer: . . . they don't believe you when you say you are Canadian?
Tche-Reth: No, I have to explain to them, oh yes, my parents came here and then after I was born here.
Interviewer: People always think you were born in Cambodia?
Tche-Reth: Well in China, I look more Chinese than Cambodian.
Interviewer: How do you feel when they say that?

Tche-Reth: I couldn't care less really, it's really not important for me . . . it's just because if I say I'm Cambodian, I don't have to explain anything. . . . It's a lot easier! I can save my breath! (Tche-Reth, Vancouver)

For these multilinguals, their identity can be experienced in contradictory ways; sometimes it serves as a marker of inclusion and at others it is a marker of exclusion. While they are able to move more easily than unilinguals across boundaries of language, ethnicity and nation, where they belong or who they are is not as easily defined.

Conclusions

Our goal in conducting this study was to document what learning languages means to multilinguals living in two distant Canadian cities with different educational and language policy contexts. We adopted this comparative lens in order to examine more closely how multilingual youth view their language repertoires and practices and to understand how specific linguistic markets influence language practices and the workings of habitus.

Our analysis of census data revealed that language policy can transform language practice within a particular linguistic market. Language policy can also shape the educational opportunities available to immigrant families who seek to acquire multilingualism. But the presence and absence of educational opportunities apparently count less in the final outcome than market forces, as was revealed by the high rate of multilingualism in Montreal (44%), where educational options are constrained, as compared to the low rate of multilingualism in Vancouver (4%), where there are more educational opportunities to become multilingual.

When we examined what multilingual youth had to say within these two linguistic markets, we found very similar ways of describing language as a resource, convertible into economic and social capital. Furthermore, students were very aware of markets other than the dominant local one and were quite able to nuance the value of the languages within their repertoire in three respects: first, they did so at a more local level, in relation to their smaller heritage/minority language communities, extended family and friendship networks in their cities; second, they referred to their languages in relation to the dominant local language community in their province, a specific field of competition; and third, thinking globally, they attributed value to their languages within an international market and from a transnational perspective.

This suggests, as Heller (1999) has argued in her ethnographic study of bilingual/multilingual students living in Toronto, that we need to acknowledge the insight youth have into the complexity of linguistic markets. We must recognize that they attribute different values to the languages in their repertoires, values that do not necessarily correspond to those held by their families, teachers or schools. We need to better understand what multilinguals do with the languages they learn throughout their life trajectories. Moreover, we must re-examine the goals of our language programs, which so often fail to take into account the rich language resources of multilingual students, focusing instead on their need to develop proficiency in the dominant language or languages within provincial and national borders.

Not surprisingly, these multilingual youth describe their identity as complex, almost always hybrid and dynamic, allowing them to claim membership within many different networks. Most view this as an advantage in the twenty-first century. We might wonder whether this optimism will persist and ask: How will their multilingual identity serve them in their life trajectories as they move through different fields? Will it facilitate movement or will they encounter barriers in higher education and the labour force despite their multilingualism? Will their multilingual identity change and, if so, in what way? Finally, we need to carefully consider how language policies aimed at protecting language status may provide or reduce opportunities for youth to build multilingual repertoires.

Acknowledgements

This study is a collaborative project, undertaken by the authors as researchers at the Montreal and Vancouver Canadian Centres of Excellence for the Study of Immigration. The research was funded by the Social Sciences and Humanities Research Council of Canada and Immigration and Citizenship Canada. The authors acknowledge the invaluable contribution of their research assistants, Marianne Jacquet and Josefina Rossell Paredes, and express gratitude to the youths who so generously shared information about their experiences as multilinguals.

Notes

1. The educational restraints of Bill 101 do not apply to post-secondary institutions such as *Cégeps*.

References

Bourdieu, P. (1977) The economics of linguistic exchanges. _Social Science Information_ 16, 645–68.

Bourdieu, P. (1982) _Ce que parler veut dire: L'économie des échanges linguistiques_. Paris: Fayard.

Bourdieu, P. (1983) The field of cultural production, or the economic world reversed. _Poetics_ 12, 311–56.

Bourdieu, P. and Wacquant, L. (1992) _An Introduction to Reflexive Sociology_. Chicago: University of Chicago Press.

Bourhis, R. (2001) Reversing language shift in Quebec. In J.A. Fishman (ed.) _Can Threatened Languages be Saved?_ (pp. 101–41). Clevedon: Multilingual Matters.

Carrington, V. and Luke, A. (1997) Literacy and Bourdieu's sociological theory: A reframing. _Language and Education_ 11, 96–112.

Cenoz, J. and Genesee, F. (eds) (1998) _Beyond Bilingualism: Multilingualism and Multilingual Education_. Clevedon: Multilingual Matters.

Dagenais, D. (2001) Investing in language education and gaining access to imagined bilingual and multilingual communities: Perspectives of immigrant parents. Paper presented at the annual meeting of the American Association of Applied Linguistics, St Louis, Missouri, February.

Dagenais, D. and Berron, C. (2001) French immersion and family language maintenance: The multilingualism project of families of South Asian ancestry. _Language, Culture and Curriculum_ 14 (2), 142–55.

Dagenais, D. and Day, E. (1999) Home language practices of trilingual children in French Immersion. _The Canadian Modern Language Review_ 56, 99–123.

Deprez, C. (1994) _Les enfants bilingues: Langues et familles_. Paris: Didier.

Heller, M. (1999) _Linguistic Minorities and Modernity_. New York: Longman.

Heller, M. (2000) Bilingualism and identity in the post-modern world. _Estudios de sociolinguistica_ 1 (2), 9–24.

Joy, R. (1972) _Languages in Conflict: The Canadian Experience_. Toronto: McClelland and Stewart.

Joy, R. (1992) _Canada's Official Languages: The Progress of Bilingualism_. Toronto: University of Toronto Press.

Lamarre, P. and Rossell Paredes, J. (2003) Growing up trilingual in Montreal: Perceptions of college students. In R. Bayley and S. Schechter (eds) _Language Socialization in Bilingual and Multilingual Societies_ (pp. 68–80). Clevedon: Multilingual Matters.

LeCompte, M., Preissle, J. and Tesch, R. (1993) _Ethnography and Qualitative Design in Educational Research_. San Diego: Academic Press.

Leung, C., Harris, R. and Rampton, B. (1997) The idealised native speaker, reified ethnicities, and classroom realities. _TESOL Quarterly_ 31, 567–76.

Levine, M. (1990) _The Reconquest of Montreal: Language Policy and Social Change in a Bilingual City_. Philadelphia: Temple University Press.

Marmen, L. and Corbeil, J.-P. (1999) _Les langues au Canada: Recensement de 1996_. Canada: Ministère des travaux publics.

Meintel, D. (1993) Transnationalité et transethnicité chez des jeunes issues de milieux immigrés à Montréal. _Revue européenne des migrations internationales_ 9, 63–79.

Ministère de l'Education du Québec (1997) Réaffirmer l'école: Prendre le virage du succès. Rapport du Group de travail sur la reforme du cirriculum. Government du Québec: Ministère de l'Education.

Mitchell, K. (2001) Education for democratic citizenship: Transnationalism, multi-culturalism, and the limits of liberalism. *Harvard Educational Review* 71, 51–78.

Norton, B. (2000) *Identity and Language Learning: Gender, Ethnicity and Social Change.* Harlow: Longman.

Schieffelin, B. and Ochs, E. (l986) Language socialization. *Annual Review of Anthropology* 15, 163–91.

Woolard, K. (1985) *Double Talk: Bilingualism and the Politics of Ethnicity in Catalonia.* Stanford: Stanford University Press.

Chapter 4
Language Crossing Among Adolescents in a Multiethnic City Area in Germany

GABRIELE BIRKEN-SILVERMAN

Introduction

Since the second half of the twentieth century multiethnicity and plurilingualism have become salient features of West European cities – in Germany, above all, as a result of labor migration predominantly from Italy and Turkey. From a linguistic point of view, basically two successive phases of migrant language contact and language acquisition can be distinguished. Schematically, these yield the picture described in Table 4.1. As this table shows, the first stage of linguistic development in migrant communities leads from monolingualism to bilingualism. In addition to their native migrant tongue as L1 the speakers acquire a more or less elaborate competence in the national language of the host country as a pressure-induced L2. Depending on the ethnic and linguistic background of the migrants, though, in quite a few instances this language already constitutes an L3 (e.g. migrants with Sicilian–Italian bilectalism, or Sardinian–Italian and Kurdish–Turkish bilingualism). During the first phase it is the official language of the host country which caused, from above, the linguistic practice of the migrant community to orientate itself toward the national prestige language. Subsequently the reverse phenomenon occurs: during the second phase migrant tongues, which are not recognized as official languages of the host country and therefore rank as nonstandard varieties, spread across their ethnic boundaries and are acquired by speakers of other ethnic groups. Especially, this is the case in multiethnic urban neighborhoods and among adolescents of the second and third migrant generations, but also among their German peers. For bilingual adolescent migrants this means the acquisition of a trilingual or plurilingual repertoire, which includes their native language, the national language of the host country and (an)other migrant tongue(s). Trilingualism need not imply an elaborate competence in all the languages, but the term is used here in the sense of a minimal qualification, the ability 'to produce complete meaningful utterances in the other language' (cf. Haugen's definition of bilingualism, 1953: 7).

So far research on migrant languages in Germany has concentrated particularly on three aspects: (1) The development of a bilingual competence with respect to the untutored acquisition of the language of the host country as target language, focusing on grammatical issues (Heidelberger Forschungsprojekt 'Pidgin Deutsch', 1975; Meisel *et al.*, 1983; Kutsch & Desgranges, 1985); (2) The bilingual communication practice and impact on the language of origin (Auer, 1984; Bierbach & Birken-Silverman, forthcoming; Kallmeyer *et al.*, forthcoming); and (3) only recently, the natural acquisition of migrant tongues by members of other ethnic groups. The latter case which is the subject of this contribution involves the acquisition of a migrant tongue as a third language in addition to one's own ethnic language and to the official language of the host country, i.e. the acquisition of a second language of inferior status in the host society, of a second nonstandard variety. In the context of migrant language research and urban sociolinguistics in 1997, a study on the language of Italian migrants in Mannheim (Germany) was initiated, which is based on an ethnographic and conversation-analytic approach and which aims at the investigation of the varying linguistic practice among Italian migrants in one of the multiethnic neighborhoods of the city. The analytical focus is on a dense network of adolescents of the second and third migrant generation, on the structure of their plurilingual repertoire and use as a communicative resource, their conversational practice in different situative contexts, the development of a group-specific communicative style

Table 4.1 Bilingualism and trilingualism among migrants

	L1	*L2*	*L 3*
Phase I	migrant tongue	national language of the host country	
	migrant tongue 1 (regional variety)	migrant tongue 2 (official language)	national language of the host country
Phase II	migrant tongue	national language of the host country	other migrant tongue

and diffusion of Italian in contact with peers of different ethnic origin. The adolescents' in-group code involves the use of dialectal and standard Italian, German and also some Turkish, acquired through contacts with peers. Parallel studies have investigated the communicative practice of adolescents in the Turkish migrant community, the largest ethnic group in the same neighborhood (Kallmeyer *et al.*, forthcoming), and the diffusion of ethnolectal patterns in youth-cultural speech styles, including also the role of Turkish (Androutsopoulos, 2000).

The purpose of the following contribution is to present the results of that part of our study which is concerned with contact Italian and contact Turkish as acquired and used by adolescents of other ethnic origin in a multiethnic urban neighborhood in Mannheim. The central question concerns what knowledge adolescents possess of the L3 and what they do with it. Therefore, our holistic approach includes studying not only the acquisition of linguistic structures, but also their occurrence in natural face-to-face interaction in situated contexts in order to gain insight into the functional use and socio-symbolic value of the third language. The results can be considered as representative for a selected group of adolescents from an urban 'ghetto', characterized by social marginalization, lacking aspirations to integrate into mainstream society and showing a strong subcultural orientation toward local street culture. Thus, current tendencies of the development of a group-specific youth language style in a multiethnic neigborhood, which can spread as ethnolectal patterns and lead to wider diffusion, become evident (Androutsopoulos, 2000; Auer, 2002).

The study is based on two sets of linguistic data which combine two methodological approaches:

(1) With the aid of a questionnaire at a *Hauptschule* (the most basic type of German secondary schooling) a qualitative language survey on marginal competence of non-native speakers in migrant tongues was monitored. The goal was to elicit spontaneous utterances in Italian, or in Turkish, in order to compile a list of words or phrases.
(2) Conversational data were tape-recorded to document the actual use of the L3 in natural communication. The recordings were carried out with a closed youth group of Italian background at their 'hang-out', the local youth center.

Previous Studies

As a particularly urban language-contact phenomenon, the acquisition and use of a minority language by members of other ethnic groups have been studied in several contexts. A selective overview of contributions in this field and the language constellations involved is provided in Table 4.2. After Hewitt's (1982, 1986) and Sebba's (1993) studies of Creole in London, the use of Stylized Asian English, Creole and Panjabi in the conversation of adolescent non-native speakers has been documented for another urban area in Britain by Rampton (1995a, b). He calls the practice of transgressing ethnic boundaries *language crossing*: 'Language crossing involves code alternation by people who are not accepted members of the group associated with the second language that they are using' (1995b: 485). Furthermore, he describes this type of language variation as 'code switching into varieties that are not generally thought to belong to them'. In reality, though, this is by no means a homogeneous practice but, depending on speakers' socio-cultural orientation and individual linguistic biography, it appears under a wide range of forms, which reach from the insertion of single words or phrases to the insertion of longer stretches of speech from the ethnic minority language into a different matrix language, and it can adopt various functions (e.g. ritual insults from Panjabi such as the words for 'fart' and 'bitch'). Taking into consideration the complexity and diversity of types of language crossing, it seems that the definition has to be modified in so far as language crossing among adolescents is not necessarily the expression of ethnic positioning, but it can also mark membership in a particular youth-cultural or sub-cultural group (cf. Auer & Dirim, 2003). Therefore, the use of elements from an ethnic minority language by non-native speakers can be due to purely pragmatic reasons or it can mark a particular social style and even indicate the development of a new code which has nothing to do with membership of the corresponding ethnic group.

In France, in a multiethnic environment in the Grenoble area, Billiez (1993) has studied the so-called *parler véhiculaire interethnique*, which implies a marginal competence of Arabic acquired by native speakers of French and of other ethnic languages in the peer group. In Germany Auer and Dirim (2000; 2003; forthcoming) have documented the spreading competence of Turkish in some multiethnic districts of Hamburg, in the Netherlands Nortier (2000) has investigated street language in Utrecht with Dutch, Moroccan, Surinamese and Turkish components, while migrant language contact among adolescents in Rinkeby, Sweden has been studied by Kotsinas (1998).[1] In the context of (Swiss) German/French/Italian trilingualism among adults in the Swiss city of Basel, Franceschini (1996a, 1999, 2000, 2001) uses the term *contact Italian*. While most of these contributions do not focus on the acquisition process, but on the functional use and on the crossing practices in adolescent peer

Table 4.2 Research on language crossing and contact varieties

Source	Area	Adults	Adolescents	Languages	
				Official	Minority
Hewitt (1982, 1986)	London, GB		X	English	+ Afro-Caribbean Creole
Sebba (1993)	London, GB		X	English	+ Afro-Caribbean Creole
Rampton (1991, 1995a, b, 1996)	England		X	English	+ Creole / Stylized Asian English / Panjabi
Billiez (1993)	Grenoble, F		X	French	+ Arab
Auer and Dirim (2000; 2003; forthcoming)	Hamburg, D		X	German	+ Turkish
Nortier (2000)	Utrecht, NL		X	Dutch	+ Moroccan / Surinamese / Turkish
Franceschini (1996a, b, 1999, 2000, 2001)	Basel, CH	X		(Swiss) German	+ French + Italian
Birken-Silverman (forthcoming)	Mannheim, D	X	X	German	+ Italian / Turkish

groups, Franceschini's study pays particular attention to marginal competence as part of cognitive aspects.

With the exception of Franceschini's study, in all these cases the acquisition of minority languages by non-members is part of a particular discourse style among adolescents in a plurilingual urban environment and not directed toward the goal of perfect language proficiency. As Rampton points out, really 'there is no target language because there is no evidence that the language crossers want to learn the language properly, being a learner is an entertaining end-in-itself' (1995a: 292). Third language acquisition in these contexts can be investigated as part of cognitive, or didactic aspects, or from a socio-pragmatic, functional perspective that is at the focus of my contribution.

Natural TLA in an Urban Multiethnic Context: Adolescents in Mannheim

In Mannheim immigrants make up 20% of the total population (317,361); among these the largest ethnic groups are of Turkish and Italian origin (34% and 14% respectively of immigrants). Also, 30.9% of the Turkish population are younger than 18, while in the case of the Italian residents the figure is 21.2%. The study was conducted in two low-income and low-prestige areas of the inner city that are most densely populated by migrants: Westliche Unterstadt/Jungbusch and the adjacent district Neckarstadt-West. In this neighborhood interethnic contacts are of particular intensity, since 46% of the population are non-Germans, and among these 43.6% are of Turkish and 12.7% of Italian origin; among the adolescents non-Germans even constitute the majority (60%, for instance, at Jungbusch and also at the local secondary school where the survey part of our study was carried out). While the social and communicative network of the Italian migrants is predominantly in-group oriented, contacts with members of the co-residing Turkish community are part of their daily interactional routine, but less intensive. Likewise, for the Turkish migrants the Italian community is a significant contact group, followed by migrants from other East European countries. As Kallmeyer and Keim (1999) have pointed out in their study of the same neighborhood, Turkish, Kurdish, Italian, Albanian and Bosnian adolescents define themselves as 'Kanaken', whose main characteristics are a low degree of school education, a sense of belonging to street society, toughness, coolness and macho behavior.

The role of school as an important place of multiethnic interaction emerges from the following figures of the local secondary school

(*Hauptschule*), where our survey on Italian and Turkish language skills was carried out: 54.4% of the students are non-Germans and, among them, 18.4% are of Italian and 51.7% are of Turkish origin.

In the interviews conducted at that school 19 adolescents (8 boys, 11 girls) participated. They are all between 14 and 17 years old, mostly second generation migrants of Turkish, Italian, Spanish and Yugoslav backgrounds, who are bilingual to differing degrees in their ethnic language and in German. Naturally, those of Italian origin were excluded from the survey on Italian language skills and those of Turkish origin did not participate in the Turkish survey. As to their socio-cultural orientation, individual profiles cannot be presented here, but generally they are rooted in the sub-cultural milieu of their neighborhood and oriented toward street culture, where skills in the predominant migrant tongues, Turkish and Italian, allow them to participate in the respective activities. Relations between the members of the different ethnic groups are such that the adolescents do not only get together at school, but also at various local meeting points, especially at the youth center. Adolescents belonging to the largest ethnic groups tend to form their own 'crews' (e.g. breakdance formations, soccer teams) and to compete with each other, whereas peers of other ethnic origin are rather peripheral members.

Special Features of TLA

Third language acquisition (TLA) of Italian and Turkish as nonstandard varieties in a migration context, as discussed here, is characterized by several distinctive features, among others the nature of the acquisitional context. In our case language acquisition is not tutored but the language is acquired in natural face-to-face interaction, a kind of immersion, since the adolescents are part of a multiethnic social and communicative network which is characterized by daily interaction between youngsters of different ethnic origin at school, during leisure activities and in their neigborhood. As Franceschini has stated, 'the multilingual context, in the way it is present in most cities, constitutes an important potential learning-field' (1999: 137). This statement brings up the issue of different learning theories with their central concepts. We can distinguish between *learning* in the sense of being goal-directed and *acquisition* in the sense of spontaneous learning ('non-focused acquisition' – Franceschini, 1999), which would be the appropriate term in our context. Moreover, we can distinguish between different explanatory models concerning the context of acquisition and use: for instance the network model from social sciences, the psychological situatedness model and the community of practice model from anthropological research (Wenger, 1998a, b; Barab & Duffy, 2000). Related to Franceschini's *learning fields* (i.e. plurilingual urban areas), a notion which highlights the spatial aspect, Wenger's concept of *practice field* seems of particular interest, since it can account for the group-specific processes that are involved.

Furthermore, the acquisition of a migrant tongue by members of other ethnic groups differs from second language learning of adult migrants (e.g. German as L2). Compared to the acquisition of the official and dominant majority language we are instead concerned with a minority language without any official status, and therefore with a nonstandard variety. Its acquisition is not pressure-driven towards a linguistic target, but the acquisition process is rather incidental and involves varieties which do not foster upward social mobility in mainstream society. With respect to mutual comprehension, there is no need of acquisition, since the official language of the host country also serves as lingua franca between migrants of different origin. Therefore, the acquisition of a migrant tongue which is not one's own functions as an additional resource that can serve as a stylistic device. Among adolescents rooted in specific milieus at the margin of mainstream society it becomes part of a locally bound and group-specific discourse style, which functions as an instrument for participation in the local street society and to get acknowledgement from below.

The acquisition process also differs from the simultaneous or sequential learning of a second language in early childhood, since the source of input is not the parents, but the peers, and that mainly during a stage in life when peer group and also cross-gender relations are of increasing influence (though exposure to other ethnic languages may already have started at pre-school age). Therefore second and third migrant generation adolescents at that time already have a fully developed knowledge of spoken and written German (mostly their dominant language) and they are more or less proficient in their ethnic home language.

Classifying this type of trilingual development with respect to conditions of exposure we can assume a high degree of exposure to other ethnic languages, but mostly fragmentary acquisition and limited use of these. Figure 4.1 shows that contact with the two dominant migrant languages is characterized less by exposure to their respective standard varieties than to 'mixed' substandard varieties as they are spoken by adolescent migrants of the second and third generation: Italo-German and Turkish German (Kanak Sprak), which include features of stylistic and regional substandard (e.g. Sicilian dialect). Such deviations from the linguistic norms of the group of origin, as well as from those of the host society,

Turkish	Turkish German (Kanak Sprak)	German
Italian (dialect)	Italo-German	German

Figure 4.1 Language exposure of trilingual migrant adolescents

and the creation of a 'new code' indicate socio-symbolical dissociation from both groups and the expression of a 'new identity' of their own which emerges from interaction in youth networks.

Survey Data

The survey part of our study involved, besides the compilation of Italian and Turkish linguistic data among non-native speakers, self-reports about the context in which they had acquired their skills. As to the different acquisitional contexts of Italian, 63% reported that they had learnt it from friends, 26.3% from schoolmates, some from television and some from songs. Girls referred explicitly to boyfriends, boys predominantly to male companions, so that, in the case of the boys, Italian as part of their in-group code and, in case of the girls, cross-gender contacts seem to play an important role.

The set of linguistic data consists of 196 Italian utterances, i.e. on average 10 per speaker (minimum 4 and maximum 18 utterances), with no remarkable quantitative difference between boys and girls (10.6 vs. 10.1 utterances). The minimal oral competence in Italian is proven by the fact that the adolescents were able to identify memorized elements as Italian, selecting them from their repertoire and naming them.[2]

Grammatical Categories

The Italian corpus was analyzed according to the occurrence of grammatical categories and according to the length of the utterances. It emerges that the category of the numerals is presented from one to six, discourse markers by *però* 'but' and *possibile* 'possible'. Certain categories of function words, however, namely prepositions and the definite article, are totally missing. Comparing our data from adolescents' speech to Franceschini's word list compiled among adult speakers in Basel (1996a), as displayed in

Table 4.3, we find that in our corpus the number of verbs or verbal expressions is rather high compared to nouns (12:17), while nouns definitely outrank the verbs in Franceschini's (1996a) corpus (44:26).

It seems obvious that these differences are due to the varying contexts of acquisition and conversational functions, which depend on age group and socio-cultural orientation. In the case of the adolescents under consideration here, the acquisition of Italian does not serve purely instrumental purposes and the vocabulary does not have a mainly referential function, but is part of a local youth street culture and of a sub-cultural style which deviates from mainstream society norms. Moreover, nouns referring to human beings prevail in our data compared to the overwhelming number of objects in Franceschini's material. These findings can be accounted for by the fact that personal addresses in form of 'offenses' – expressing antagonism or also particular closeness among peers – and 'sweet-talk' are characteristic of the adolescents' verbal activities and speech style and constitute an instrument to position the other in terms of exclusion and inclusion. The number of adjectives is extremely limited compared to Franceschini's findings (4:15). In conclusion, a good deal of these differences can be explained by the different acquisitional and interactional contexts, in our case part of the particular communicative style of a plurilingual youth group in a marginalized social milieu.

Yet such an analytical procedure is of limited usefulness here because simple single word utterances are not predominant, and the phrases or sentences produced either cannot be segmented easily into their single lexico-semantic components, or they remain unanalyzed by the speakers. The large bulk of the data consists of speech act-bound adjacency pairs (i.e. relatively fixed conversational routines distributed over two conver-

Table 4.3 Grammatical categories in the Basel and the Mannheim corpus

Grammatical category	Basel (Franceschini, 1996)	Mannheim
Nouns	44 1. <concrete objects> 2. <human>	17 1. <human> 2. <concrete objects>
Verbs	26	12
Adjectives	15	4

sational turns, of which the second one is more or less prefabricated and therefore predictable) and of more than one-word phrases, i.e. formulaic speech.[3] This reflects a holistic type of language acquisition: the conversational format is preferred to the word format, short interactions are activated, and production of mini-dialogues is not uncommon. Illustrative examples are the following ones:

> – *Ti amo. Dumi biacci bella* [st.it. ti amo. Tu mi piaci bella] [I love you. I like you beautiful (girl)]

> – *wafangulo cornutto* [st.it. va fa un culo cornuto] [piss off cuckold]

Communicative Patterns

The type of language proficiency outlined above reveals a high degree of pragmatic competence in certain domains. By and large the corpus reveals five different types of communicative patterns such as greetings, apologies, thanks, love declarations, personal insults (see Table 4.4). The most striking result to emerge is that 19.4% (38) of the utterances are lexemes and lexical expressions with a strong expressive load, maledicta – a result which corresponds to the findings of Auer and Dirim (2000), Billiez (1993)[6] and Rampton (1991).[7] These are overwhelmingly personal insults, often directed towards females. With such a lexical stock of vulgar terms, it could be assumed that this type of TLA is restricted to the acquisition of a certain register, but there are also cases of adolescents acquiring a higher degree of language proficiency which have to be treated separately, though. It can be considered as part of a new speech style: 'dissing'[8] – verbal assaults according to certain rules – i.e. they can be used in a ludic and competitive function. Most of these terms fit into the category of derogatory personal addresses, which are used by the adolescents to establish hierarchical order (cf. Phoenix 1997).

Lexical Types

The Italian corpus shows 56 different lexical types including formulaic expressions. Lexical items are acquired less in order to express a referential message, such as the content words *pizza* (three occurrences), *spaghetti* (two occurrences), *lire* and *matematica*, which are borrowings in German and internationalisms. Instead they are acquired mostly as appropriate for a situation. Besides the particles *sì* 'yes' and *no* 'no', which are always named together, and the cardinal numbers from one to six and a few discourse markers, routine formulas predominate and include greetings,

Table 4.4 Communicative patterns

Utterance type	Percentage of use	Examples
Greeting formulas	6.1 (12)	*ciao* 'hi; bye'[4]
Question–answer sequences	10.7 (21)	*come stai? – bene* 'how are you? – fine' *come ti chiami* 'what's your name?' *che ore sono?* 'what time is it?'
Routine formulas/adjacency pairs	5.1 (10)	*bon appetito* 'enjoy your meal' *scusa* 'excuse me; sorry' *aspetta* 'wait' *grazie – prego* 'thanks – you 're welcome; please'
Love language	13.8 (27)	*ti amo* 'I love you' *amore* 'love' *dammi un baccio* 'give me a kiss'[5]
Swearing (maledicta)	19.4 (38)	*bastardo, cornutto* 'cuckold' *troia* 'sow' *porca* 'id.' *vafangulo* 'lick my ass'

positive politeness formulas, i.e. love declarations, and 'negative' politeness formulas, i.e. seemingly bald face-threatening acts (12 different types of insults). In addition to that we find 12 types of 'address formulas'. Based on a model on the development of a fused lect (cf. Thomason & Kaufman, 1988: 74–6), the dynamics of the acquisition process can be described as subsequent stages of growing language proficiency which correlate to the degree of contact intensity. Applied to the Italian language corpus of our study, Table 4.5 sets in relation stages of increasing language contact and stages of language acquisition with respect to lexic, pragmatic functions and grammar.

It emerges from the specific stock of Italian lexemes that the language is attached to a set of social values which the others can adopt and which they can identify with: expression of social power from below, macho performance and street power, and an instrument that gives the speaker control of the situation. Compared to Italian, Turkish is particularly associated with male power and competition.

Grammatical Structures

As to the acquisition of grammatical structures, the Italian corpus reveals the following: all the nouns are given in the singular, occasionally with the indefinite article, a generalized *uno* (corresponding to the numeral), while this form in standard Italian is subject to certain constraints (initial z-/s- + consonant). The appropriate forms are *una* (f.), *un* (m.), the latter appearing only in one unsegmented utterance. Particularly high is the number of those nouns which also can be used as adjectives. There are signs of gender differentiation (*bello* (m.), *bella* (f.) 'beautiful'), but plural forms are missing.

Among the personal pronouns the first and second person singular forms have been acquired[9] as well as the corresponding unstressed object pronouns (*mi* 'me' and *ti* 'you'). As to the verbs, there is a large number of imperatives, i.e. second person singular and first person plural, often embedded in syntagmas which enable the speaker to perform directive speech acts: e.g. *aspetta* 'wait', *veni cca* (sic.) 'come here', *bacciamo* 'let's kiss'.

Variability

Another salient feature is the variability of the items, and the fluctuation from one speaker to the other (cf. Franceschini, 1999). Not only the variation in input (such as different dialectal varieties depending on the origin of Italian native speakers) contributes to variability, but also different L1s and L2s, which influence particularly the graphic reproduction: *come* vs. *komme* 'how' (identification with German *komme* 'come'), and *da mi un bacio* vs. *daj mi uno baccio* 'give me a kiss' (the latter already the result of an analytic process, the identification of the article with the numeral).

Among the major problems to be resolved there is the classification of this variety with regard to formal and functional aspects. As to the first issue, the acquisition of these minimal skills in an out-group minority language does not result in a pidgin, since it is not pressure-driven and does not serve to facilitate communication. Since the acquisition is not goal-directed, but incidental, it cannot be called a learner variety, interim- or interlanguage either. It is rather part of an emerging ethnolect which is based on German as lingua franca and marked by several phonetic, morpho-syntactic, lexical and pragmatic peculiarities, among these a stock of prefabricated elements from migrant languages which serve as a stylistic device.

As to the functional aspects, several hypotheses have been suggested. Studies such as Auer and Dirim (2000), Hewitt (1986), Cutler (1997, 1999) support the hypothesis that crossing to an ethnic minority language can be explained by a hidden prestige function due to the socio-symbolic value which is attributed to it by the speaker. Moreover, one can assume that the adolescents' use of an ethnic language which is not their own constitutes an instrument to distinguish themselves not only from the dominant host culture, but also from their specific ethnic background, and to position themselves in a 'global' sub-cultural milieu. As Hargreaves formulates it: 'By injecting liberal doses of slang, and expressions imported from other tongues, they re-appropriate the language so as to make it perceptibly their own' (1995: 104).

Summarizing, we can say that this kind of plurilingual repertoire enables these adolescents to resolve rather undemanding communication tasks requiring some routine skills to interact with peers, to participate and to converge. What appears particularly interesting is that these minimal skills in Italian reflect the stereotypic features of the Italian: those of the Latin lover and mafioso, the tough guy, that are not unwelcome in street society. Therefore the appropriation of the other's code can also be explained as the acquisition of verbal competence in the local street society which leads to the creation of a local and group-bound street code.

Table 4.5 Stages of language contact and language acquisition

Degree of contact intensity	Transference	Consolidation	Function	Examples (no. of occurrences)
1 little ▼	lexical	content words	referential	pizza (3), spaghetti (2), lire (1), matematica (1)
2 medium ▼▼	lexical/pragmatic	particles cardinal numbers discourse markers routine formulas	discourse functional phatic expressive/emotional	sì no (9) 1–6 (39) però, possibile (2) greetings (12) personal relationship positive politeness formulas / compliments (27) insults (38)
3 strong ▼▼▼	grammatical	grammatical structures		bello (m.) (8), bella (f.) (1) 'beautiful' ti amo (1sg.pres.), mi ami (2) 'I love you', 'you love me' io 'I' du (it. tu) 'you'

Turkish Elements

As to the Turkish part of the survey, our results indicate the acquisition of a primarily male code which largely corresponds to the stock of ritual insults known as verbal duels, i.e. obscene sexual offenses and boasts as described by Tertilt (1996, 1997) and by Dundes *et al.* (1972). It seems that this genre, part of a ludic enculturation practice among Turkish males (cf. Rampton, 1995a: 19; Hieronymus, 2000: ch. 5), is acquired also by boys of other ethnic origin. Symptomatic may be the list of 23 lexical items produced by a boy of Bosnian origin who notes explicitly 'Moslem Power' as his affiliation, including e.g. *sikter lan* 'piss off man' (cf. Androutsopoulos & Keim, 2000), *otusbir* 'masturbate' and, furthermore, *çeckmeck* 'masturbate', *anana sikim'* I fuck your mother', *sikeven* 'I fuck you', *götinen sikim* 'I fuck your ass' and *orusbugoigu* 'son of a bitch'. In that respect the linguistic stock differs from Franceschini's findings among adult native speakers in the Swiss city of Basel: a limited set of Turkish routine formulas in opposition to the acquisition of an Italian 'life style vocabulary' (1996a: 99). In our context, though, the data confirm Billiez's hypothesis about the *parler véhiculaire interethnique* among adolescents: 'elles [ces injures proférées assez fréquemment au cours des interactions verbales dans le groupe de pairs] jouent beaucoup plus le rôle d'insultes rituelles que personnelles, et que, outre la fonction ludique, elles servent de preuves de "virilité" chez les garçons' (1993: 119).

Equally, Rampton's statement that a certain proficiency in the other's ethnic language is part of the adolescents' local identity seems to hold also for the youth community investigated in Mannheim: a certain proficiency in Italian and to a minor degree in Turkish. Beyond that, though, it is above all the adolescents' socio-cultural identity which thus finds its socio-symbolic expression. Therefore, the enlargement of the speech repertoire can be interpreted as part of the development of a patchwork identity, including the following prestige components that guarantee acknowledgement and success in the ghetto milieu:

(1) a cross-sex component stereotypically conveyed by Italian love language, exploited to increase the degree of expressivity;
(2) a social component necessary to control one's territory, expressed by threatening Italian expressions as they are conveyed also by mafia movies; and
(3) a masculinity component conveyed by Turkish ritual insults.

Conversational Data

Conversational data have been recorded regularly in a group of adolescents – all of them of Sicilian descent and members of a hip hop crew. The following extracts from in-group conversation will provide some evidence for the actual use of Turkish as a second ethnic language and substandard variety as part of their plurilingual communicative practice. These interactional sequences document alternation between four language varieties which characterize their group-specific communicative style: local German, mostly the matrix language, which shows features of an adolescents' ethnolect as described by Auer (2002), Sicilian dialect as marked choice, standard Italian (preferred by the girls), and fragments of Turkish. This plurilingual code characterized by switching, mixing and crossing is the socio-symbolic expression of their local and socio-cultural life world. As part of a socio-symbolically meaningful plural-voicing practice, Turkish serves to mark 'exclusion' and 'otherness', while Italo-German and particularly Sicilian express in-group solidarity, especially among the males. Therefore, the respective communicative situations do not involve an ethnically mixed group but an ethnically closed friendship network. Though switching to another migrant tongue seems to be less frequent in in-group talk than in the conversation of ethnically mixed youth groups, these extracts demonstrate not only how the youngsters exploit their Turkish language skills, but also the particular functions and the socio-symbolic value attributed to Turkish language. Compared to other studies, the decisive role of socio-cultural orientations becomes evident in so far as the members of the Italian group are oriented toward socio-cultural models such as street culture and hip hop. The members of the 'crew' are Gio (17), Flavio (17), Carmine (16), Franco (17), Sina (16), her boyfriend Pino (16) and his cousin Dani (15). A marginal member linked to the group by family and friendship ties is the student Sara (22).

In Extract 1 *otuzbiri* 'masturbate' illustrates the communicative function of Turkish as part of the male in-group code.

Extract 1 *otuzbiri* [vulg. 'masturbate']¹⁰

01	**Sara:**	Flavio dove sei?	[Flavio where are you?]
02	**Gio:**	viene qui *sofot*!	[come here immediately!]
03	**Pino:**	#LAUGHS#	
04	**Flavio:**	>*isch komm gleisch*<	[I'm coming in a minute]
05	**Sina:**	>vieni qui *sofot*<	[come here immediately]
06	**Sina:**	#LAUGHING#	

07 **Gio:**	chi sta fannu **ótuzbiri** ?	[what are you doing,
	fora intra *falu deine* *	masturbating? outside,
	dein volla Sack	inside your * your full
		purse]
08 **Flavio:**	**otuzbiriti** unu ca	[masturbate that the
	l'autri hannu |(. . .)|	others have (. . .)]
09 **Gio:**	| sì |	[yes]
10 **Sara to Gio:**	*was has=du gesagt* ?	[what did you say?]
11 **Flavio:**	*mit äh*	[with eh]
12 **Gio:**	**otuzbiri** vol diri	[otuzbiri means]
13 **Sara:**	*ach* **otuzbi**/	[ah otuzbi/]
14 **Gio:**	vol diri trentuno	[means 31]
15 **Sara:**	*jetz rede ma a scho*	[now we're already
	türkisch > isch weiß	talkingTurkish too >
	was **otuzbiri**/ *ja* |*isch*|	I know what otuzbiri/
	hab n türkischen Freund	yes, I have a Turkish
		boyfriend]
16 **Gio:**	| *gut* |	[alright]
17 **Sara:**	*also bitte<*	[so please]
18 **Gio:**	*oh > tut mir leid*	[I'm sorry]

The Turkish element *otuzbiri* (lines 7, 8, 12, 13, 15), a widespread ritual insult, corresponds to the tough code of the male group members. It is used here in a cryptic function, apparently only including the males. The one-word transfer inserted in Sicilian utterances is part of a jocular challenge, a verbal duel among boys as described by Dundes *et al.*: 'If one does not or cannot retort a phallic insult, one essentially admits that he is reduced to the female receptive role' (1972: 136). Thus Flavio becomes part of the competitive game between the males which asserts the challenger's hierarchical position.

Extract 2 *yakalarsam* ['if I catch you']

01 **Pino:**	*eh Sara wie wars denn*	[ey Sara, how was that
	eigentlisch bei dir wie lange	with you, how long did
	hats bei DIR gedauert bis	it take YOU till it was
	=s offiziell war?	official (having a
		fiancé)]
02 **Sara:**	*bei mir war=s =n TÜRKE*	[in my case it was a Turk
	* *un= kein Itaka*	and not an Itaka (deroga-
	|*aus Sizilien*|	tory German term for
		Italian) from Sicily]

03 **Gio:**	I tolli bin ata I	
04 **Gio:**	#IMITATING TURKISH, SINGS ON A TURKISH TUNE#	
05 **Sina**	=*s hat Folgen*	[there will be consequences]
06 **Gio:**	**elina ba kucidim** #IMITATING TURKISH, WHIPS SOMETHING#	
07 **Pino:**	**kucidim (. . .)**	
08	#LAUGHTER#	
09 **Gio:** ·	**prima annici** #IMITATES KISSING# #IMITATING TURKISH# **cimiha (. . .) krimi** #IMITATING TURKISH#	
10 **Pino:**	*ey der sagt* **yakalarsam**	[ey he says **yakarlasam** 'if I catch you']
11 **Y:**	(. . .)	
12 **Gio:**	=*s geht so hhö* (. . .) **zi pot kille alle alle**	[it goes like that]
13 **Franco:**	*d= sagt* **yakalarsam** *wenn isch dich fange*	[he says yakalarsam 'if I catch you']
14 **Pino:**	<< **yakalarsam** >	
15	# IN A DEEP THREATENING VOICE#	
16	#COUGHING, LAUGHTER#	
17 **Gio:**	**ciliman hale buri buri vdik** * (. . .) # IN A DEEP THREATENING VOICE# * *allora indi andai iaiai*	[then I went home]
18	#SINGING#	
19	#LAUGHTER#	
20 **Franco:**	*der Vadda wird da ma* (. . .)	[the father will (. . .) her]
21 **Sina:**	*okay des hat voll viel mit zu tun desweg=n aba wie lange hat=s* I *gedauert* I	[okay that has a lot to do with it therefore but how long did it take]
22 **Sara:**	I *ja drei Jahre* I	[yes 3 years]
23 **Pino:**	*bis du/ bist du dann*	[are you/ are you then]
24 **Franco:**	<< a < *tschou* > =*sch bin net ma=/einhalb Jahre mit der zamme*	[I've been with her not even one year and a half]

25 **Gio:**	*ou bist du mit eim Türke*	[ou, you are with a
	zamm? ja	Turk? yes]
26	#NOISE#	
27 **Dani:**	#LAUGHS#	

Extract 2 is a multilingual sequence which consists of local German, i.e. an ethnolectal variety of youth language, of an inserted Sicilian phrase (l. 17) and several Turkish and pseudo Turkish elements[11] used not only with referential function, but also for derision and parody to indicate distance. Turkish is activated after Sara, who does not belong to the 'crew', emphasizes that her boyfriend is a Turk and not an *Itaka*, a German derogatory term for 'Italian'. This means a double infraction of social rules in the group: first because group members and close friends are free of national labels – considered exceptions from their ethnic groups – and second because Sara challenges the boys with her jocular abuse. The reaction to her 'offense' is a stylized performance which ridicules the Turkish milieu and is in part based on the song (and video) *Simarik* 'bad girl' by the Turkish pop singer Tarkan (l. 10, *yakalarsam* 'if I catch you'). Therefore this example, which demonstrates quotations from a Turkish song and their re-contextualization, is not only instructive of contact-induced crossing, but also of media-induced crossing.

Similarly, in Extract 3 Turkish is used in responding to another 'offense' of Sara's – calling the boys of the breakdance crew *Italian Fisch Boys*.

Extract 3 *çak* ['gimme five']

01 **Sara:**	aspetta *dann redet jetz ers=*	[wait then Carmine talks
	mal der Carmine |Italian	first Italian Fish boys.
	Fisch Boys. *Warum Ital/*	Why Ital/(. . .)]
	(. . .) |	
02 **Gio:**	|no iddu nun parra no|	[no he won't talk no]
03	#LOUD LAUGHTER, SHOUTING#	
04 **Gio:**	Sara super Sara **çak**	
05 **Carmine:**	yeah	
06 **Sara:**	|=*s war keine Absicht*	[it wasn't on purpose
	Carmine|	Carmine]
07	# |LAUGHTER| #	
08 **Carmine:**	ma	[whatever]
09 **Sara:**	ah scusa Italian B-Boys	[ah excuse me Italian
		B-Boys]
10 **Carmine:**	*egal =s macht nix * ey isch*	[doesn't matter * ey I'm
	bin stolz auf den Namen	proud of the name > yes
	> ja isch hab/ wir ham ein	I have/ we have taken a

national=n Namen　　national name from our
genommen von　　na/ nationality]
unze Na/ Nationalität<

The name Italian Fisch boys is their self-denomination and used only by the males as part of their in-group code: for outsiders it means as *Fisch* in the local German youth variety 'coward, dummy', while it has assumed a positive meaning for the crew which Sara is not a member of, though. Reacting with *çak* 'gimme five' to the 'insult', Gio enacts the voice of a Turk and thus indicates ironically an outside alliance.

Conclusion

Language crossing among migrant adolescents as documented above involves a trilingual or plurilingual repertoire which includes German as the official standard language of the host country with different varieties (such as the local ethnolect) and one or more nonstandard languages, i.e. their native migrant tongue and another one. In the multiethnic urban neighborhood under consideration here these are Italian and Turkish, the languages of the two largest migrant communities. As our study documents, language crossing in this specific socio-cultural milieu is primarily a contact-induced and to a minor degree a media-induced phenomenon, i.e. skills in these languages have been acquired mainly through direct verbal interaction in peer groups, but they are also mediated by the ethnic pop music culture. Sharing a subcultural orientation and therefore a particular life style of their own, these adolescents acquire a verbal instrument which is the condition of participating in street society. TLA is directed toward lexical and pragmatic skills, including certain functional registers and certain communicative patterns mainly related to street culture. These conversational everyday routines are specific of interaction in street culture: hustling, verbal duels, playing the 'macho' man and fights. In the case of Italian these refer predominantly to the social functions of cross-gender contacts and power from below; in the case of Turkish the function of ritual insults stands out.

Finally the question arises as to whether we are dealing with a flexible and dynamic multilingual system or even with an emerging new language. In the youth networks under consideration here, we seem to be concerned more with a special group code implying the use of elements from different languages as a communicative strategy and less with a dynamic multilingual system, as described by Franceschini (1999) in a quite different situative context, where Italian seems to be a communicative necessity.

As the case study of the Italian youth group shows, their acquisition of Turkish is closely bound to subcultural orientation and the corresponding style which exploits the socio-symbolic value of Turkish as 'tough' street code. What is expressed here is above all the relation between symbolic inclusion and exclusion, solidarity and distance, which are enacted by plurilingual voicing. Thus, in the conversational extracts from in-group talk in the Italian youth group, German as interethnic lingua franca constitutes the dominating and preferred matrix language; and whereas Sicilian marks solidarity among the males, Turkish instead marks distance and antagonism. Not only with regard to functional aspects, but also with regard to formal aspects is this particular type of youth language of interest: on the one hand, we find that code switching and mixing between varieties of German and Italian, and on the other hand, that the inserted Turkish elements, which are mostly discourse-functional one-word transfers, constitute examples of crossing, the result of contact-induced acquisition of an ethnic nonstandard language.

As the current state of research on migration-induced third language acquisition and use in natural contexts suggests, further case studies will have to take in consideration the wide range of parameters, such as social network structure, socio-cultural orientation and gender, in order to provide deeper insights into ongoing language variation processes and into developing new 'globalized' speech styles in adolescents' peer groups.

Notes

1. In a narrower context, i.e. limited to two languages, Cutler's studies of the acquisition of Black English by white adolescents in Yorkford, New York (1997, 1999) are also of interest since they, too, deal with crossing to a nonstandard variety.
2. The few instances which were not classified correctly show interferences with Spanish: *te giero* (sp. *te chiero*) 'I love you', which the informant names in addition to the it. equivalent *ti amo*; frequently the numbers *dos, tres, sinco* (sp. *dos, tres, cinco*) 'two, three, five' instead of it. *due, tre, cinque*; and, moreover, in the case of a half-Spanish student who remarked explicitly that Italian and Spanish are very similar, *holà* 'hallo' and *cetal* (sp. *che tál*) 'how are you?'. The instance *Idiot* suggests rather the corresponding German form than the it. *idiota*, but can also be explained by elision of the final vowel which is frequent in certain Italian dialects. A particular – interesting case is *lilly putaner* (three occurrences), a hybrid form of it. *puttana* 'whore', which must have been identified with German *Lilliputaner* 'Lilliputian', i.e. an instance of folk etymology. Only one student rendered the approximately correct form *filiputtana* 'son of a whore'.

3. What was not listed – interestingly enough – is pseudo-italianisms which are widespread in colloquial German (e.g. *alles paletti* – *nul problemo*). Particularly instructive in the context of youth language and wider distribution are two forms that have been taken up by the media: *ciao bella* and *idiota*, which figured in TV commercials at the time of the survey. These examples are not only instructive with respect to the expanded use of Italian and the connections between spoken language and the media, but they reveal also stereotypic views behind the routine formulas, the cliché of Italians as Latin lovers and Mafiosi. As our studies reveal, these heterostereotypes are taken up in a playful manner by Italians of the second and third generation and they are adopted by adolescents of other ethnic origin as elements of their own patchwork lifestyle.

4. cf. Franceschini's results (55.9%).

5. Besides the category of greetings, Franceschini lists as well *come ti chiami* 'what's your name ?, *ti amo* 'I love you', *amore* 'love' and *ciao bella* ' hi baby' (1996a: 99).

6. 'Les innovations linguistiques réalisées en arabe couvrent plusieurs domaines, et en premier lieu celui des insultes, jurons, injures. [. . .] L'autre domaine parfois investi par l'arabe dialectal est celui des salutations ou formules de politesse' (1993: 119).

7. In Panjabi language-crossing (1991: 394). He mentions, among others, nouns referring to the body, bodily functions and animals. Among Rampton's data figure also it. *basta* (in our data *bastardo*) and *puttana* 'whore' mixed with creole – in our data mixed with German. In the same extract *fuddu* 'idiot' is classified as an instance of crossing from Panjabi, but cf. sic. *fuddu* 'id.'.

8. Originally an abbreviation of *disrespect(ing)*. This new type of ritual insult has lately gained currency with young people.

9. *io* 'I' and *du* 'you' instead of st. it. *tu*, possibly due to the identification with germ. *du* or due to the widespread substitution of germ. *t-* by dialectal *d-*, a feature of the Rhine-Franconian dialect area which Mannheim belongs to.

10. Transcription conventions: normal type = Italian/Sicilian; *italics* = German; **bold** = Turkish; (. . .) unintelligible; # metalinguistic comment#; > piano<; <forte>; = elision; | . . . | parallel sequences; / break-off; * pause.

11. In the context of his similar findings for Panjabi, Rampton speaks of 'ephemeral invention and nonsensical improvisation' (cf. Rampton 1995a: 167).

References

Androutsopoulos, J. (2000) From the streets to the screens and back again: On the mediated diffusion of ethnolectal patterns in contemporary German. In *LAUD Linguistic Agency*, Series A: No. 522., University of Essen. On WWW at http://www.rzuser.uni-heidelberg.de/~iandrout/iclavedraft.htm.

Androutsopoulos, J. and Keim, I. (2000) 'Hey lan, isch geb dir konkret handy': Deutsch-türkische Mischsprache und Deutsch mit ausländischem Akzent: Wie Sprechweisen der Straße durch mediale Verarbeitung populär werden. *Frankfurter Allgemeine Zeitung* 21. On WWW at http://www.rzuser.uni-heidelberg.de/~iandrout/papaers/tuerkde.html.

Auer, P. (1984) _Bilingual Conversation._ Amsterdam and Philadelphia: John Benjamins.

Auer, P. (2002) 'Türkenslang': Ein jugendsprachlicher Ethnolekt des Deutschen und seine Transformationen. On WWW at http://wwwfips.igl.uni-freiburg. de/auer/FS+Burger2.pdf.

Auer, P. and Dirim, I. (2000) Das versteckte Prestige des Türkischen: Zur Verwendung des Türkischen in gemischtethnischen Jugendlichengruppen in Hamburg. In I. Gogolin and B. Nauck (eds) _Migration, gesellschaftliche Differenzierung und Bildung: Resultate des Forschungsschwerpunktprogramms FABER_ (pp. 97–112). Opladen: Leske + Budrich.

Auer, P. and Dirim, I. (2003) Socio-cultural orientation, urban youth styles and the spontaneous acquisition of Turkish by non-Turkish adolescents in Germany. In J. Androutsopoulos and A. Georgakopoulos (eds) _Discourse Constructions of Youth Identities_ (pp. 223–46). Amsterdam: Benjamin.

Auer, P. and Dirim I. (forthcoming) Zum Gebrauch türkischer Routinen bei Hamburger Jugendlichen nicht-türkischer Herkunft. In V. Hinnenkamp and K. Meng (eds) _Sprachgrenzen überspringen: Sprachliche Hybridität und polykulturelles Selbstverständnis._ Tübingen: Stauffenberg.

Barab, S.A. and Duffy, T. (2000) From practice fields to communities of practice. In D. Jonassen and S.M. Land (eds) _Theoretical Foundations of Learning Environments_ (pp. 25–56). Mahwah, NJ: Lawrence Erlbaum Associates.

Bierbach, C. and Birken-Silverman, G. (forthcoming) Tutto misto? Combining codes: Communicative practices and members' concepts in the Italian community in Mannheim. In J. Gvozdanović, B. Cornillie, J. Lambert and P. Swiggers (eds) _Communicative Practice and Language Choice._ Berlin: Mouton de Gruyter.

Billiez, J. (1993) Le 'parler véhiculaire interethnique' de groupes d'adolescents en milieu urbain. In Agency for Cultural and Technical Cooperation (ed.) _Actes du Colloque International des langues et des villes, org. conjointement par le CERPL_ (pp. 117–26). Paris: Didier Érudition.

Birken-Silverman, G. (forthcoming) Urban language contact in the migrant community of Mannheim (Germany): Italian–Turkish networks and communicative practice. In B. Cornillie _et al._ (eds) _Linguistic Identities, Language Shift and Language Policy in Europe._ Orbis/Supplementa. Leuven and Paris: Peeters.

Cutler, C. (1997) _Yorkville Crossing: A Case Study of the Influence of Hip Hop Culture on the Speech of a White Middle Class Adolescent in New York City._ CALR Occasional Papers in Language and Urban Culture 8. London: Thames Valley University Centre for Applied Linguistic Research.

Cutler, C. (1999) Yorkville Crossing: White teens, hip hop, and African American English. _Journal of Sociolinguistics_ 3 (4), 428–42.

Dundes, A., Leech, J.W. and Ötzkök, B. (1972) The strategy of Turkish boys' verbal dueling rhymes. In J.J. Gumperz and D. Hymes (eds) _Directions in Sociolinguistics: The Ethnography of Communication_ (pp. 130–60). New York: Holt, Rinehart and Winston.

Franceschini, R. (1996a) Die Reaktivierung von latenten Kompetenzen bei Gelegenheitssprechern. _Scolia. Sciences cognitives, linguistique & intelligence artificielle. Sémantique et cognition_ 9, 85–109.

Franceschini, R. (1996b) Il parlante occasionale e processi cognitivi: Risultati di un test in situazione naturale. _Linguistica e Filologia 3. Quaderni del dipartimento di linguistica e letterature comparate_, 49–72.

Franceschini, R. (1999) Sprachadoption: Der Einfluss von Minderheitssprachen auf die Mehrheit, oder: Welche Kompetenzen der Minderheitensprachen haben Mehrheitssprecher? *Bulletin suisse de linguistique appliquée* 69 (2), 137–53.

Franceschini, R. (2000) A multilingual network on the re-activation of Italian as the third language among German speakers: Evidence from interactions. *Zeitschrift für Interkulturellen Fremdsprachenunterricht* 5(1) on WWW at http://www.ualberta.ca/~german/ejournal/frances3.htm.

Franceschini, R. (2001) I margini linguistici della città: L'italiano in una città germanofona (per una sociolinguistica urbana plurilingue (SLUP)). In G. Held, P. Kuon and R. Zaiser (eds) *Sprache und Stadt. Stadt und Literatur* (pp. 119–37). Tübingen: Stauffenburg.

Hargreaves, A.G. (1995) *Immigration, 'Race' and Ethnicity in Contemporary France.* London: Routledge.

Haugen, E. (1953) *The Norwegian Language in America: A Study in Bilingual Behavior.* Philadelphia: University of Philadelphia Press.

Heidelberger Forschungsprojekt 'Pidgin Deutsch' (1975) *Sprache und Kommunikation ausländischer Arbeiter. Analysen, Berichte, Materialien.* Kronberg: Scriptor.

Hewitt, R. (1982) White adolescent Creole users and the politics of friendship. *Journal of Multilingual and Multicultural Development* 3 (3), 217–32.

Hewitt, R. (1986) *White Talk Black Talk: Interracial Friendship and Communication Amongst Adolescents.* Cambridge: Cambridge University Press.

Hieronymus, A. (2000) Bo lan, das ist der Kral. Qualitativ-heuristische Explorationen in urbane Lebenswelten. Vielsprachige Jugendliche in Sankt Pauli und Altona. PhD thesis, University of Hamburg. On WWW at http://www.sub.uni-hamburg.de/disse/228/Diss.

Kallmeyer, W. and Keim, I. (1999) Deutsch-türkische Sprachvariation und die Herausbildung kommunikativer Stile in dominant türkischen Migrantengruppen. Unpublished manuscript. Mannheim: IDS.

Kallmeyer, W., Keim, I., Aslan, S. and Cindark, I. (forthcoming) Linguistic variation and the construction of communicative social styles in Turkish migrant youth groups in Germany. In J. Gvozdanović *et al.* (eds) *Communicative Practice and Linguistic Choice.* Berlin: Mouton de Gruyter.

Kotsinas, U.-B. (1998) Language contact in Rinkeby, an immigrant suburb. In J. Androutsopoulos and A. Scholz (eds) *Jugendsprache – Langue des jeunes – Youth language. Linguistische und soziolinguistische Perspektiven* (pp. 125–48). Frankfurt: Peter Lang.

Kutsch, S. and Desgranges, I. (eds) (1985) *Zweitsprache Deutsch – ungesteuerter Erwerb: interaktionsorientierte Analysen des Projekts Gastarbeiterkommunikation.* Tübingen: Niemeyer.

Meisel, J., Clahsen, H. and Pienemann, M. (1983) *Deutsch als Zweitsprache: Der Spracherwerb ausländischer Arbeiter.* Tübingen: Narr.

Nortier, J. (2000) Influence of ethnic minority languages on adolescent speech. In A. Fenyvesi and Klara Sandor (eds) *Working Papers of the Bilingual Language Use Theme Group* (pp. 67–84). Szeged: University of Szeged.

Phoenix, A. (1997) Youth and Gender: New issues, new agenda. *Young: Nordic Journal of Youth Research* 5 (3), 2–19.

Rampton, B. (1991) Interracial Panjabi among British adolescents. *Language in Society* 20, 391–422.

Rampton, B. (1995a) *Crossing: Language and Ethnicity Among Adolescents*. London: Longman.

Rampton, B. (1995b) Language crossing and the problematisation of ethnicity and socialisation. *Pragmatics* 5 (4), 485–513.

Rampton, B. (1996) Crossing: Language across ethnic boundaries. In H. Coleman and L. Cameron (eds) *Change and Language* (pp. 89–102). Clevedon: Multilingual Matters.

Sebba, M. (1993) *London Jamaican: Language Systems in Interaction*. London: Longman.

Tertilt, H. (1996) *Turkish Power Boys: Ethnographie einer Jugendbande*. Frankfurt: Suhrkamp.

Tertilt, H. (1997) Rauhe Rituale: Die Beleidigungsduelle der Turkish Power Boys. In SPoKK (ed.) *Kursbuch JugendKultur: Stile, Szenen und Identitäten vor der Jahrtausendwende* (pp. 157–67). Mannheim: Bollmann.

Thomason, S.G. and Kaufman, T. (1988) *Language Contact, Creolization and Genetic Linguistics*. Berkeley: University of California Press.

Wenger, E. (1998a) Communities of practice: Learning as a social system. In *The Systems Thinker*. Part of the Pegasus Communications Community Forum online. On WWW at http://www.co-i-l.com/coil/knowledge-garden/cop/lss.shtml.

Wenger, E. (1998b) *Communities of Practice: Learning, Meaning, and Identity*. Cambridge: Cambridge University Press.

Chapter 5
A Survey of Language Ability, Language Use and Language Attitudes of Young Aborigines in Taiwan

HUI-CHI LEE

Introduction

In Taiwan, there are two main ethnic groups, Chinese and aborigines. The majority of the population is composed of Chinese people who have migrated from mainland China since the eleventh century. The earliest inhabitants, aborigines, have become the minority in Taiwan. According to the statistical data provided by the Taiwan Department of Interior Affairs in 2001, the total population of aborigines in Taiwan is 414,000. They constitute 1.9% of the population in Taiwan. Among the Taiwanese aborigines, there are 10 main tribes nowadays. They are Amis, Atayal, Paiwan, Bunun, Puyuma, Rukai, Tsou, Yami, Saisiat and Shou. The languages of Taiwanese aborigines all belong to the Austronesian family. Being minority people, their native languages are vanishing gradually in the predominantly Chinese society.

The Language Environment of Taiwan

The language situation and language policy of Taiwan can be seen as reflecting its history. Some linguists (e.g. Tsao, 1999) divide the long history of Taiwan into three main periods: the period prior to the Japanese occupation (pre-1895), the period during Japanese occupation (1895–1945) and the post-war period (post-1945).

The Austronesian people are known to be the earliest inhabitants of Taiwan Island. The aborigines have been on Taiwan for several thousand years. In the past, they spoke more than 20 different kinds of Austronesian languages, but nowadays there are only about a dozen such languages left. The Chinese began to migrate from mainland China to Taiwan at the end of the eleventh century. Goddard (1966) believes that most immigrants at that time were Hakkas. Hakka people speak Hakka, one of the Chinese dialects. Since the fifteenth century many Chinese who came from Fujien, the closest area to Taiwan on mainland China, have migrated to Taiwan. These migrants were Southern Min speakers. Because of trade interests, Dutchmen and Spanish people once occupied some parts of Taiwan and Dutchmen even encouraged Chinese migration to the island from 1624 to 1661. In 1661, a Chinese general drove the Dutch out of Taiwan and, under his rule, the Chinese population increased. About 40,000 to 50,000 Chinese had settled on Taiwan (Hsu, 1980). Chinese immigration to Taiwan continued during the eighteenth and nineteenth centuries, and the large numbers of immigrants, including Hakkas and Southern Mins, became the main body of the population. The number of Southern Mins was much greater than that of Hakkas.

At the end of the eighteenth century, Taiwan became a Japanese colony, because the government of the Tsing dynasty ceded the territory. Kelman (1969, 1971) and Fishman (1968) indicate that developing nations often promote a national language in order to unite an ethnolinguistically diverse population. As Japan occupied a dominant position, it attempted to educate Taiwanese people to identify themselves as Japanese. During the 50 years of the colonial period (1895–1945), Japanese became the national language. Japanese was prestigious as it was the only official language, so Taiwanese people were encouraged to learn Japanese at school. Southern Min, Hakka and the Austronesian languages all remained as vernacular languages of everyday communication among their own ethnic groups.

In 1945, Chinese people from mainland China took over Taiwan from Japan after The Second World War. The languages used by these Mainlanders consisted of many varieties, including Mandarin, Wu, Hsiang, Kan, Hakka, Yueh and Min. The common language used by Mainlanders was Mandarin, which is one of the dialects of Chinese, spoken widely in northern and southwestern parts of China. However, the major language spoken by the Taiwanese at that time was Southern Min, which is another dialect of Chinese. In 1945, as soon as the Mainlanders took over the government of Taiwan, and in order to consolidate their political power and out of fear of Taiwanese independence, the central authorities implemented a language policy to promote a national language, Mandarin. Therefore, the National Language Movement was started and proceeded vigorously. Public use of Southern Min, Hakka or aboriginal languages in the armed forces, schools and government was disallowed officially and the Movement forced all the ethnic groups in Taiwan to learn Mandarin. The very first step the Movement took was to adopt a policy of 'de-Japanification': to remove Japanese influence on Taiwan (from 1945 to 1969). The next step was to depress all vernacular languages spoken in Taiwan and to support Mandarin as the only language allowed to be used in public (from 1970 to 1987). Proficiency in Mandarin became an important requirement for getting employment or entering school. Teachers and administrative staff and students were required to use Mandarin whenever communication took place in public. Most of the press was published in Mandarin, and its use became a sign that the user was educated, elegant and civilised. Other languages, such as Southern Min, Hakka and the aboriginal languages, were reduced to being used only in private speech. The aim of the Movement was to unite all the various language groups in Taiwan and create a sense of nationhood among its multicultural and multilingual peoples. As a result, Gao (1984) found in his survey that 91.7% of aborigines could communicate without difficulties in Mandarin. As a language policy, the National Language Movement was very efficient and successful (Smith, 1992). It promoted monolingualism in Mandarin and it became clear that the more highly educated people were, the more often they spoke Mandarin; and the younger they were (about under the age of 40), the better they could speak it (Research Development and Evaluation Commission, 1981). Huang (1993) indicates that, at the time of this study, 87% of the Taiwanese population were able to speak Mandarin. From 1987 on, owing to the gradually changing political environment, Taiwanese society became more open and democratic. Taiwanese people began to pay attention to their ethnic identity. The government also started to lay stress on native language education. In 1993, the legislative Congress passed a new measure to protect the uses of native languages in the media. Southern Min and Hakka are now obviously common in the mass media, but aboriginal programmes are still a long way behind. There are few TV programmes using aboriginal languages, even though many discuss (in Mandarin) how to promote the aboriginal languages and cultures.

Formosan Austronesian Languages

Ever since the study by Klaproth (1822) was published, the aboriginal languages in Taiwan have been generally recognised to be part of the Austronesian family. Several arguments have been adduced in favour of the claim that the aboriginal languages of Taiwan belong to the main branch of Proto-Austronesian, or that all the other Austronesian languages have split off from the Austronesian languages of Taiwan. However, Blust (1995) points out that the sub-relationships of these languages, both to one another and to their relatives outside Taiwan, remain controversial even today. Two fundamentally distinct views have been put forward. First, Formosan aboriginal languages are thought to be very different from all the other Austronesian languages. Haudricourt (1965) proposes a tripartite structure: (1) Western Austronesian, which includes the islands of Southeast Asia apart from Taiwan, together with Madagascar, parts of mainland Southeast Asia, Palauan and Chamorro in western Micronesia, and Yami of Botel Tobago Island (Lan Yu), (2) Northern Austronesian, which includes the Formosan languages, and (3) Eastern or Oceanic Austronesian, which includes the Austronesian languages of Melanesia and Polynesia, together with most of the languages of Micronesia (Blust, 1995). This view seems to be widely, but not universally, accepted. The second view (e.g. Tsuchida, 1976) suggests that Formosan Austronesian languages are in a sub-group together with other western Austronesian languages. Blust (1995) called the second view the 'Formosan-Philippine Hypothesis'. The Formosan Austronesian languages are believed to form a sub-group with the languages of the Philippines. These two views, the 'Primary Branch Hypothesis' and the 'Formosan-Philippine Hypothesis' still remain controversial.

Motivation and Purpose

According to Huang (1993), Southern Min speakers make up 73% of the population of Taiwan; 13% are Hakka speakers; Mainlanders account for a further 12%; and aborigines for only 2%. The Chinese majority forced aboriginal speakers to gradually abandon their native languages so as to adapt themselves to the larger 'Chinese-based' environment. This is one of the reasons why several of the aboriginal languages are dying. The successful National Language Movement caused the young aboriginal generation to adopt Mandarin and discard their own native languages. Therefore, young aboriginals today seldom use their languages or are even able to speak them. In this survey we ask how often they use their native languages; how well they manipulate them; in what situations they use them; and what attitudes they have towards them. If they have become near-native Mandarin speakers, do they really consider their aboriginal languages useless and low-class? In Taiwan, studies exploring the language ability and language use of Taiwan aboriginal people have been undertaken. On the basis of such previous research, we now concentrate on finding out more about language attitudes in order to obtain further insights into the aboriginal language situation in Taiwan.

Tsao's Study of Aboriginal People on Taiwan

Tsao (1997) used questionnaire-based methods to investigate the language ability and language use of eight aboriginal tribes in Taiwan. He found that 'age' and 'educational level' are the main factors that influence language ability and language use. The younger the respondents were, the better their Mandarin language abilities were and the less often they used their native language. Similarly, the higher their educational level, the better their Mandarin language abilities were and the more often they used Mandarin. Tsao's survey was completed in 1995 and his work comprised all age levels (under 31, 31–50, over 50). The present survey tries to use up-to-date data to find out whether there is any significant difference in the aboriginal language situation now as compared to several years ago. The data collected is focused on the younger age group (from 16 to 31). In addition to Tao's two main survey dimensions, the study adds one other, namely language attitude, so as to investigate aborigines' attitudes towards three languages: Mandarin, their own native language and Southern Min. Since Southern Min is a Chinese dialect widely spoken in Taiwan, most people in Taiwan, including aboriginal people, can speak or at least understand it. This research tries to find out whether there are significant differences in attitude towards these three languages. The reason why we introduced the factor of language attitude into our research is that attitudinal factors are known to influence language maintenance, shift and use.

Young's Study of Chinese People in Taiwan

Young's (1989) study was limited to entholinguistic Chinese in Taiwan. He excluded the aboriginal population from his study. He mentioned that all ethnolinguistic groups in his survey agreed on the importance of the maintenance of dialects, the instrumental value of Mandarin, and the personal value of both Mandarin and other Chinese dialects. He investigated three ethnic groups in Taiwan: Southern Min, Hakka people and Mainlanders. He found that many sociocultural factors did influence language use, maintenance and shift. As he put it:

> More females tended to use Mandarin than males. Older Hakka and Southern Min respondents tended to use less Mandarin than

younger respondents. More Hakkas and Southern Mins of higher socioeconomic status tended to use Mandarin than those of lower socioeconomic status. There was more of a shift toward Mandarin for those who received more formal education. Those Hakka and Southern Min who started their Mandarin education earlier tended to use Mandarin more often. Mandarin was used most frequently by those in the following occupations: police/military, civil service, and education. Southern Min was used most frequently in other occupations. People that live in urban areas indicated that they used Mandarin more than those that live in rural area. Ethnic background of neighbourhood was a large influence on usage where those who live in ethnic areas tended to use the neighbourhood language while those who live in mixed areas tended to use Mandarin. (1989: 93)

From Young's survey, we can see that Mandarin has positioned itself prestigiously. Southern Min and Hakka are both used less and less. Southern Min could be considered to be the majority language of Taiwan, as 71% of the population use it. Aboriginal speakers are a small minority – less than 2% of Taiwan's population. If Southern Min is facing a crisis of language loss, we can imagine how very much faster the aboriginal languages will be lost.

Methodology

In this survey a questionnaire design based on Chan (1994) and Han (1996) has been adopted. Tsao and Chan collaborated on a project sponsored by the National Science Council of Taiwan in 1995 and Han was one of the assistants in the project. Their aboriginal survey was a part of this project. Our survey makes reference to their research, but it is an independent piece of work. The first part of our questionnaire includes respondents' background information (sex, age, education, mother tongue, etc.) and the respondents' self-evaluation of how well they can speak their native languages. The second part of the questionnaire is about the respondents' language use. Questions in the second part are concerned with the relationship between language use and the interlocutors, locales and topics. The last part of the questionnaire deals with language attitudes. A seven-point scale was used for respondents to express their attitudes towards the languages regarding their difficulty, intimacy, value, usefulness, etc.

Respondents

Valid data from 195 respondents has been included in the survey. As we were most concerned with aspects of language relating to the young aboriginal generation, the age level of the study ranged from 16 to 31, and most of the respondents were in fact under the age of 18, as shown in Table 5.1.

The tribes of the respondents are spread throughout Taiwan Island, and they include eight tribes in all. Most of our respondents belonged to the Amis tribe, the second most numerous group to the Atayal tribe, and the third to the Paiwan tribe. The tribe distribution of the survey reflects the tribe distribution of the population in Taiwan. Details of the respondents' tribes are shown in Table 5.2.

Table 5.1 Age distribution

Age	Frequency	Percentage
16–18	143	73.3
>18	52	26.7
Total	195	100.0

Table 5.2 Tribes' distribution

Tribe	Frequency	Percentage
Amis	70	35.9
Atayal	41	21.0
Paiwan	34	17.4
Bunun	18	9.2
Rukai	7	3.6
Teluku	18	9.2
Tsou	1	0.5
Saisiat	6	3.1
Total	195	100.0

Social variables

According to Tsao's study, age is an important factor that causally relates to linguistic behaviour. Age level, therefore, is the main variable in this survey. The respondents were all under 35. They had received the usual compulsory education for nine years. In other words, they had all been taught in Mandarin for at least nine years from elementary school to junior high school. According to Tsao's analysis of this young generation, they had good Mandarin ability and they used Mandarin frequently. Our survey was intended to ascertain whether the same results could be replicated six years later.

Data analysis

The interaction between language ability, language use and language attitude was the main focus of our research.

Language ability was measured by respondents' self-evaluation on a five-point scale, with a maximum score of 5 (very fluent), score 4 (being able to communicate with others), score 3 (being able to communicate with difficulties), score 2 (being able to understand, but not able to speak) and a minimum score of 1 (having no idea at all). In this part, a t-test was applied to compare the subgroups' means to see if the differences between means were significant.

The language use data were measured by a three-point scale with a maximum score of 3 (usually used), score 2 (sometimes used) and a minimum score 1 (never used). This part was divided into three subgroups: role relationship, locale and topic. Frequencies for the language chosen when interacting with different persons, at different locales and on different topics were calculated. A t-test was applied to see if the differences between the means of native languages and Mandarin were significant.

The data on language attitude was measured by a seven-point scale with nine dimensions: (1) The maximum score 7 was given for 'difficult' and the minimum score for 'easy', (2) The maximum score was for 'rough' and the minimum score for 'smooth' and (3) The maximum score was for 'loose' and the minimum score for 'precise'. The other question pairs were (4) 'elegant–vulgar', (5) 'fast–slow', (6) 'intimate–cold', (7) 'gentle–harsh', (8) 'useful–useless' and (9) 'educated–uneducated'. Respondents were asked to answer on the scale respectively for Mandarin, the native languages and Southern Min. A t-test was used to compare the subgroup means to see if the differences between the means of three languages were significant.

Results and Findings

Language ability

The native language ability score ranged from 1 to 5 (1 = having no idea at all; 5 = very fluent). The mean score for respondents between the age of 16 and 18 was 2.83, whereas the mean score for respondents older than 18 years was 3.75 (see Table 5.3). Through the t-test we found that there was a significant difference in native language ability between different age levels ($p<0.05$). In view of these results, we concluded that younger respondents had worse native language ability.

In Taiwan, young male people at the age of 18 are required to serve in the army for a year and ten months. It is customary to think that young people become more mature and adult-like as a result of having served in the army. Perhaps after 18, the young aboriginal people tend to identify themselves with their aboriginal origin and, possibly, this self-identity helps them to learn their own native languages better.

Table 5.3 Comparisons of native language ability

	Age	*Mean*	*Std Deviation*
Native language ability	16–18	2.83	0.98
	>18	3.75	1.01

Language use

From the statistical analyses, we derived three findings: (1) There is a significant difference in language use between different role relationships ($p<0.05$), (2) there is a significant difference in language use between different locales ($p<0.05$) and (3) there is a significant difference in language use between different topics ($p<0.05$). The results showed that younger aboriginals tend to speak in Mandarin no matter with whom they talk, no matter in what location they talk and no matter what topic they talk about. The only exception (although this difference is not significant) is that, when they speak with grandfather and grandmother, the young generation tend to speak in their native languages.

From the t-test results we found that there exist significant differences with different interlocutors[1] (from pair 1–17[2]), at different locales[3] (from pair 18–26), and about different topics (pair 27–29).

From the t-test, it is easy to see that most items of language use are significantly different (*p*<0.05). The scores of Mandarin within almost all the items in the section on language use are overwhelmingly statistically higher than the scores of native languages. This means that the aboriginal young generation seldom use their native languages in many situations. In Figure 5.1 we can clearly see that, except 'with grandpa' and 'with grandma', young aboriginals use more Mandarin than native languages. This is probably because their grandparents do not understand Mandarin very well, since the National Language Movement came after their grandparents' period of schooling. Still, many of the grandparents do understand Mandarin, even if they do not speak it well. But if the young people need to communicate with their grandparents, they know it is better to try to use their native languages rather than Mandarin. Otherwise, they are likely to choose Mandarin as their first choice when communicating with someone who knows Mandarin. Also, we find that in the item 'at home' the Mandarin score is significantly higher than that of native languages. Home is supposed to be the place that makes people the most relaxed. If they use Mandarin at home, then we can imagine that they will use Mandarin in other contexts, too. Mandarin is mainly used in teaching, and it is not easy for the young aboriginal generation to use their native languages at school because most of the teachers are Chinese.

Language attitude

We looked into young aborigines' language attitudes towards the three languages: Mandarin, their native language and Southern Min. The respondents were asked to answer nine questions for every language. A seven-point scale was used to assess these three languages according to attributes such as 'difficulty', 'elegance', 'value' and 'intimacy'. The statistical results of the comparison between Mandarin and native languages are shown in Table 5.4, where it can be seen that there are six items (*) with significant differences (*p*<0.05). The six significantly different items are difficulty, smoothness, preciseness, intimacy, usefulness and educated–uneducated. The descriptive statistics show that aborigines consider Mandarin to be easier than their native languages. Moreover, Mandarin is smoother than native languages, more precise than native languages, more useful and more educated. However, native languages are more intimate than Mandarin. None of the 195 respondents chose point 6 to show that they consider their native languages the coldest. It is obvious that, even if young aborigines cannot speak or understand their native languages any more, they still consider their native languages psychologically close to them.

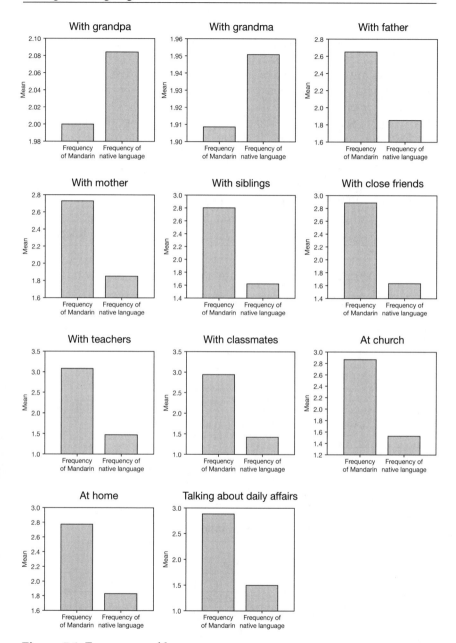

Figure 5.1 Frequency of language use
Note: right bar = native language use; left bar = Mandarin use

In addition to the comparison of Mandarin and native languages, a comparison was made between native languages and Southern Min, and the statistical results are shown in Table 5.5. There are eight significantly different items (*) in language attitudes between native languages and Southern Min. They are: smoothness, preciseness, elegance, intimacy, gentleness, usefulness and educated–uneducated. The results show that native languages are considered to be smoother than Southern Min, more precise, more elegant, more intimate, gentler, more useful and more educated than Southern Min.

Taking the statistical results on language attitudes, we combined the results of Mandarin, native language and Southern Min to show the significantly different items more clearly in Figure 5.2.

For the young aboriginal generation, Mandarin is smoother than their native language, and native languages are smoother than Southern Min.

Table 5.4 Attitude towards Mandarin and native languages

		Std deviation	*t*	*Sig.*
Pair 1	Mandarin: easy–difficult Native language: easy–difficult	2.19	–14.947	0.000*
Pair 2	Mandarin: smooth–rough Native language: smooth–rough	2.38	–12.408	0.000*
Pair 3	Mandarin: precise–loose Native language: precise–loose	1.97	–2.180	0.030*
Pair 4	Mandarin: elegant–vulgar Native language: elegant–vulgar	1.68	–1.624	0.106
Pair 5	Mandarin: fast–slow Native language: fast–slow	2.18	–1.771	0.078
Pair 6	Mandarin: intimate–cold Native language: intimate–cold	1.61	4.493	0.000*
Pair 7	Madarin: gentle–harsh Native language: gentle–harsh	1.77	0.121	0.904
Pair 8	Mandarin: useful–useless Native language: useful–useless	1.61	–3.638	0.000*
Pair 9	Mandarin: educated–uneducated Native language: educated–uneducated	1.78	–11.847	0.000*

Second, Mandarin is more precise than native languages, and native languages are more precise than Southern Min. Third, Mandarin is the gentlest and Southern Min is the harshest among the three languages. Fourth, Mandarin is the most useful, while Southern Min is the least useful and, fifth, Mandarin is the most educated, while Southern Min is the least educated. Also, we found that none of the 195 respondents chose the extreme score of 7 to show that their native language appears cold to them. This fact tells us that, although young aborigines are not able to speak their languages well, they feel a special affection for their languages.

In Taiwan, Taiwanese who speak Southern Min are the majority of the population. Therefore, Southern Min is a language widely spoken in Taiwan. Interestingly, aborigines tend to speak Southern Min for making fun of other aborigines, not for daily communication with other aborigines.

Table 5.5 Attitude towards native languages and Southern Min

		Std deviation	*t*	*Sig.*
Pair 1	Native language: easy–difficult Southern Min: easy–difficult	2.58	–2.028	0.044*
Pair 2	Native language: smooth–rough Southern Min: smooth–rough	2.50	–2.955	0.004*
Pair 3	Native language: precise–loose Southern Min: precise–loose	2.25	–6.108	0.000*
Pair 4	Native language: elegant–vulgar Southern Min: elegant–vulgar	1.86	–14.383	0.000*
Pair 5	Native language: fast–slow Southern Min: fast–slow	2.00	–0.251	0.802
Pair 6	Native language: intimate–cold Southern Min: intimate–cold	2.00	–13.394	0.000*
Pair 7	Native language: gentle–harsh Southern Min: gentle–harsh	2.07	–9.060	0.000*
Pair 8	Native language: useful–useless Southern Min: useful–useless	2.00	–4.688	0.000*
Pair 9	Native language: educated– uneducated Southern Min: educated– uneducated	1.64	–5.273	0.000*

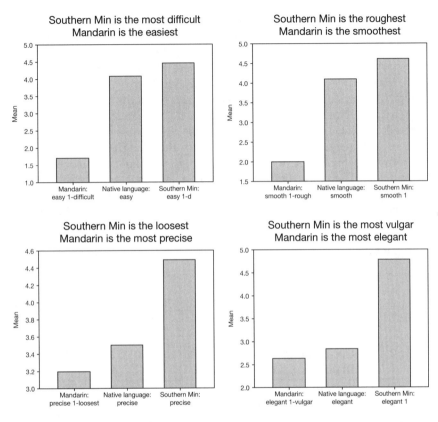

Figure 5.2 Attitudes towards Mandarin, native languages and Southern Min

Discussion and Conclusion

As regards language ability, it is regrettable that native language teaching does not appear to be effective – 73% of the respondents had native teaching for two hours a week during one year, but their native language ability did not improve very much. Native language teaching was not enough to counteract native language loss.

As for language use, our survey shows results that are different from Tsao's. His survey showed that his subjects, who were members of the young generation, used their native languages with family and close friends some eight years ago. However, nowadays young aborigines speak Mandarin most of the time. If aborigines do not speak their own lan-

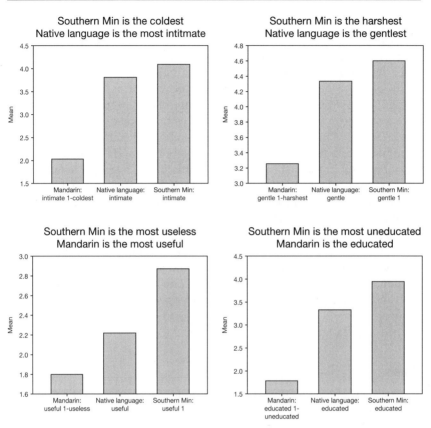

Figure 5.2 Continued

guages even at home or with close relatives, language loss is proceeding at a much faster pace than previously thought.

As far as language attitudes are concerned, respondents look up to Mandarin and they look down on Southern Min. This situation is possibly because of the National Language Movement, which required students not to speak different dialects or languages in public. Mandarin was the only acceptable language at school, and Austronesian languages and Southern Min were repressed at the time. Speaking Southern Min was considered to be 'vulgar, uneducated and low-class'. This is perhaps the reason why Mandarin is thought to be the most useful and the most educated language. Mandarin has become the new mother tongue for the young aboriginal generation in Taiwan.

In order to improve the language ability of the young aboriginal, the government devised new curricula in 1994 for the teaching of native languages and cultures in elementary and junior high school (Chen, 1998). Since then, more and more schools offer native language classes. However, many of these native language lessons are taught as one of the extra-curricular activities. Generally, students attend the language class once, or perhaps twice, a week and the lesson takes only one or two hours every week. Teachers are mostly aboriginal members of staff at the school, or aboriginal parents or priests from the neighbourhood. There are still no formal or well-organised materials available for such language teaching – teachers and related persons produce their own independent teaching materials. Until now it has not proved possible for native languages to become languages used in class or languages used daily at school. Aboriginal languages are only target languages taught in class.

In recent years, the Taiwanese government and people have been trying very hard to preserve aboriginal cultures and languages. Quite apart from the language revival achieved up to now, one positive result is that racial discrimination against aborigines has disappeared. The two main ethnic groups, Chinese and aborigines, now tend to respect one another's cultures and languages.

Notes

1. Questions of 'different interlocutors' also include 'neighbors, strangers, and people in different tribes'. These questions have all produced a significant difference to show that Mandarin is used more than native languages.
2. Among the question items of interlocutors, 'with spouse' and 'with sons and daughters' obtained few answers because most of the respondents were unmarried.
3. Questions of 'different locales' also include 'at school, at the working place, in the department store, in the market, in the governmental offices, in the private offices'. Under these circumstances, the questions all have produced a significant difference to show that Mandarin is used more than native languages.

References

Blust, R. (1995) The position of the Formosan languages: Method and theory in Austronesian comparative linguistics. *Austronesian Studies Relating to Taiwan* (*Symposium Series of the Institute of History and Philology*). Taipei: Academia Sinica.

Chan, Hui-chen (1994) Language shift in Taiwan: Social and political determinants. Unpublished PhD thesis, Georgetown University, Washington, DC.

Chen, Mei-ru (1998) *The Review and Prospect of the Policy of Linguistic Education in Taiwan*. Kaoxiong: Fuwen Book Publishing Co.

Fishman, J.A. (1968) Sociolinguistics and the language problems of the developing countries. In J. Fishman and J. Das Gupta (ed.) *Language Problems of Developing Nations* (pp. 3–16). New York: John Wiley and Son Inc.

Kelman, H.C. (1969) Patterns of personal involvement in the national system: A social-psychological analysis of political legitimacy. In J.N. Rosenau (ed.) *International Politics and Foreign Policy* (2nd edn) (pp. 276–88). New York: Free Press.

Kelman, H.C. (1971) Language as an aid and barrier to involvement in the national system. In J. Ruben and B. Jernudd (ed.) *Can Language Be Planned?* (pp. 21–51). Honolulu: East-West Center Book, University Press of Hawaii.

Gao, De-yi (1984) The investigation of the national policy on aborigines. Unpublished MA thesis, Institute of Politics, National Cheng-Zhi University.

Goddard, W.G. (1966) *Formosa: A Study in Chinese History*. London, Melbourne, Toronto: MacMillan.

Han, Shi-fen (1996) A survey of language ability and language use of the aborigines in Taiwan. Unpublished MA thesis, Institute of Linguistics, National Tsing Hua University.

Haudricourt, A.G. (1965) Problems of Austronesian comparative philology. *Lingua* 14: 315–29.

Hsu, W. (1980) From aboriginal island to Chinese frontier: The development of Taiwan before 1683. In R.G. Knapp (ed.) *China's Island Frontier: Studies in the Historical Geography of Taiwan* (pp. 3–29). Honolulu: University Press of Hawaii and Research Corporation of the University of Hawaii.

Huang, S. (1993) *Language, Society and Ethnic Identity*. Taipei: Crane Publishing Co.

Klaproth, J.H. (1822) *Sur la langue des indigenes de l'Ile de Formose*. Paris: Asia Polyglotta.

Research Development and Evaluation Commission (1981) *The Review of the Policy of National Language*. Taipei: Executive Yuan.

Smith, R. (1992) The educational role of Chinese almanacs: Past, present, and future. (ERIC Document Reproduction Service No. ED 368603).

Tsao, Feng-fu (1997) *The Comparison of Language Policy between Taiwan and Mainland China*. Taipei: Crane Publishing Co.

Tsao, Feng-fu (1999) The languages spoken by the four major ethnic groups in Taiwan: their history and present state. *Hanxuei Yenjiou (Chinese Studies)* 17 (2), 313–43.

Tsuchida, Shigeru (1976) *Reconstruction of Proto-Tsouic Phonology*. Studies of Languages and Cultures of Asia and Africa Monograph Series 5. Tokyo: Institute for the Study of Languages and Cultures of Asia and Africa.

Young, R. (1989) *Language Maintenance and Language Shifts Among the Chinese on Taiwan*. Taipei: Crane Publishing Co.

Chapter 6

Trilingual Input and Children's Language Use in Trilingual Families in Flanders

ANNICK DE HOUWER

Introduction

There are many children all over the world who grow up in a bilingual environment and who themselves actively speak two languages. At the same time, there are also many children who grow up hearing two languages in their environment but who in fact do not end up speaking those two languages themselves (although they will generally be able to comprehend two languages). While in itself this lack of active language use in bilingual settings goes undisputed, it is not always clear what might be the explanations for it (see, e.g., De Houwer, 1999).

We know even less about children growing up in a trilingual environment. Whether young children who hear three languages in their environment normally end up speaking three languages is an open question, and we know little about the reasons for children's active trilingual usage or their lack of it.

Bilingual homes or a combination of home and school environments where different languages are used are typical settings in which children become bilingual. Given this pivotal role of the home setting, I have suggested elsewhere (De Houwer, 1999) that one major cause of children's active vs. passive bilingualism may lie in the specific patterning of language use by parents in the home. The same reasoning may be applied to trilingual situations. Specific parental input patterns may, to a large extent, determine whether children who hear three languages on a regular basis actually end up speaking those three languages or not.

The study presented in this chapter aims to investigate the relationship between parental input patterns and child language use in trilingual settings. The data for this study come from a large-scale survey on the home language use of 18,046 families with young children in officially monolingual Dutch-speaking Flanders. The survey was not specifically designed for the study presented in this chapter. Rather, in the absence of language census data in Flanders, the overall aim was to explore the presence of languages other than Dutch in the lives of school-age children growing up in Flanders. This was accomplished by simply asking respondents to state which language(s) they and their family members used at home.

As it turned out, in about 2% of the families surveyed children's global language input (combining school and home) consists of three languages. Since the survey gives information on parental input patterns as well as children's language use in the home, it becomes possible to analyse what the relationship is between these two for those families in which the children hear three languages on a regular basis.

After presenting some general information on the survey, I will give a characterisation of parental and child language use in the trilingual families in the sample. In the ensuing analyses of possible relationships between parental input patterns and child language use I will, on the whole, pay more attention to the possible relationships between parental input patterns and the *lack* of active trilingual usage in the children, rather than to those between input patterns and children's active trilingualism.

Method

Setting

The data for this study were collected throughout Flanders, the officially monolingual Dutch-speaking region of Belgium. Although Brussels is the official capital of Flanders, it is not part of the Flemish region and as such was not covered in the data collection.

According to the Belgian Institute of Statistics, NIS, there were 5,898,824 individuals living in Flanders on 1 January 1997 and 288,307 of these, or 4.9% have non-Belgian citizenship. Like many other Western European countries, Belgium, including Flanders, has a recent history of attracting 'guest-workers' from other countries. Many of these workers from countries such as Italy, Greece, Morocco and Turkey decided to stay in Belgium and brought their families to join them there. Larger Flemish cities such as Ghent and Antwerp now have many neighbourhoods where people of very diverse cultural backgrounds live in close proximity. They also have much higher proportions of non-Belgian citizens than more rural areas do. Today, many young people are 'second generation' immigrants.

The fact that Flanders is officially Dutch-speaking means, among other things, that all non-private schools, colleges and universities, other educational services, health services (including speech therapy) and public administration have to use Dutch and only Dutch. Television and radio programmes broadcast out of Flanders are officially Dutch-speaking, although about half of all television programmes are imports from English-speaking countries and transmitted in English (with Dutch subtitles). Service encounters tend to take place in Dutch. On the whole, then, public life in Flanders is very much oriented towards Dutch.

[handwritten in margin: Influential!]

Data collection: The survey

Basic aim

[handwritten in margin: Background]

In Belgium (and thus also in Flanders) it has been illegal since 1947 to ask about home language use in official census questionnaires. The prohibition was a result of the Belgian 'language wars' between the Dutch- and French-speaking communities in Belgium and continues to be in place, because knowing the linguistic reality might upset the carefully constructed political balance between the separate language-defined regions (cf. De Houwer, 2003; see also Verdoodt, 1996). The lack of empirically founded information or even informed estimates on home language use in Flanders makes it impossible to verify to what extent educational or social services should take into account the possibly bilingual or even trilingual backgrounds of their clients, whether they be children or adults.

The survey undertaken in this study was designed as a very first step towards gaining some information on home language use in families with young children in Flanders, so that there would at least be some idea of the incidence of multilingualism and of the languages involved. The focus of the survey was on children in mainstream schools, where a Dutch-speaking home background is typically taken for granted and where multilingualism is not expected by teachers or the local community. This means that children attending international or European schools or schools with a large proportion of children from non-Flemish backgrounds were not part of the targeted population. The reason for excluding these schools was that there is a public acknowledgement in Flanders that children in these schools have a home language that is different from the school language (any precise statistical information is lacking, however).

Recruitment

In a series of three data collection phases spanning twelve months the principals of Dutch-medium primary schools throughout Flanders were contacted by telephone and asked whether they were prepared to cooperate with the survey. If they were, a set of questionnaire forms was sent to the principals, who then organised the distribution of the forms to each student in the school in first, second and third grade (children aged 6 to 9). The children were asked to take the questionnaire home, have their parents fill it out and return the form to the school. Schools then sent the completed questionnaires back to the investigator.

All returned and completed questionnaires thus concern families in Flanders with at least one child aged 6 to 9, and all school-age children in the sample hear Dutch at school. Most children in Flanders start going to (pre-)school at age two and a half.

The questionnaire and yield

The questionnaires consisted of a single page in Dutch. They were designed to require as little knowledge of written and spoken Dutch as possible. (See the Appendix at the end of this chapter for a copy of the original instrument and a translation into English.)

The information requested on the questionnaire concerned (1) the family's place of residence and (2) for mother, father and each child living in the same household (space for up to five children): the language(s) spoken at home, family members' ages and citizenship.

The questions about age, place of residence and citizenship were asked to allow later analyses of possible relationships between home language use and any of these variables. None of these factors will be discussed in the present chapter, which will focus exclusively on language use within the family.

It should be noted that the questionnaire gives only a picture of one particular moment in time and that the information requested does not furnish any information about previous and possibly different language use patterns or family composition.

The total number of returned questionnaires suitable for data analysis amounted to 18,046. These 18,046 questionnaires give information on the home language use, citizenship, age, family position and place of residence of 74,690 individuals living in Flanders (children and adults combined).

Analyses and Results

Trilingual families: A characterization

For the purposes of the present analysis, only the language use in the trilingual families in the sample is taken into account. An overview of language use in the entire sample can be found in De Houwer (2003).

Families are here considered to be trilingual if within the family unit at least two languages X and Y are spoken, either in addition to or instead of Dutch. So, even if within the family unit only two languages X and Y are present, the family in question is still considered trilingual. The reason for this is that at least one child in such a family will have trilingual input, namely Dutch at school and X and Y at home. All school-age children in the families counted as trilingual thus hear at least three languages in their day-to-day lives (of course, children may hear many other languages at school or from other sources, but this possibility is not considered here any further).

Under the above definition there are 308 trilingual families in the sample (1.7% of all families surveyed). These families represent a total of 1333 individuals (not counting preverbal infants under the age of one). Not all of these individuals speak a language other than Dutch at home, though: 15% of them speak only Dutch. However, only 7% of all the parents in the trilingual families are monolingual Dutch-speaking, whereas three times as many, or 22%, of all the children in trilingual families are monolingual Dutch-speaking. Thus, it is mostly the children rather than the parents in the trilingual families that do not speak a language other than Dutch at home, in spite of being exposed to trilingual input.

The actual languages other than Dutch that are spoken in the trilingual families cover a very large range. There are about 25 different languages represented in the trilingual sample, ranging from Western European languages, such as French and English, to non-Indo-European languages, such as Kiswahili, Berber and Urdu.

In the following analyses the data from 64 of the 308 families first counted as trilingual will be excluded. There are two main reasons for this. First, in 24 families counted as trilingual the parental input consisted of only one language X other than Dutch. Yet at least one child in each of these families was reported to speak two languages other than Dutch at home. If the information was filled out correctly, it is clear that the source of the third language spoken by any of the children cannot lie in parental usage at the time of completion of the questionnaire. The source of the input in a third language, if any, cannot be traced. Hence these 24 families will be discarded from further analysis.

Then there are 40 families who reportedly offer quadrilingual input. For 12 of these there is a strong suspicion that the parents indicated which languages they are skilled in, rather than which languages they actually speak at home. All families concerned have Belgian citizenship, and the languages listed besides Dutch are those that university-educated

Flemings are typically expected to know, namely French, English and German or Spanish. In none of these 12 families do the children speak anything but Dutch. In the other 28 multilingual families there are nearly as many different parental input patterns as there are families. In addition, the patterns of language use for the children vary considerably as well: the children in these 28 multilingual families either speak just Dutch, two languages, three languages or four languages at home. Because of the low numbers and the huge variability here, any further analyses of relationships between parental input patterns and children's language use seem rather pointless.

For the remaining 244 families, the global language input to the children is trilingual. Either the children receive trilingual input at home from their parents, including Dutch, or they get bilingual parental input at home, but the school provides Dutch, the third language. Families where there is trilingual input at home account for 69% of the 244 trilingual families. Those with bilingual input at home in languages X and Y that is supplemented by Dutch at school account for the remaining 31%. There are thus more than twice as many families offering trilingual input in comparison to bilingual input.

All in all there are 14 individual input patterns present in the data. A parental input pattern is a configuration of reported spoken home language use by mother and father combined (the parent pair), or by either mother or father in single parent families. The 14 patterns are all the patterns that are theoretically possible. As is to be expected on purely mathematical grounds, there are twice as many patterns for the families with trilingual input than there are for the families with bilingual input. The most frequent individual pattern is the one where both parents speak the same three languages at home, namely Dutch and two languages other than Dutch. A close second is the pattern where both parents speak two languages other than Dutch at home but no Dutch. Table 6.1 lists all the patterns that are present in the data in their order of frequency of occurrence.

The children in the 244 families exhibit five different home language use patterns: (1) Dutch and two other languages X and Y, (2) two languages X and Y but no Dutch, (3) Dutch and one other language X, (4) one language X only and (5) only Dutch (note, however, that we only know that children are reported to speak a particular language; we have no information on children's levels of proficiency). Pattern (1) is the only trilingual pattern, but children exhibiting home pattern (2) are most likely also actively trilingual, since they must use their third language, Dutch, at school. Patterns (3) and (4) both mean that children use two languages, X and Dutch, whether the latter is used at home or not. Pattern (5) means that children are at best passively bilingual, but that as far as active language use goes they are monolingual.

If we look at the children's total language use across home and school, we find that even though the children all receive trilingual input they are certainly not all actively trilingual: not even half of the 608 children in the 244 trilingual families are active trilinguals (see Figure 6.1). More than a third are actively bilingual rather than trilingual, and more than a fifth speak only one language, namely Dutch.

Only about two fifths of the children in the survey who could have been speaking three languages actually do so. Thus, trilingual input clearly is no guarantee for actually speaking three languages. However, it may matter quite a bit in what particular fashion the trilingual input is offered to children. There might well be particular parental input patterns

Table 6.1 Parental input patterns in 244 trilingual families

Parent 1	Parent 2	No. of families	Home input B or T? *
D+X+Y**	D+X+Y	38	T
X+Y	X+Y	36	B
D+X+Y	D+X	34	T
D+X	X+Y	27	T
D+X+Y	D	23	T
X+Y	X	23	B
D+X+Y	X+Y	15	T
X	Y	13	B
D+X+Y	– ***	12	T
D	X+Y	8	T
D+X	D+Y	6	T
D+X+Y	X	3	T
D+X	Y	3	T
X+Y	– ***	3	B

Notes:

* B = Bilingual input at home (no Dutch); T = Trilingual input at home (includes Dutch)

** X and Y refer to any two languages spoken at home excluding Dutch; D stands for Dutch

***single parent family

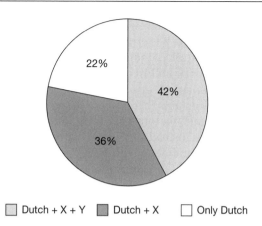

Figure 6.1 Children's global active language use under trilingual input conditions

that foster active trilingual usage, and others that do not. Given the large variation in the individual parental input patterns (see above) this is an issue that can certainly be explored on the basis of the available data.

Parental input patterns and children's language use

In order to investigate the possible relationship between parental input patterns and children's language use, the analyses in the following will be focused on the family unit rather than on individual children. The main reason for this is that parental input patterns are considered to operate on the family level. In order not to over-complicate the analyses, children's language use will be categorised as falling into either of two categories: (a) actively trilingual and (b) not actively trilingual. Actively trilingual children speak Dutch, and two languages X and Y (patterns (1) and (2) above). They represent 42% of the children studied. Not actively trilingual children speak Dutch, and may also speak one other language X. They account for 58% of the children (patterns (3), (4) and (5) in the previous subsection).

Failure or success at being actively trilingual will be decided on the basis of the 'best' behaviour of any one child in the family. Thus, for instance, a family will be considered as having actively trilingual children if at least one child in the family speaks three languages, and regardless of the language use of the other children in the family. This analytical decision does not unnecessarily boost or lower the rates of successful language transmission for a particular parental input pattern, since earlier analyses have shown that, on the whole, all children in the same family exhibit similar language use patterns (cf. De Houwer, 2001). In addition, the approach here gives all parental input patterns a similar 'chance' regardless of the number of children that parents happen to have.

Within this 'family-oriented' approach, 45% of the 244 families have actively trilingual children and 55% of them do not. The small differences between these figures and the ones for individual children above (45% instead of 42%, and 55% instead of 58%) are attributable to the fact that families have different numbers of children.

As noted before, there is a multitude of individual parental input patterns (see Table 6.1 above). Not one of them is uniquely associated with either of the two child language use patterns (i.e. active trilingual usage or not). However, the 14 individual patterns can be put into broader categories which may help to address the issue of whether and/or to what extent children's trilingual language use is correlated with parental input patterns.

A first obvious division in the input patterns is the one between families where the parental input includes Dutch (in addition to two languages X and Y) and those where it does not (see the distinction between 'trilingual' and 'bilingual' home input above). As Figure 6.2 shows, the families with actively trilingual children are about equally divided between those that have Dutch in the parental input and those that do not. However, families in which the children do *not* actively speak three languages are almost exclusively families in which the trilingual parental input includes Dutch: more than four fifths of the families where the children do *not* actively speak three languages have Dutch in the parental input.

We can also look at the data starting from the difference in parental input. Of the families in which the parental input includes Dutch 69% have children who are not actively trilingual. Only 31% of the trilingual families where at least one of the parents speaks Dutch at home have children who speak three languages. On the other hand, three quarters of the families in which the parental input does not include Dutch have children who are actively trilingual. The difference between the two types of input in relation to child active trilingual usage is statistically highly significant (Chi^2 = 39.416; p<0.001).

There is a strong correlation, then, between the presence of Dutch in the parental input (the 'Dutch factor') and children's active trilingualism or, rather, the lack of it. The presence of Dutch in the parental input is strongly associated with a lack of active trilingualism in the children, whereas the absence of Dutch in the parental input is strongly associated with child active trilingualism.

We find a small confirmation of the role of the 'Dutch factor' even in the limited subsample of the 15 single parent families that are part of the 244 trilingual families. In 12 of these 15 single parent families the single parent speaks Dutch and two languages X and Y at home. In 7 (that's just more than half) of these 12 families no child is actively trilingual. Two of the three families in which the single parent just speaks two languages X and Y at home have actively trilingual children. These data, then, follow the general trend for the Dutch factor as outlined above.

The Dutch factor can account for the child language use patterns in 71% of the 244 trilingual families. This percentage combines, on the one hand, families with Dutch parental input but no children who speak three languages and, on the other hand, families without Dutch in the parental input who do have actively trilingual children. In 29% of the families, however, parents do not have the type of children that might be expected on the basis of the Dutch factor: here either the parents who speak Dutch at home do have actively trilingual children or the parents who do not use Dutch at home do not. It is clear, then, that the Dutch factor is not the only one that can help explain the absence or presence of active trilingualism in the children.

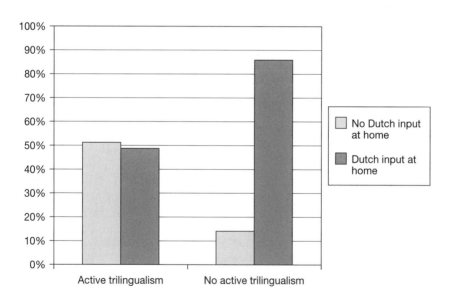

Figure 6.2 Relationship between use of Dutch in parental input and incidence of active trilingualism in children

Another parental input factor that might help explain the absence or presence of active trilingualism in the children is whether both parents in the parent pair use two languages X and Y or not. In 39% of the families with two parents the parents both speak languages X and Y, regardless of whether they use Dutch or not. In the other 61% of dual-parent families the parents do not both speak X and Y at home. There are three sub-patterns here: the main sub-pattern (108 families) is the one where one parent speaks languages X and Y and the other parent just language X. The second most frequent sub-pattern (31 families) is represented by those parent pairs in which only one parent speaks languages X and Y (the other parent speaks Dutch). In the third group of families (22 in total) one parent speaks language X and the other parent language Y. For the 15 single-parent families in the trilingual sample we can of course make no comparisons between the language use of the parents.

The number of dual parent families amounts to 229. When we look at the factor 'two languages X and Y used by both parents or not', we find a picture that is rather similar to the one for the factor 'Dutch in the parental input or not'.

As Figure 6.3 shows, the families with actively trilingual children are equally divided between those where both parents speak both languages X and Y and those where they do not. However, families in which the children do *not* actively speak three languages are mostly families in which not both parents speak both languages X and Y: in 70% of the families where the children do *not* actively speak three languages the parents differ from each other in their use of languages X and Y.

When we look at the same data in another way and consider the families in which the parents differ in their use of languages X and Y, 64% have children who are *not* actively trilingual. Only 36% of the trilingual families where parents differ from each other in their language use have children who speak three languages. Families in which both parents speak both languages X and Y have actively trilingual children in 57% of the cases. The difference between the two types of input in relation to child active trilingual usage is statistically significant (Chi^2 = 8.7718; $p<0.005$).

Again, then, we find a correlation between a characteristic of the parental input patterns and children's active trilingualism or the lack of it. In this case, the fact that parents differ from each other in the X and Y language choices they make at home is associated with a lack of active trilingualism in the children. The converse is not quite true: the fact that both parents both speak two languages X and Y at home shows no strong association with active trilingualism in the children. As indicated above, in 57% of the families in which both parents each speak languages X and

Y the children are actively bilingual. However, in the other 43% of these families the children are not. This rather small (14 points) difference does not warrant any statements regarding any strong beneficial effects of the use of the same two languages X and Y by both parents. Rather, this factor appears to be fairly neutral.

So far we have identified two separate aspects of parental input patterns that are associated with a lack of active trilingualism in the children, namely the use of Dutch by at least one of the parents, and the use of different language choices for X and Y in the parent pair. If we combine both these inhibiting factors, 93% of the cases where there is no active trilingualism in the children are accounted for (see total of boxed percentages in Table 6.2). That is, in 93% of the 135 families in which, in spite of trilingual input, the children do not speak three languages, at least one of the parents either speaks Dutch and/or the parents differ in their use of the two languages X and Y. In nine of the ten remaining families (the other 7%) without actively trilingual children the parents both speak

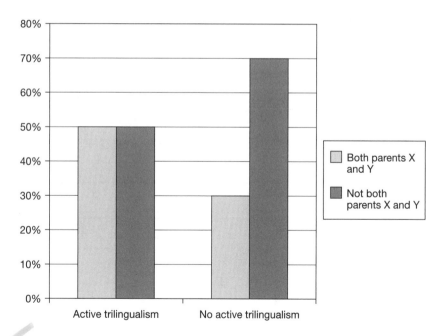

Figure 6.3 Relationship between use of X and Y in parental input and incidence of active trilingualism in children

exclusively X and Y at home. One might expect the children in these nine families to be actively trilingual, and one can only guess at the possible reasons for why they are not. In the 27 other families where the parents both speak exclusively X and Y at home the children do speak three languages (see Table 6.2).

The validity of the two factors associated with the lack of active trilingualism in children, namely the presence of Dutch in the parental input and the use of different languages X and Y in the parent pair, is further supported by the association of their counterparts with active trilingualism. Those families where Dutch is not present in the parental input and/or in which both parents use both languages X and Y account for 74% of all families with actively trilingual children (total of shaded numbers in Table 6.2).

Active child trilingualism is thus not expected when there is Dutch in the parental input and when parents do not both speak languages X and Y. Indeed, when this pattern obtains (namely D + NOT 2x (X+Y) – see top row in Table 6.2), 77% of the 104 families do *not* have actively trilingual children. For the 24 families with this input pattern that do have actively trilingual children, obviously other features must play a role.

Table 6.2 Parental input patterns and child active trilingualism in 244 trilingual families

Input pattern	No actively trilingual children (%)	Actively trilingual children (%)
D + NOT 2x (X+Y)	59	22
D + 2x (X+Y)	2	22
D + X + Y (single parent)	5	4
no D + NOT 2x (X+Y)	7	25
no D + 2x (X+Y)	6	25
no D, only X + Y (single parent)	1	2
total number of input patterns	135 (100%)	109 (100%)

Notes:
D = Dutch used by at least one parent
2x (X+Y) = both parents speak languages X and Y

For the entire group of 244 trilingual families, the parental input patterns identified above that are associated with children's active use of three languages, or the lack of it, can account for 84% of the variation in whether children speak three languages or not. For the other 16% (39 families) the type of data available through the survey cannot be used to explain either the absence or the presence of active trilingualism in the children. A first group of families consists of the 24 with actively trilingual children in spite of the fact that one of the parents speaks Dutch *and* both parents do not both speak two languages X and Y (input pattern 'D + NOT 2x (X+Y)'; see previous paragraph). A second group consists of the 9 families with no actively trilingual children, in spite of doubly favourable input conditions, namely no parent speaks Dutch at home and both parents each speak X and Y (input pattern 'no D + 2x (X+Y)' – see the fifth pattern in Table 6.2 and discussion previously). Finally, there is the third group consisting of 6 single-parent families (see discussion previously).

Discussion and Conclusion

Trilingual usage by children growing up in a trilingual environment in Flanders is not the 'default' option: in even less than half of the 244 families surveyed in which children could have grown up to speak three languages, they actually do. Since children need language models to learn from, and since their primary socialisation context typically is that of the family, it makes sense to investigate to what extent language input patterns as used by the children's parents might be correlated with children's language use (see also De Houwer, 1999). In this case, even though of course we can always only measure correlations and never observe causation, it can also be assumed that we are dealing with a potential effect situation in which parental input patterns actually have an influence on children's language use.

As shown in the analyses, there are two main conditions that do not favour the active use of three languages in children growing up in a trilingual environment: the fact that either one or the other of their parents speaks Dutch at home, and the fact that not both their parents speak the same two languages X and Y. On the other hand, when parents do not speak Dutch at home and/or both speak two languages X and Y, there is a three in four chance that they have at least one child who speaks three languages. Parental input patterns, then, certainly seem to affect child language use: the factors 'presence of Dutch' and 'usage of two languages X and Y by each parent' can explain a large proportion of the data.

Why the parental input patterns identified here should play a role in children's use of three languages or the lack of it can only be guessed at. However, parental input that includes Dutch might be an inhibiting factor because of the fact that, if parents use Dutch at home, it becomes a strong competitor for the other home languages: after all, Dutch in Flanders has the advantage of being used in the environment at large and at school. When home language choices have to be made, children have three possibilities rather than just two, and there may be no real communicative need for the use of languages X and Y, since the parents speak Dutch themselves and so allow it for home language use. Another argument could be that, given the same total amount of talk (not a realistic proposition though!), there is less home input in each of three languages (Dutch, X and Y) than there is in two languages X and Y. Thus there might be less opportunity for children to learn languages X and Y if, in addition, Dutch is spoken by the parents at home. Conversely, children who hear both their parents speak languages X and Y might have more balanced and varied opportunities to learn and use these languages than children whose parents each speak different languages. Also, as I pointed out in De Houwer (1999: 79), it might matter to children whether their parents project a similar or a dissimilar linguistic identity. Parents who both speak two languages X and Y at home (regardless of whether they use Dutch as well) project a more similar linguistic identity than parents who do not. This might be another underlying reason for the supportive nature of the 2x (X+Y) factor.

Other potentially important factors that might play a role in the establishment of active trilingual usage in children may be the relative frequencies with which the home languages are spoken. Differences here might account for the differences in failure and success rates for the very same individual parental input patterns. Another very important factor could be the interactional strategies (see Lanza, 1997) that parents use in communicating with their children.

The exclusive focus here on parental language use does not imply that children's home language input is fully dependent on parental language: children's language input at home may also come from siblings, visitors, relatives and many other people besides. The totality of this input will play a role as well, of course.

Doubtless there is a multitude of factors that can help to explain children's active trilingual usage under trilingual input conditions. It is clear that the factors identified so far do not tell the whole story. However, more than four-fifths of the variation in the survey presented in this chapter can be attributed to just two main factors, namely the use of Dutch (the environmental language) in the parental input, and the use of the non-environmental languages X and Y by both parents. More large-scale surveys and analyses of the type presented here are needed to further substantiate the results of this study. If indeed more evidence from populations in different regions confirms the results obtained in Flanders, this will be good news for parents wishing to promote active trilingualism for their children raised in a trilingual environment: while a 100% success rate cannot be guaranteed, their children will stand a very good chance of speaking three languages if parents do not use the environmental language at home but instead each use their two languages X and Y.

Acknowledgements

This research is based on data collected under direct supervision of the author by L. Cox, L. Debouck, S. De Preter, S. De Witte, M. Marti, S. Stockmans, P. van Aarle, I. Van Luchene and A. Wagemans. Financial help for the main portion of data collection was made available by the Department of Political and Social Sciences, UIA/University of Antwerp. Dr J. Van Borsel, University of Ghent, was instrumental in helping this project 'take off'. Many thanks to all, and to the many schools and individuals who invested their time and effort.

I would also like to thank Wolfgang Wölck and the editors for helpful comments on a draft version of this chapter.

Appendix: relevant part of one page questionnaire used for survey

Original version (in Dutch)

Geachte ouders,

Wij doen een onderzoek naar de taalachtergronden van jonge kinderen in Vlaanderen. Zouden wij u daarom mogen verzoeken onderstaand formulier in te vullen?

U kan dit formulier terug meegeven aan uw kind. De school zorgt er dan voor dat het terug bij ons komt.

Heel hartelijk dank!

(name of student helping in data collection)

Uw woonplaats: ....

Gezinsleden die in huis wonen:

	thuis gesproken taal/talen	_leeftijd_	_nationaliteit_
moeder			
vader			
kind 1			
kind 2			
kind 3			
kind 4			
kind 5			

English translation

Dear parents,

We are doing a study of the language backgrounds of young children in Flanders. We would greatly appreciate it if you could help us and fill out this form.

The form can go back to the school with your child. The school will then see to it that the form gets back to us.

Very many thanks!

(name of student helping in data collection)

Place of residence: ....

Family member living at home:

	language(s) spoken at home	_age_	_citizenship_
mother			
father			
child 1			
child 2			
child 3			
child 4			
child 5			

References

De Houwer, A. (1999) Environmental factors in early bilingual development: The role of parental beliefs and attitudes. In G. Extra and L. Verhoeven (eds) *Bilingualism and Migration* (pp. 75–95). Berlin: Mouton de Gruyter.

De Houwer, A. (2001) When do children speak their parents' language? A macro-level investigation of language use in bilingual families in Flanders. Paper presented at the Third International Symposium on Bilingualism, Bristol, United Kingdom, April 18–20.

De Houwer, A. (2003) Home languages spoken in officially monolingual Flanders: A survey. In K. Bochmann, P. Nelde and W. Wölck (eds) *Methodology of Conflict Linguistics* (pp. 71–87). St Augustin: Asgard Verlag.

Lanza, E. (1997) *Language Mixing in Infant Bilingualism: A Sociolinguistic Perspective.* Oxford: Clarendon Press.

Nationaal Instituut voor de Statistiek (NIS) (1997) *Bevolkingsstatistieken.* Ministerie van Economische Zaken, Koninkrijk België.

Verdoodt, A. (1996) Belgique. In H. Goebl, P. Nelde, Z. Stary and W. Wölck (eds) *Contact Linguistics: An International Handbook of Contemporary Research* (pp. 1107–23). Berlin: Walter de Gruyter.

Part 3: Language Policy and Education

Chapter 7

Creating and Implementing a Language Policy in the Israeli Educational System

ANAT STAVANS AND DORON NARKISS

Introduction

Lambert (1995) states that language policy may be motivated by one or a combination of six domains: its official status and use in different aspects of societal organizations; norms for national language; linguistic hegemony; language teaching in the formal education system; instruction and use of language in informal education; and language planning process. The present study is concerned primarily with the domain of language in formal education. Yet is it clear that through the educational community a reflection of all other five domains is evident.

Once a decision is made regarding which language will be taught by whom, for how long, and in what manner, it will also involve issues of the official status of a language, the norms of the language within a society, whether there will or will not be a language hegemony, whether languages are going to be taught equally in formal and informal education, and above all how the planning and policy making occurs.

Lambert proposes an ethnic language planning typology, which is construed from a national perspective rather than from an individual ethnic group's perspective. In this typology Lambert proposes three categories. The 'homogeneous' category constitutes a vast linguistic majority and small and marginal linguistic minorities (e.g. most of the countries in Western Europe, Latin America, the USA, Russia and Japan). The 'dyadic' category includes countries divided into two or three ethnolinguistic groups (e.g. Canada, Belgium, Yugoslavia and Singapore). The third category is that of 'mosaic' countries which contain a substantial number (five or more) of constituent ethnic minorities (e.g. Nigeria, Ethiopia and India).

Each of these types of countries addresses different domains of language policy, which in turn shape the country's typology. For example, homogeneous countries are primarily concerned with the domain of the norms of the language in the society – namely, the purification and codification of the traditional language. If these countries are large and powerful they seek to 'propagate' their language abroad, creating what Phillipson (1992) calls 'language imperialism' (see Ngũgĩ, 1986; Pennycook, 1994, 1995). To do so such countries must address seriously their entire language education planning (mostly formal and partially informal).

Dyadic countries are primarily concerned with the domain of societal organizations, namely, the use of the two or three ethnic languages in governmental and educational institutions as well as teaching of foreign languages.

Mosaic countries attend primarily to their internal linguistic diversity by giving attention mostly to the domain of language instruction. In doing so most of the educational emphasis is placed on the standardization of the languages and preparation of pedagogical materials to spread literacy.

Lambert's typology does not mention Israel as an example of any of the three types of countries. This is not accidental. Israel behaves like a homogeneous type of country in terms of the language policy, in that there is a strong hegemonic use of Hebrew in almost every aspect of life, imposed by the official social institutions. At the same time Israel declares that it has two official languages (Hebrew and Arabic), thus complying with the dyadic type of country. Lastly, Israel is first and foremost a young country containing a diverse population, many of them immigrants from around the world, making the languages of Israel an integral part of a societal heterogeneity and requiring a language policy of the type of mosaic countries. Therefore, Israel does not fall clearly into any one of Lambert's categories, but rather into all three.

This is why Israel provides a unique 'lingual-cultural laboratory'. It has two official languages, Arabic and Hebrew; a very active and strong presence of English as the language of wider communication; and a variety of ethnolanguages such as French, Spanish, German, Yiddish, Russian, Amharic, Rumanian, Hungarian etc. (Ben-Rafael, 1994; Ben-Rafael & Brosh, 1991; Shohamy & Donitsa-Schmidt, 1998).

Israel's lingual-cultural texture comprises a 20% Arabic-speaking minority and a large number of languages used by a relatively large Jewish immigrant population – roughly 600,000 Russian speakers and 50,000 Ethiopians have arrived in the last few years. Yet Hebrew is the dominant language for official, public and private use for most its 6,000,000 citizens. While the official language policy has implicitly supported the 'hegemony' of Hebrew or 'monocentricism', there has been a parallel 'existential' need for Hebrew–Arabic bilingualism among the minority Arab-speaking population. This Hebrew–Arabic bilingualism is highly skewed in favor of Hebrew, with Arabic being used as a social, educational, literary and cultural language only among Israeli Arabs. Hebrew is used for communication at places of work (except in the Arab sector) and in governmental transactions, unless the target population utilizes a minority language. In the legislative system, laws are published in Hebrew, with English and Arabic translations occasionally provided (upon request and often with delay) and the representation in court is in Hebrew unless otherwise required, in which case interpreters are used. As far as education is concerned, the main language of education is Hebrew, with the exception of the predominantly Arabic-speaking sector.

Inevitably this amalgam of languages and ethnicities creates linguistic and cultural tensions and inequalities. Such tensions are the result of the different speech communities' ideology, rooted in beliefs and attitudes, further complicated by practice and the lack of a language policy rooted in realistic planning, implementation and evaluation.

Creating and implementing an official language policy is a multifaceted enterprise (Kaplan, 1994). Such an enterprise may take any shape, from a declared legal statement to producing a document containing recommendations for further actions. The latter is the case of the Israeli policy for language in education as described by Spolsky and Shohamy (1996, 1997, 1999). Spolsky and Shohamy make a distinction between policy, ideology and practice, suggesting a relationship between the linguistic 'ideal' and 'real'; between the goals and beliefs of the producers (i.e. the policy makers), the product – the 'policy', the consumers (i.e. those for whom the policy was created and who partake in its implementation) and the market (i.e. the speech community which shares attitudes and beliefs, and which uses the languages and assigns value to various aspects of the linguistic varieties within it).

These elements and processes are, roughly speaking, applicable to all attempts to create a language policy in multilingual societies. As a result of the study reported below, we believe that improvements could be made both to the model and to its application under certain conditions, so that the following study may be of assistance in isolating the 'dos and don'ts' of a successful language policy. The planning measures in Israel over the past decade can serve as a case study, and the critique that we offer – its methods and results – will perhaps be of use not only to planners in Israel but elsewhere as well.

Schiffman challenges conventional wisdom about creating and implementing an official language policy, which he expresses by what he calls 'laws' of language policy:

(1) There is *no such thing* as no language policy. If there doesn't seem to be an explicit language policy, the policy is implicit, covert, de facto, unwritten, customary.

(2) Language policies, however explicit, are typically underspecified. That is, no matter how specific they are, they are never explicit enough to cover all contingencies.

(3) When language policies fail . . . it is typically when it comes to implementation of the policy. Language policy planners typically fail to anticipate all the ramifications of the implementation (costs, time, follow-up, cultural factors) and often act as if vaguely-worded policies will somehow take care of themselves. They thus fail to deal with unintended consequences or unanticipated developments, or factors beyond their control.

(4) Language policies have a cost, whether this be the financial costs of implementation, enforcement, verification, testing, etc., or the typically unreckoned human costs (confusion, wasted human resources, inconvenience, suffering, alienation . . .). Policies often fail to balance costs with benefits, or ignore certain costs or certain benefits.

(5) Policy planners tend to think a policy can be developed, set in stone, enshrined in law, and that the issue is solved once and for all . . . people act as if policies developed years ago will remain valid, and must be treated as if still valid (even if conditions have changed). They fail to see the evolutionary aspects of policy, and that policies typically evolve and change (or that if they fail to evolve, that they will fail). (2001)

For many years the Israeli education system had no official, structured language policy. Each language program for each age group was developed and planned independently and without a general vision as to what is or should be the language landscape of the country in general, and without specific reference to the needs of the citizens. Language policy was a haphazard affair, at best, since the end of the British Mandate over Palestine in 1948. Sources show that the attitude of the British towards Jewish immigration to Palestine during the Mandate years (1917–48) was in general very favorable, and British governments supported the cause of a 'national Jewish homeland' over Arab protests for several reasons. One of these may have been a perceived linguistic affinity, for most of the immigrants in the pre-State period were Jews of European origin, many of them English speakers (Lockard, 1997). During these years and even earlier a *Kulturkampf* over the linguistic identity of the country's Jewish population took place, ending with the total victory of Hebrew, particularly in education, over all other contenders, including English, French, German and Yiddish. These languages were henceforth subsumed within the culture, and survived with varying degrees of success. After the establishment of the State and in the wake of the Second World War, waves of immigrants arrived, many from Arabic-speaking backgrounds. The authorities in Israel at the time, composed mainly of Jews of European origin, were unwilling to accept the languages and cultural patterns of these later immigrants, seeing Islamic and Arabist culture as inferior, and so consciously adopted a 'melting pot' rationale, according to which all immigrants had to learn the official language, Hebrew, which now became the identifying national language (Shohat, 1988). As a sop to the Arab population that remained within Israel's borders after 1948, Arabic was also added as an official language, but its identification with the non-Jewish residents of the country blocked its acceptance as a wider lingua franca, even though, as mentioned, Arabic was spoken by a large proportion of Jewish immigrants as well. Since the collapse of the Soviet Union, great numbers of immigrants from its constituent republics have arrived in Israel. The demands of this highly educated group, the growth in interest in language policy research, epitomized by the establishment in 1993 of a Center for Language Planning and the need to provide a coherent formal policy on language teaching in schools that would take into account demographic and political issues, led in 1996 to the publication of a Ministry of Education Circular on language policy.

The Ministry of Education funded several studies, and several academic products emerged in the form of official reports, academic publications and books. Amongst these, Spolsky and Shohamy (1997) state that a number of fundamental changes took place in a piecemeal fashion in the policy concerning the place of languages in Israeli education. Such changes were crystallized in the first formal statement of a Policy for Language Education in Israel, in a document, a 'Circular', issued by the Ministry of Education's Director-General, dated 1 June 1995 and, in a revised form, reissued on 15 April 1996 (Ministry of Education, Culutre and Sport, 1996). The policy, with new features addressing the teaching and maintenance of various native languages as well as second and foreign language education, has been officially in effect since September 1996. This circular is available to every school principal, who in turn must make its contents known to the relevant language teachers. This document specifies the language situation in Israel as it pertains to all educational sectors in Israel (i.e. Jewish, Arab, Bedouin, religious, secular etc.), explaining, describing and defining a variety of terms, purposes, objectives, facts and vision. Despite this seeming inclusiveness, this document supports Schiffman's Law (2) – that a language policy, no matter how specific, is never explicit enough to cover all contingencies.

To the best of our knowledge, since the launch of the official language policy in 1995, there has been no follow-up study or assessment as to the implementation of the policy, and so no attempt to prove or disprove Schiffman's Law (3) regarding the failure to implement. Clearly, any document which intends to establish guidelines or serve as a blueprint for a policy is geared to a certain audience and is rooted in some authoritative knowledge that is generated by a set of attitudes, purposes and principles. Hence, such a document stands as a representation of a language policy within the educational system in the complex lingual-cultural arena of Israel, as well as a wider blueprint for other multilingual cultures. As Spolsky and Shohamy state:

> The process of making a language policy is complex. It depends first on the existence of a policy-maker or a policy-making group, a person or body empowered (or claiming the power) to issue rules that can be expected to influence the language behavior of other people. Sometimes policies have no effect because they ignore the sociolinguistic reality, or because of refusal or resistance on the part of the people who are expected to change. (1997: 39)

We claim that among other things, this document was interpreted – as illustrated graphically in Figure 7.1 – by the language education community as 'the product' whose 'producers' (linguists and sociolinguists, educators, ethnolinguists and other academics, as well as Ministry officials such as inspectors) set the guidelines for the different 'consumers' (i.e. teachers, pupils, parents, principals and teacher trainers) to prepare and lead the speech communities of Israel into the linguistic 'market' dictated by internal ideological pressures and by external geopolitical, economic and technological forces. In other words, as Schiffman's Law (4) suggests, the costs and benefits of a specific language policy always reach beyond what the policy envisions.

With this in mind, we set out to investigate to what extent the only formal Israeli document designed to make the education system aware of a language policy was implemented and how it changed the perspectives of the different parties involved. We wanted to examine to what extent this document (the product) is known, understood and implemented by some of its immediate consumers (the teachers), in order to elicit and statistically determine the response to the ideals and assumptions of the Director-General's Circular as revealed in the text of the document, and

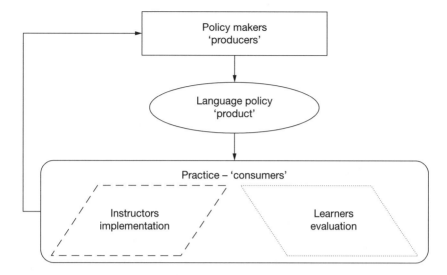

Figure 7.1 Operational plan of policy making

Source: Interpreted from Spolsky and Shohamy, 1997

to elicit views on the necessity of having a language policy, and on the shape such a policy should have in the future.

Since the document is concerned with developing language education programs for several languages in Israel and the establishment of curricula for all languages taught in schools, it is of vital concern to all Israeli citizens; but most crucial to the process of implementing the policy are the teachers. In this study we report on the results of a questionnaire distributed to language and non-language teachers of different grade levels – kindergarten (abbreviated as K hereafter), elementary school (E), middle school (M) and high school (H) in two sectors (Arab and Jewish), all of whom are subject to the directives of the Ministry of Education in Israel (including this language policy). The primary aim is to describe the perceived educational linguistic reality in terms of teachers' beliefs and attitudes towards language teaching and use, in the light of the under-lying elements encrypted in the policy in terms of principles, purpose, attitude, and practice (planning, implementation and evaluation). These elements are not independent entities but rather part of a complex as illus-trated in Figure 7.2.

Figure 7.2 provides a revised version of the process by which a language policy should be created, with its main tenet being the inver-sion of the process. That is to say, a language policy in a country like

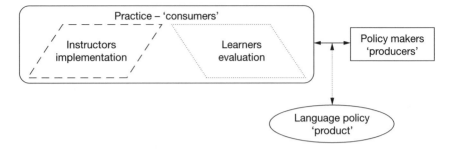

Figure 7.2 Revised operational plan of policy making

Israel, which is simultaneously homogeneous, dyadic and mosaic, and which is primarily concerned with the educational domain of the policy, should begin by a thorough analysis and consultation with the implementing parties (the teachers).

Research Question

Our main research question is: 'To what extent is the language policy as proposed by the Israeli Ministry of Education known and implemented in schools by the teachers?' Various aspects of the Director-General's Circular – the official document detailing the Ministry's language policy – were examined by means of a questionnaire distributed among many teachers. We wanted our results to be as representative as possible of the actual attitudes among teachers in Israel towards the language policy and the document that details it. We therefore set out to investigate the differences in attitude among teachers of various age groups (kindergarten, primary, middle and high school); differences between teachers of different languages (Hebrew and Arabic, the official languages, as well as of non-official languages, such as English, French and Russian) and teachers of other subjects; and, most importantly, given Israel's unique demographics, differences between teachers in the Arab sector and teachers in the Jewish sector.

Methodology

Subjects

The study sampled 244 teachers, 135 from the Jewish sector and 109 from the Arab sector. Table 7.1 illustrates the characteristics of the subjects

Table 7.1 Subjects

	Jewish	Arab
Gender (%)		
Male	13.3	54.6
Female	86.7	45.4
Age (years; months)		
X	36.9	29.3
sd	8.9	5.5
Birth place (%)		
Israel	80.6	99.1
Other	19.4	0.9
Grade level (n)		
Kindergarten	23	30
Elementary school	25	14
Middle school	46	38
High school	41	27
Proportion of subjects (%)	55.3	44.7

and the sampled groups. All subjects were practicing teachers of different age groups and taught different topics. For the middle school and high school teachers a further distinction was made – whether the teachers were of 'languages' (e.g. Hebrew, Arabic and English) or 'subjects' (sciences, humanities or social studies). This distinction is only relevant for the upper grades, as it does not exist in kindergarten and elementary school.

Material

A questionnaire consisting of 30 items was composed. Each item was drawn from the text of the Director-General's 1996 Circular and consisted of a single or of multiple statements. The items were either quoted directly from the Circular or paraphrased into a statement format. The subjects were asked to respond to the statements in one of two ways: (a) a binary Yes (1)/No (2) response to factual questions, e.g. 'Arabic has become a compulsory language for pupils in Junior High'; or (b) (in most cases) a five-level scaled response ranging from 'total disagreement' to 'total agreement'.

Procedure and data analysis

The questionnaires were distributed – during the academic year of 2001 – to teachers in different schools around the country, teachers of different subjects and of different age levels. The questionnaires were then collected and coded. Distribution and frequencies were calculated and ANOVA tests were performed to find significant differences within and across each sector, each teaching specialization and each age group. The results discussed in the following section draw only on comparisons that turned out to be statistically significant either across sectors (Arab vs. Jewish) or across age groups (grade level) or across subject taught (language or non-language subjects).

Results and Discussion

It is important to remember that our primary goal in this study was to achieve a synchronic picture of the response to the policy as perceived and understood by one of the key links in the process of implementation, namely, the teachers. We will present the statistically significant findings and provide a comprehensive profile in our discussion to follow.

First we were interested in teachers' knowledge of a language policy in the Israeli education system. The results showed that most teachers know that there is a language policy in the educational system in both sectors (Arab and Jewish), irrespective of the teacher's area of expertise (language vs. non-language) or the grade level they teach (K, E, M or H). However, when asked whether they are familiar with its details or whether they thought there should be an official language policy, we found that there were significantly more teachers in the Arab sector who were not familiar with the details of the policy as compared to their Jewish sector colleagues (J = 1.8, A = 1.6; $p = 0.02$); whereas there are more Jewish teachers than Arab teachers who think there should be a language policy in the Israeli educational system (J = 1.1, A = 1.3; $p = 0.017$).

Teachers' attitudes towards languages in Israel

In looking at teachers' attitudes towards the knowledge of languages (more specifically English, Hebrew and Arabic) in Israel, we found significant differences between the Arab and Jewish teachers with regard to: (a) whether knowledge of languages enhances the development of one's native language (A = 4.1, J = 3.8; $p = 0.05$); and (b) whether knowledge of various languages promotes economic cooperation (A = 4.1, J = 4.5; $p = 0.04$).

We suspected that there would be divergent attitudes towards the different languages from different teachers. To that end we asked the teachers to rank which of the languages (in a list of ten languages) was an official language of Israel. The option for possible answers ranged from very transparent alternatives (Hebrew, English and Arabic) to extremely idealized ones (sign language). Yet all possible languages carry a social value and to some extent 'real life' stereotypification. Sign language provided a neutral option in that it does not represent any religious, national or ideological entity and caters to a small minority within each sector's community. The results showed a significant difference between Arab and Jewish teachers' opinions as to whether Hebrew is an official language (A = 4.89, J = 4.95; p = 0.04), perhaps a form of mild protest, and no significant difference in the perception of Arabic as an official language by both sectors (A = 4.3, J = 4.2). Granted, both Arabic and Hebrew are the official languages of Israel.

In order to bring out more clearly and strikingly a differential sectorial approach as to the status and need of the language of the 'other' within a society that contains a majority and a large minority, we proceeded to ask for the attitude towards the need for developing a high proficiency in the 'other's' language. While the attitude towards the need to develop high proficiency in Hebrew for Arab speakers showed no significant difference, sectorial or otherwise, the need to develop high proficiency in Arabic among Hebrew speakers brought out a significant difference, the Arab teachers claiming that it is very important that Hebrew speakers learn Arabic, and the Jewish teachers downplaying Arabic's importance for native Hebrew speakers (A = 4.0, J = 3.1; p = 0.0001).

Teachers in the Arab sector are aware of their minority status, and Hebrew is the language of the more privileged majority, so it is an important language to know – mostly for professional reasons, but to some extent also in order to integrate into Jewish society. Hebrew's majority status allows Arabic – first among many other cultural manifestations – to be snubbed, even though it is the language of a large minority within Israel, as well as of an overwhelming majority outside it. The Ministry of Education's Circular is a reflection of this collective majoritarian attitude: the number of hours allotted to Arabic language studies for Jewish pupils is less than that allotted to English, and often even these hours are not devoted to Arabic. Schools, groups of pupils within schools and individual students can opt out of studying Arabic almost entirely by choosing a second European tongue or, in some cases, the language of a specific immigrant community.

One immediate result of this is that Arab graduates are usually trilingual (Arabic, then Hebrew, then English), with English the weakest of the three, whereas Jewish graduates, whether bi- or trilingual (usually the former), have much better proficiency in English. This gives graduates an edge in the business, academic and high tech areas, thus further reducing the chances of the less privileged to get even. In response to the statement 'Study of Arabic for pupils whose mother tongue is Hebrew is essential, given the geopolitical situation in Israel', there was also a significant difference between the response of the Arab sector versus the Jewish one with the Arab sector teachers agreeing more with the statement than teachers in the Jewish sector (A = 4.3, J = 3.9; p = 0.01).

We went one step further to inquire about the teachers' opinions on statements (again drawn from the language policy document) as to which languages are necessary from two different standpoints – that of a citizen and that of a pupil. The status of 'citizen' is more inclusive – it includes the teacher him- or herself, as well as the pupil. The status of the language for pupils is more restricted, and places the teacher in an authoritative position (as educators and stakeholders of the future of the children).

Figure 7.3 shows sectorial differences between Arab and Jewish teachers with regards to knowing Arabic, Hebrew or English. These differences are not surprising, given that the Arab sector teachers see in Hebrew a language of greater need to learn while living in Israel (where they are in a linguistically dominated and threatened position) and working within the 'local' geographic boundaries. The Jewish sector teachers on the other hand see as more important the learning of English, because: (a) there is no immediate threat to their native language (Hebrew) which is required for living and working in Israel (as well as being part of the majority's culture), and (b) English is a commodity, the language of wider communication and the one that enables upward mobility crossing the 'local' geographical boundaries of Israel. Sectorial differences between Arab and Jewish teachers were also found in relation to the languages necessary to learn as a pupil.

Figure 7.4 shows that, while both Arab and Jewish teachers may agree on the importance of Hebrew for their schooling, they disagree as to the importance of the need of learning Arabic (A = 4.82, J = 4.15; $p<0.05$). The Arab teacher regards Arabic as important for the pupils, while the Jewish teacher regards it as important but not as important as the Arab teacher.

A fascinating result came up when dealing with sign language. As mentioned, initially sign language seems to be a neutral language devoid of ideological, religious or political attributes as far as teachers are concerned. While across the board sign language is regarded as absolutely

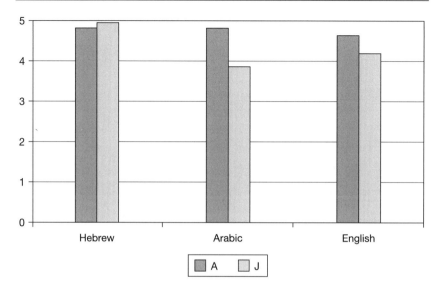

Figure 7.3 Sectorial differences regarding the languages a citizen of Israel must know

unnecessary or partially necessary, there were statistically significant differences among the teachers across the sectors and the grade levels. The Jewish teachers are more open to the inclusion of sign language in the linguistic arena than their Arab counterparts, for deafness, like other handicaps, carries a heavy social penalty, not only for the individual but for the family – it is a disgrace in the Arab sector, while in the Jewish one it is a handicap in need of treatment.

Moreover, a statistically significant ($p = 0.02$) sectorial difference in relation to teacher's specialization was observed regarding the perceived need for English for students in Israel. The results show that in the Arab sector language teachers feel more strongly about the need for their pupils to learn English as compared to their Jewish counterparts (A = 4.8, J = 4.4). Yet in the Jewish sector, non-language teachers give greater importance to the teaching of English than their colleagues do in the Arab sector (A = 4.5, J = 4.8).

The Director-General's Circular shows uncertainty (and ambiguity) as to the implied audience of the policy, so that the document seems unaware of areas of dissent or conflict towards its assumptions and intentions – e.g. whether knowledge of languages enhances the development of one's native language, which teachers in the Arab sector agreed with

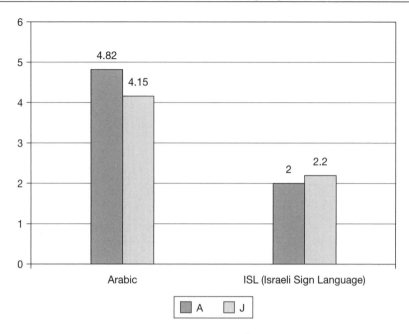

Figure 7.4 Sectorial differences regarding the languages a pupil in
    Israel must know

far more than Jewish teachers (A = 4.1, J = 3.8; p = 0.05); and whether
knowledge of various languages promotes economic cooperation (A = 4.1,
J = 4.5; p = 0.05), which Jewish teachers accepted significantly more than
teachers in the Arab sector. Sectorial issues emerge as the most chal-
lenging both for the Ministry of Education and for the researcher.

   One notable finding concerns sectorial differences between Arab and
Jewish teachers with regards to the languages a citizen should know.
Hebrew is the only language for which Jewish teachers' agreement was
higher than that of teachers in the Arab sector (A = 4.83, J = 4.96; p = 0.002).
Arabic was seen as nearly as important as Hebrew by most Arab teachers
and by nearly one-third of the Jewish teachers (A = 4.82, J = 3.88; p =
0.0001). English was also ranked high – third by Arab teachers and second
by Jewish teachers. But there was a difference between Arab and Jewish
teachers as to the importance of English, with Arab sector teachers agreeing significantly more as to its importance. Jewish teachers were more
insular, as it were, maintaining the importance of Hebrew over Arabic and
English, and did not give English as high a degree of agreement (A = 4.61,

J = 4.20; p = 0.02). This suggests that English has become a means by which an underprivileged, marginalized population gains power, by means of circumventing the official languages. There is reason to believe that the same is true of the position of English among the underprivileged Jewish population as well. Being a language teacher seems to reinforce these conflicting positions: Jewish sector language teachers enact insularity by finding English less important than non-language teachers in the sector do; and Arab sector language teachers, aware of the potential of linguistic proficiency, find English more important than Arab sector teachers of other subjects.

Teachers' beliefs about fostering mono- and/or multilingualism as competing systems

Teachers' beliefs and concerns about whether a language should be introduced, which language this should be, and how and when it should be introduced are a fascinating facet of their understanding of the linguistic capacity and scope of the society. These convictions become a viable source for possible interpretation and implementation of the language policy on the one hand and for professional empowerment on the other.

We began by asking teachers which languages they thought should be taught and strengthened: the mother tongue, before learning an additional language; or the two official languages of Israel, Arabic and Hebrew. Here a significant difference emerged between the Arab and the Jewish teachers as to the need to learn the mother tongue before another language is introduced (A = 4.7, J = 4.4; p = 0.02), and the same trend prevailed with regard to the need to learn all official languages (A = 3.7, J = 3.1; p = 0.01). Teachers responded to the linguistic situation in the sense that Lambert would call a 'dyadic' culture, in which the integrity of one of the languages (Arabic) was seen as being threatened by the dominance of the other (Hebrew) – a prime area for language policy intervention, and one unaddressed by the Circular. Of course, for the majority, the native Hebrew speakers, this poses less of a threat, and the inclusion of Arabic is seen as less important. But, for the minority, questions of language are more affective, and so their responses show a desire to strengthen the mother tongue before embarking on the language of the majority, and they also place more emphasis on the status of Arabic as an official language, thus leading to a greater insistence on a more equal study of both languages. Thus, in terms of monolingualism and bilingualism, teachers in the Arab sector are more inclined to reify the formal status of Arabic as an official language, to grant it the standing in public discourse that is legally its due, whereas teachers in the Jewish sector lean more to Lambert's homogeneous, monoglot model.

These beliefs then structure and explain other responses to the questionnaire and to the hidden assumptions made by the Circular. These other responses include answers to such issues as the optimal age to begin learning an additional language, how it should be taught – with or without recourse to the mother tongue – and whether proficiency should be emphasized equally in mother tongue and additional language. With regard to the incipient age of learning another language, teachers were offered these choices to rank: kindergarten, first grade (the initial grade of formal schooling), third grade (the canonical age of foreign language instruction), middle school and high school.

As shown in Figure 7.5, two types of differences were observed in this respect. First, sectorial differences as to the incipience of new language acquisition show a consistent pattern of the Jewish teachers' higher willingness to introduce another language as early as kindergarten and first grade, as well as the third grade, as compared to that of their Arab counterparts. This does not contradict the earlier finding that in the Arab sector there is a greater response to a dyadic language culture, but expresses

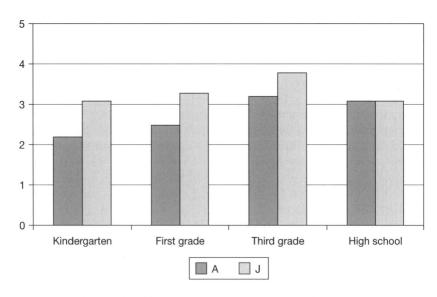

Figure 7.5 Sectorial differences as to incipient age of language
               instruction

anxiety that dyadism may be lost if Arabic as mother tongue is not strengthened. In the same manner, the Jewish sector's willingness to begin study of 'another' language does not indicate willingness to share Hebrew's hegemony with Arabic: in all probability, the additional languages envisioned by teachers in each of the sectors are different. Teachers in the Jewish sector are not thinking of Arabic as the additional language that pupils will study, but probably of English, whose very distance, linguistically and culturally, from Hebrew on the one hand, and great global importance on the other, make its acquisition at once non-threatening and extremely desirable.

Second, as far as introducing another language at high school level is concerned Arab teachers are more forthcoming than their Jewish counterparts. This response may be the outcome of two different motivations for the study of languages other than the mother tongue. In the Jewish sector the high school graduate commonly goes on to the army, and then to integrate into civil society, both navigated primarily in Hebrew, so there is no particular need to strengthen another language in high school. The native Arabic speaker in contrast will often need Hebrew, and possibly other languages as well, in order to function as an adult, and so there is room for more languages precisely in the last years of schooling. This again points to the multiplicity of conceptions of Israel as a linguistic community, between a homogeneous, monolingual society at one extreme and a mosaic culture at the other. Our research did not analyze responses according to immigrants' country of origin, but it is possible that among the large immigrant population the beliefs are that Israel is or should be a mosaic linguistic culture.

Another significant result concerns the question as to whether a language teacher must use only the target language when teaching a language, or should teach the target language in the mother tongue. The underlying assumption is that teachers' attitudes towards language instruction will show whether they think the language is a subject matter which is taught in the native tongue or whether it is another linguistic system which is used as it is taught. The Jewish teachers tend to think it is necessary to use the target language while teaching it more than their Arab colleagues (J = 3.7 > A = 3.2). These differences were across sectors and class levels. In general, there are differences among teachers of different grade levels as to the use of only the target language in the language classroom – with kindergarten, middle and high school teachers ranking highest and elementary school ranking the lowest.

When addressing not only language instruction but also other subjects taught at school, teachers were asked whether different subjects should be taught in different languages. There were sectorial differences between the Arab sector teachers who agreed more strongly with this statement compared to their Jewish counterparts.

Specifically, our study shows that the Circular does not address the possible sectorial *response* to its edicts, but it does reinforce existing patterns of inequality between the Arab and Jewish sectors, primarily by the relegation of Arabic, an official language, to an officially marginal language. By doing so the Circular disregards the rights – and opinions – of the large Arab minority, and caters to and reinforces the majority's dictates towards images of the minority's language, thus further marginalizing Arabic and mother tongue Arabic speakers. Another example of this is the way the Circular places Arabic on a par with some of the languages of the new Jewish immigrants to Israel, permitting the study of non-language subjects in these native tongues, and thus treating Arabic as if its speakers, too, like new immigrants, are destined to be finally absorbed into the Hebrew mainstream. Ironically, all teachers themselves reveal the absurdity of this position by responding with agreement to the use of Arabic in the Arab sector as the language of general instruction, and with far less and differing degrees of agreement to the use of immigrant languages for this purpose.

Equally important, there is no awareness of the conflicts among Israeli teachers over when to start teaching another language. The possibility of lowering – or indeed of raising – the incipient age of second or third language acquisition is not considered. A lower age is a possibility almost unanimously accepted by Jewish teachers; teachers in the Arab sector would welcome a higher one. This is only one indication of the kind of educational climate of opinion the Ministry of Education could use to urge changes that would be accepted by a majority of the teachers. But it is also a sign of the deep rifts among teachers and between sectors which the Circular, and by analogy its producers, do not take into account.

Important findings relate to the place of mother tongue acquisition in Arab and in Jewish sectors. Thus teachers in the Arab sector are more convinced of the need to learn the mother tongue before another language is introduced (A = 4.7, J = 4.4; $p = 0.02$), and are more prone than Jewish teachers to accept the need to learn all official languages (A = 3.7, J = 3.1; $p = 0.01$).

The Circular outlines a general procedure, or makes recommendations, which will not be implemented and which will themselves be taken as signs of lack of consideration towards different teacher and pupil populations. Thus, although Jewish teachers agree more that it is necessary to use the target language while teaching it, it should be recalled that Arab pupils are required to be trilingual (Arabic mother tongue, Hebrew and English), whereas most Jewish-sector pupils are bilingual (Hebrew and English), therefore instruction in the target language is more feasible.

Closely connected to this are issues of priority in the proficiency of the native language and another language. While teachers in the Arab sector, as well as all language teachers, find it feasible and necessary to teach two languages simultaneously, teachers in the Arab sector believe far more strongly than Jewish teachers that the native language should be taught prior to other languages. This captures the anxiety of the teachers in the Arab sector who want and require proficiency in several languages, but who at the same time are worried about the need to provide a strong foundation and identity in the mother tongue. Arab teachers emphasized more than their Jewish counterparts the need to encourage parents to maintain and promote their children's native language.

This is matched by another interesting statistical difference. High school teachers insist more than others on the priority of the mother tongue, suggesting again that identity politics play an important role in thinking about language policy: the closer the pupil is to graduating, the more important the native language is seen.

Linguistic and cultural identity and ideology with implications for a revised language policy

Once we had covered the issues of which languages are official, which should be learned first, second, or learned altogether, we asked the teachers who they think should make the decision as to which language will be learned. The options we gave ranged from the traditionally authoritative to the individual, from the Ministry of Education, via the school, to the teacher, the parent and the pupil. Stating the weight the various parties have is a highly loaded sociolinguistic issue, which funnels elements of social and cultural identity often leading to or stemming from an ideological position.

As shown in Figure 7.6, the responses revealed a sectorial difference: teachers in the Arab sector prefer that the decision be taken by the highest authority, as compared to teachers in the Jewish sector, who would allow the pupil greater autonomy in deciding which languages to study. One interpretation of this result is that Palestinian society is more authoritarian in most fields than Jewish society, and the difference is an example of this. But given the asymmetric relations between the sectors, and the anxiety associated with language loss in the Arab sector, the preference for the decision to lie with a higher power might be explained by a desire to limit the competition with Arabic among the Arabic-speaking population. Jewish sector teachers, confident of Hebrew's hegemony, can well indulge in allowing the individual pupil more autonomy in this area. The statistics can be shown to reinforce a generally more conservative approach towards language teaching and maintenance, particularly of the mother tongue.

In general teachers agree that in planning a language policy emphasis should be placed on the maintenance of immigrants' language. However, there were sectorial differences where the Arab teachers emphasized more than their Jewish counterparts the need to encourage parents to maintain and promote their children's native language. Moreover, when looking at all the respondents, the only significant differences were observed among the teachers of different grade levels (see Figure 7.7).

Teachers agree that a language policy should foster a variety of skills and abilities, ranging from the formal (encrypted as an educational construct) to the functional (encrypted as a cultural construct). Teachers attribute not only formal needs and motivations to learning another language but also believe that language learning must be accompanied by language maintenance of the learner's mother tongue (in cases where it is other than Hebrew). When asked whether, beyond a basic formal

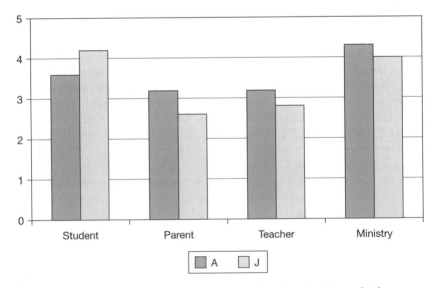

Figure 7.6 Sectorial differences in relation to who decides which languages will be learned

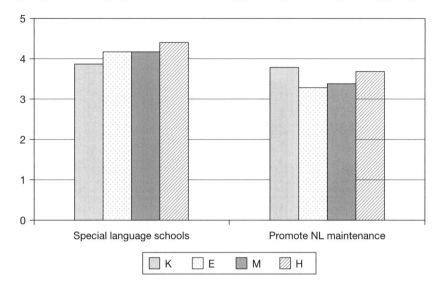

Figure 7.7 Teachers of different grade levels consider that a language policy must ensure mother tongue maintenance and special schools for language instruction

proficiency in another language, the policy should strive to foster further abilities, such as professional/vocational, commercial, academic, literary, or all of them together, teachers of different grade levels agree on all but fostering professional/vocational ability. The results show that the higher the grade taught, the more appropriate it is seen to teach another language for professional purposes.

Language knowledge for purposes of developing commercial skills is regarded differently by teachers of different sectors and grade levels (see Figure 7.8). While in the Jewish sector there is a gradual increase in the importance for teaching another language for commercial purposes, with the highest supporters being high school teachers and the lowest being kindergarten teachers, Arab sector teachers emphasize other language teaching during most of the school years of the child, especially elementary and middle school teachers. Looking at these two graphs comparatively, Jewish sector teachers regard the importance of other language teaching for professional and commercial purposes equally, while Arab sector teachers put commercial purposes above professional ones. This might be explained by the fact that most Arab villages have a predominantly commercial enterprise and children at very young ages are introduced to and actively involved in family commerce.

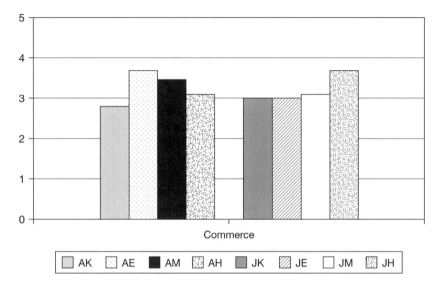

Figure 7.8 Grade level and sectorial differences regarding incipient age
for learning a language for commercial purposes

The concentration on commercial or professional purposes in language
teaching requires the development of certain language skills. All teachers
agree that the spoken aspects of language should be taught formally.
However, as shown in Figure 7.9, differences were found with regard to:
(a) promoting writing skills – with Arab sector teachers supporting this
practice more than the Jewish sector teachers, (b) promoting comprehension skills – with sectorial and class level differences, and (c) promoting
appreciation of literature and culture in the language – in which both
sectorial and language versus non-language differences were observed.

Writing, comprehension, literary and cultural appreciation are all seen
as more important by the teachers in the Arab sector and, within that
group, by HS teachers more than others. The diametrically opposed
pattern of agreement of Jewish and Arab sector teachers (A: E-M-K-H/J:
H-K-M-E) as to the comprehension requirement may not be entirely
meaningful or explicable (see Figure 7.10). However, when we narrow
the focus to the two extreme members of this statistic result – the elementary and high school teachers' responses in the Jewish and Arab sectors
– we can definitely point to two very different ideas of where the
emphasis on comprehension must fall – as a skill learned early with less
emphasis in following years, or as a process whose most important point
is at the end of formal education.

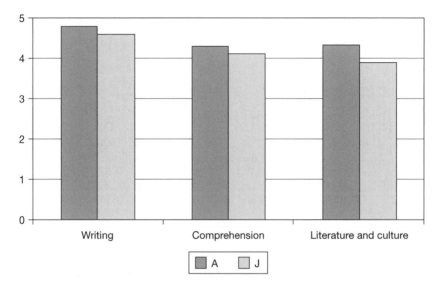

Figure 7.9 Sectorial differences as to which aspects of language must be emphasised in a language policy

Language teachers are, as a group, more ready to adopt new ideas related to language teaching, because they are more aware of the problems with prevailing systems. Kindergarten and elementary school teachers also embrace these new concepts, because they have more flexibility in curriculum and assessment than in higher grades, and teach children of a younger age who are less in need of the strict standardization that still, despite the language policy Circular, characterizes middle and high school teaching. As the grade level rises, then, teachers have diminishing control over their pupils, and there is a return to more coercive, traditional means of teaching and assessment, which stress the teacher's authority over the learning subject. As pupils approach the end of the educational process, they are inducted, as it were, into the 'real' values of the society: its brutality, antagonisms and conflicts. This is true in a way of the language policy Circular itself: it dictates to and legislates for a very large group of 'consumers'. Its regimentation of teachers provides yet another model or representation for relations between those in charge and those who happen to be in a subordinate position: teachers and pupils, men and women, majority and minority.

As part of the establishment of a policy the perception of the 'decision makers' and their relative weight plays a significant role in the way such

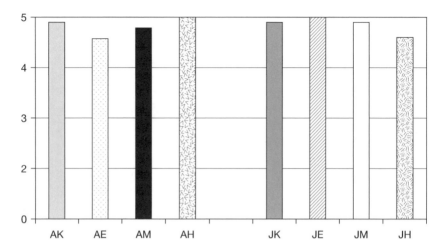

Figure 7.10 Sectorial and grade level differences as to the emphasis placed on language comprehension as established in a language policy. For key see p. 160

policy will be treated once launched. While among Jewish teachers the pupil is believed to have sufficient autonomy to decide which language to study, in Arab society, which is much more conservative in the roles it assigns its members and more concerned with the perils of its linguistic and cultural identity, the voice of authority alone is allowed to decide such questions, here being the Israeli Ministry of Education, but the (male) teacher receives some reflected glory in being associated with this power.

This, we have seen, is of a piece with other responses. Teachers in the Arab sector prefer strengthening of, and instruction in, the mother tongue before other languages are introduced. For them, language is far more an identity issue than for Jewish teachers, and languages are seen as far more important in the way they carry, contain and transfer cultural identity, which explains why, for teachers in the Arab sector, written proficiency, listening comprehension and literary and cultural appreciation are so much more important than they are to Jewish teachers.

Conclusion

The differences examined above, most of which emerged in the different conceptions of language teaching in the Arab and Jewish sectors, are not only representative of two different ideas, they imply two different pedagogical approaches, and moreover two – or more – different policy planning approaches. While the teachers surveyed showed moderate cognizance of the official language policy underlying the Director-General's Circular, they often showed biases and preferences that are absent in this document. The Circular lacks in its informative nature in terms of both its existence and content; while it tries to present a pluralistic language teaching prospect it does not account for the resistance it may arouse, and although this pluralistic prospect may seem flexible to the 'producers' and feasible institutionally it leaves little to no room for operative choices. This study provides some idea of tensions within both Jewish and Arab sectors – about which languages should be or are being learned, for what purposes, to what extent and by whom – that the Circular tries to provide but cannot in its current form.

While the Circular (the 'product') does not provide a full and realistic framework as perceived by the consumers – represented in our study by the teachers – this does not necessarily mean that there should not be an official language policy. On the contrary, it means that teachers from both sectors, all grade levels and all subjects want, and should be responsible for drafting, a future language policy. It does mean that a language policy must not try to impose ideal relations on the complex reality of language communities. The first and necessary step in envisioning a successful language policy must start from understanding the pitfalls of existing language policy structures. In this sense the present language policy framed by the Israeli Ministry of Education is a vital document, for it enables the generation of a discussion on what a language policy should and should not be.

There are still many lacunae regarding language policy, but there is also much interest in the subject. Teachers can contribute to policy making and implementation and deserve to be consulted. After all they are the 'brokers' between the 'ideal' and 'real' of language education practices. Israeli teachers of all the sectors, grade levels and subjects agree on these issues, even though there is a sectorial division between the Jewish and the Arab sector teachers as to the nature and implementation of such policy. The Arab sector teachers want a language policy that is 'equal but separate' – namely, equality in conditions and segregation in practice. The Jewish sector teachers desire a policy of 'limited pluralism' with little to no change in recognition of multilingualism, yet maintaining a linguistic pseudo-hegemony of the majority language (Hebrew) and the language of wider communication and high prestige (English).

Schiffman's fifth Law states that 'policies typically evolve and change' and 'if they fail to evolve, they will fail' (Schiffman, 2001). A language policy in a complex cultural and linguistic situation, such as the one described in this study, can be a means to a continued status quo. In Israel this means perpetuating the non-egalitarian history of language education practices, in which case it would be far better that it continue to be disregarded as it mostly has been to date. We believe that while 'evolution' in this respect means providing leverage for new approaches to complex multilingual and multicultural identity, 'revolution' means accepting and implementing a language policy that encompasses such complexity.

References

Ben-Rafael, E. (1994) *Language, Identity and Social Division: The Case of Israel*. Edited by P. Mülhäusler and S. Romaine. Oxford Studies in Language Contact. Oxford: Clarendon Press.

Ben-Rafael, E. and Brosh, H. (1991) A sociological study of language diffusion: The obstacles to Arabic teaching in the Israeli school. *Language Planning and Language Problems* 15 (1), 1–23.

Kaplan, B.R. (1994) Language policy and planning: Fundamental issues. *Annual Review of Applied Linguistics* 14, 3–19.

Lambert, R.D. (1995) *Language Policy: An Overview*. Paper read at the International Symposium on Language Policy, 20 December, Bar-Ilan University, Israel.

Lockard, J. (1997) Welding these residents together: Modernization, neutralism and ideologies of English in mandatory Palestine 1917–1948. *Journal of Commonwealth and Postcolonial Studies* 4, 18–34.

Ministry of Education, Culture and Sport (1996) *Policy for Language Education in Israel*. Office of the Director-General. (In Hebrew.) Jerusalem, Israel.

Ngũgĩ wa Thiong'o (1986) *Decolonising the Mind: The Politics of Language in African Literature*. Oxford: James Currey and Portsmouth, NH: Heinemann.

Pennycook, A. (1994) *The Cultural Politics of English as an International Language*. New York: Longmans.

Pennycook, A. (1995) English in the world/the world in English. In J.W. Tollefson (ed.) *Power and Equality in Language Education* (pp. 34–58). Cambridge: Cambridge University Press.

Phillipson, R. (1992) *Linguistic Imperialism*. Oxford: Oxford University Press.

Schiffman, H.F. (2001) Schiffman's 'laws' of language policy. On WWW at http://ccat.sas.upenn.edu/~haroldfs/540/laws.html. Last modified 13 February 2001.

Shohamy, E. and Donitsa-Schmidt, S. (1998) *Jews vs. Arabs: Language Attitudes and Stereotypes*. Tel-Aviv: The Tami Steinmetz Center for Peace and Research.

Shohat, E. (1988) Sepharadim in Israel: Zionism from the standpoint of its Jewish victims. *Social Text*/19–20, 1–35.

Spolsky, B. and Shohamy, E. (1996) National profiles of languages in education: Israel: Language policy. In P. Dickson and A. Cumming (eds) *National Profiles of Language Education in 24 Countries*. Slough: National Foundation for Educational Research.

Spolsky, B. and Shohamy, E. (1997) Planning foreign language education: An Israeli perspective. In K. de Bot and T. Bongaerts (eds) *Perspectives on Foreign-language Policy: Studies in Honour of Theo van Els* (pp. 99–111). Amsterdam: John Benjamins.

Spolsky, B. and Shohamy, E. (1999) *The Languages of Israel: Policy, Ideology and Practice.* Clevedon: Multilingual Matters.

Chapter 8
Trilingualism in Guinea-Bissau and the Question of Instructional Language

CAROL BENSON

Introduction

The setting for this discussion of multiple languages in education is Guinea-Bissau, a small West African country characterised by societal trilingualism in indigenous languages, a creole that serves as lingua franca, and an official ex-colonial language. This paper draws on educational, ethnographic and sociolinguistic data which was gathered by the author over a period of eleven months from 1992 to 1993 (see Benson, 1994), a follow-up visit in 1995, and ongoing correspondence with Guinean colleagues in the field.

The purpose of this paper is to address some issues in trilingualism that have been raised by a number of European researchers. I will examine models and frameworks that have been developed in other multilingual contexts and determine their applicability to an African one. Following precedents established by Cenoz *et al.* (2001), I will address four areas of interest:

- Sociolinguistic context for trilingualism.
- Psycholinguistic processes in the acquisition of two or more languages.
- Linguistic characteristics of the languages involved.
- Pedagogical aspects of third language learning.

Cenoz *et al.* (2001) point out that further research is needed to determine how research in bilingualism and second language acquisition relates to more complex linguistic situations. Their working definitions of third language acquisition in school (learning the third language as a subject) and trilingual education (use of three languages for instruction) are presented with the understanding that different contexts will produce different models (Cenoz *et al.*, 2001: 3). In the case of Guinea-Bissau, we will examine a bilingual experiment that has been proposed as an alternative to a monolingual school system in a trilingual society. The next section provides a brief description of the setting, after which the linguistic and pedagogical implications will be discussed.

Research Setting

The Republic of Guinea-Bissau, with a population currently estimated at 1.2 million (World Bank, 2001), is one of the poorest countries in the world. Like a number of other developing countries, its primary education system is plagued by low overall enrolment, low female participation, and high repetition and dropout rates (Ahlenhed *et al.*, 1991). Based on 1985 census figures, 95% of the population over age seven is primarily orate, with no access to literacy skills in any language, and only 0.2% finish six years of primary school (Galli & Jones, 1987). More recent figures indicate some improvement, with 52% enrolment in primary school and 37% adult literacy, but obviously these figures are still overwhelmingly low, and female participation (39% of primary enrollees and 17% of literate adults) is particularly limited (UNDP, 2001).

In this context, education development efforts have been directed toward both quantitative objectives, which include extending basic schooling to the entire school-aged population, and qualitative ones, which involve overall improvement of primary instruction to increase student success rates. My research focused on a bilingual schooling experiment that functioned from 1986 to 1994 and was designed to improve school quality by changing the language of instruction. The experiment involved initial instruction in Kiriol, a widely spoken lingua franca and second language for most children, with a transition to Portuguese, the official language that is foreign to most Guineans. Whether due to lack of resources or failure to see indigenous languages as viable school media, the experiment for the most part ignored the mother tongue of the students, but used the second language in an effort to solve the communication problems inherent in the national all-Portuguese system. The national system would be categorised as submersion by most counts (see models as summarised in Baker, 1996) since there is little explicit instruction of Portuguese, despite its clearly assimilationist goal that children should become highly literate, native-like speakers of the official language. Research methods included participant observation, interviews, classroom observation, community language surveys involving the families of 950 students, and individual oral and written language assessment of 1012 students in Kiriol and Portuguese. The guiding research question was whether or not Kiriol, a second language for most Guineans, could function as an effective language of beginning literacy and content area instruction in a transitional bilingual program.

Although the field data discussed here were collected a number of years ago, it is unlikely that the linguistic situation has changed significantly since then, nor is there any reason to believe that the less-than-optimal schooling conditions discussed here have changed for the better. On the contrary, a civil war from 1998 to 1999 has caused further breakdown in the public educational system, which leads me to believe not only that the implications of this study still hold, but also that they are even more important today for efforts in improving the quality of primary schooling for Guinean children.

Sociolinguistic Context

Although it is a small country, Guinea-Bissau has a surprisingly diverse population. Most Guineans speak at least one of 30 indigenous languages as a mother tongue. The largest ethnolinguistic groups are Balanta (27%), Fula (23%) and Mandinga, Manjaco and Papel (10–12% each), with the remaining 17% representing 25 other groups and their languages (MICEP, 1981)[1]. A total of 15 ethnic groups self-identified in our sociolinguistic surveys, which were limited to five regions of the country including Bissau, the capital. Despite this diversity, ethnic and linguistic groupings are generally distinguishable by region; for example, the dominant ethnic groups participating in this study were the Manjaco and Mancanha in the north, the Bijagó in the western island archipelago of the same name, and the Balanta in the south.

As mentioned in the introduction, there are two additional languages present in Guinean society, and these are layered on top of the indigenous languages. They are a creole, known as Kiriol, which functions as the country's lingua franca; and Portuguese, the official ex-colonial language, which is used in formal institutions such as schools and government. The concept of layers is invoked here to represent both the sequence of acquisition and the existence of differences in prestige and function from a Guinean perspective. As Sridhar explains regarding societal multilingualism, multiple language use is usually asymmetrical depending on conditions such as 'the status and roles of the languages in a given society, attitudes toward languages, determinants of language choice, the symbolic and practical uses of the languages, and the correlations between language use and social factors such as ethnicity, religion, and class' (1996: 47). I am by no means the first to discuss this type of three-language hierarchy in an African context; for example, the term triglossia was used as early as 1972 to describe the case of Tanzania, where the three languages include a local language for intra-group communication, a lingua franca (Kiswahili) for wider communication, and a European or 'world' language in official domains (Abdulaziz-Mkilifi, 1972; see also Brann, 1981 and Rubagumya, 1991). Trilingualism in Guinea-Bissau is portrayed in a similar way in Figure 8.1.

Regarding the first language or L1 level, most Guineans are born into a speech community whose primary language is indigenous to the region, as mentioned above. Use of this language establishes what Sridhar calls the native place network, meaning that it establishes an ethnic identity but is 'often restricted in its functional range' (1996: 52). The L1 is used at home and at traditional ceremonies such as weddings, funerals and harvest festivals. Regional politicians address communities in their L1 whenever possible to invoke the in-group spirit, and those of the same group who meet in the city will at least greet in the L1 to acknowledge their shared background. The latest census data available on language repertoires show that 54% of Guineans are monolinguals, and that most are monolingual in an indigenous language (MICEP, 1981).

Exposure to the L2 layer depends on various conditions such as ethnic or linguistic pride, linguistic heterogeneity of the community or family, proximity to different groups and need for trade. Guinean children are often exposed to Kiriol, the lingua franca, at an early age. Some Guineans acquire the L1 and Kiriol simultaneously, but most acquire Kiriol subsequent to the L1. The language repertoire data show that 30% of Guineans are bilinguals, and that most bilinguals speak an indigenous language

Figure 8.1 Three layers of language in Guinean society

and Kiriol (MICEP, 1981). More recent estimates indicate an increase in Kiriol language skills, which will be discussed further below.

The third language, or L3, is accessed only by those few who participate in formal schooling or have contact with foreigners. Portuguese is learned subsequent to L1 and L2 acquisition, if at all, and most often through study rather than by communicative means. Although only a small percentage of Guineans claim to speak Portuguese (9% total according to the 1991 census, MICEP, 1993), there is a widespread, unquestioning belief in its value for future employment and other opportunities. The language reper- toire data show that 12% of the population is trilingual, and that two-thirds of trilinguals speak an indigenous language, Kiriol and Portuguese; the remaining trilinguals speak two indigenous languages and Kiriol (MICEP, 1981).

In summary, while Guinean society is characterised as trilingual, most individuals are not exposed to Portuguese and do not have access to that third language level. This triglossic situation has a number of implica- tions for educational language use. As Ytsma (2001: 14) points out, there is a fundamental contrast between settings where all three languages are spoken and settings where this is not the case. In the latter setting, as exemplified by Guinea-Bissau, the L1 and L2 are spoken but the L3 is a foreign language. Logically, Ytsma argues, the educational goals for foreign language teaching should be relatively lower than those for L1 and L2 teaching. However, in Guinea-Bissau as in many post-colonial nations we find the reverse to be true: L3 speaking and literacy skills are highly valued, and native-like proficiency is the goal of schooling, while the L1 and L2 are relatively ignored by the national system, except for their unsystematic oral use when teachers can find no other way to communicate with their students.

Without going into detail regarding post-colonial politics and language attitudes, it seems clear that planners in Guinea-Bissau are far from estab- lishing the ideal type of trilingual schooling envisaged by Ytsma which 'deliberately aims to promote additive trilingualism among its students' (2001: 12). However, as I will attempt to show below, inclusion of Kiriol, the L2, in primary schooling is a first step in the slow process of recog- nition that Portuguese is not the only viable language for use in official domains. The successful aspects of bilingual Kiriol–Portuguese schooling, even though a less-than-ideal 'weak' transitional model was used, demon- strate the pedagogical advantages of using a language which students have already acquired and which is part of their experience.

Psycholinguistic Processes in the Acquisition of Two or More Languages

The processes involved in acquiring second and third languages are another aspect of trilingualism to be considered. Two important questions that have been raised by Cenoz *et al.* (2001: 6) are the following:

- Does L3 acquisition follow the same stages as L2 acquisition?
- Do L3 learners have advantages over L2 learners?

To explore these questions we need to know at what point in the individual's linguistic development these languages are acquired. Figure 8.2 depicts two different theoretical models for the acquisition of three languages over time, along with a third model depicting acquisition of the three languages in the Guinean context. As discussed above, Guineans who acquire Portuguese as an L3 do so in formal learning situations subsequent to acquiring the L1 and L2. In contrast, the Kiriol L2 is in many cases acquired relatively soon after the indigenous L1 and usually through informal means.

Cenoz *et al.* (2001: 5) find that there are differences between acquiring a second or additional language through contact and learning a foreign language; this is arguably an important distinction to be made between Kiriol and Portuguese in Guinea-Bissau. This distinction is demonstrated by our oral test data, which were cross-sectional in that primary students grades 1 to 4 were tested during one school year (1992–3) and longitudinal

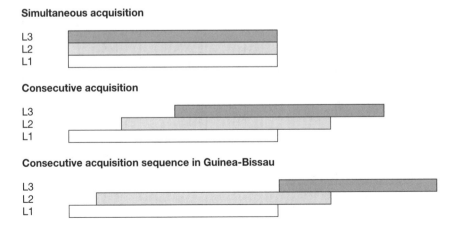

Figure 8.2 Acquisition of three languages

in that the same students were tested at the beginning and end of that year. Both experimental and 'control' students (i.e. those in status-quo Portuguese classrooms) were tested individually in Kiriol and Portuguese by my Guinean colleagues, using a series of questions or requests which increased in difficulty. Based on students' responses they were given a language level of 1 (no communicative skills), 2 (receptive language only), 3 (survival skills), 4 (intermediate language) or 5 (proficient native-like language).

Individual test data on oral Kiriol skills indicate that most students entering grade 1 at age seven are already competent Kiriol L2 speakers, as shown in Table 8.1. Since there was no significant difference between experimental and control students on these tests, they are aggregated here. Lack of scores at some levels indicates only that there were no students studying at those levels during the 1992–3 school year.

The only exception to early Kiriol competence was in one more monolingual (L1) area in the rural north, where grade 1 students had between 'receptive' and 'survival' skills upon school entry. Whether or not they

Table 8.1 Average levels of spoken Kiriol (beginning/end of school year)

Regions	Students tested	Grade 1	Grade 2	Grade 3	Grade 4
Rural communities (experimental sites):					
North	198/153	2.4/3.5	3.6/4.3	4.4/4.3	
South	116/108		4.8/5.0		
Archipelago	174/161	4.7/4.9	4.8/4.9	4.9/4.8	5.0/5.0
Suburban:					
North	162/–	4.7/–	4.9/–	5.0/–	
Archipelago	193/138	5.0/5.0	5.0/4.0	5.0/5.0	
Bissau (outer)	–/ 97	–/5.0	–/4.9	–/5.0	
Urban:					
Bissau (centre)	–/ 72	–/5.0	–/5.0		

were in experimental bilingual schools, however, these students' Kiriol skills improved significantly in grades 1 and 2; in fact, since the 1992–3 school year was subjected to a series of prolonged interruptions caused by teachers' strikes and political unrest, it seemed that most of their Kiriol acquisition probably took place outside the classroom (Benson, 1994). While the Kiriol skills of rural grade 3 students took a slight (0.1 point) downturn, possibly due to lack of school exposure, these students were already intermediate to advanced speakers. Meanwhile, they had virtually no Portuguese skills upon school entry, and gained little Portuguese competence thereafter (see Table 8.2). As shown by the Portuguese test averages here, none of the students tested, no matter what the form of schooling or proximity to the city, ever reached a 'survival' level (3) in Portuguese, even after four years of schooling. There was even a significant (0.5 point) downturn in the Portuguese skills of grade 3 students in the north, which I believe resulted from lack of exposure to Portuguese due to the above-mentioned interruptions in the school year (Benson, 1994).

Cenoz *et al.* (2001: 6) comment that, in an ideal world, bilingual (and biliterate) learners are well equipped to learn the L3 because they have

Table 8.2 Average levels of spoken Portuguese (beginning/end of school year)

Regions	Students tested	Grade 1	Grade 2	Grade 3	Grade 4
Rural communities (experimental sites):					
North	198/153	1.0/1.1	1.4/1.6	2.9/2.4	
South	116/108		1.2/1.3		
Archipelago	174/161	1.1/1.1	1.2/1.3	1.3/1.9	2.5/2.3
Suburban:					
North	162/–	1.2/–	1.5/–	2.1/–	
Archipelago	193/138	1.2/1.4	1.3/1.6	2.3/2.8	
Bissau (outer)	–/ 97	–/1.3	–/1.4	–/2.5	
Urban:					
Bissau (centre)	–/ 72	–/1.5	–/2.4		

gained learning strategies, metalinguistic awareness and communicative
sensitivity. I am unsure that Guinean students gain the range of learning
strategies Cenoz *et al.* are referring to since, as mentioned above, L3 exposure in Guinean classrooms does not come in the form of 'comprehensible
input' as Krashen (1982) and other second language learning specialists
would recommend (Cummins, 2001: 61). However, it could be argued
that multilingual Guinean society already promotes the latter two skills,
at least in terms of oral communication. The daily linguistic practices of
Guineans with whom I had contact would indicate great mutual interest
in communication and the making of choices in pursuit of that interest.
These choices usually draw upon the first or second language layers. For
example, in a village or monolingual community, a Guinean visitor is
often greeted in the local language, but the greeter is usually prepared to
switch to Kiriol at the first indication that the visitor is not a competent
speaker of the language, judging by such things as failure to properly
continue the conversation following the ritual greeting. In cases where
physical characteristics do not reveal the ethnicity of the speaker,
Guineans do not readily make assumptions about language; more often
they will ask in Kiriol where the person is from (birth village), what
her/his ethnicity is, or simply, 'Do you speak X?' In many situations I
observed, the addition of a single non-speaker to a group was enough
stimulus for a rapid, unmarked switch to Kiriol. If this is not practical,
i.e. if there are monolinguals in the group, someone inevitably appoints
him or herself translator for the others. I was often impressed by the
linguistic skills of average Guineans. One example from my experience
took place in a Mancanha village at the funeral of a colleague's mother,
during which a heated discussion arose in Mancanha concerning distribution of the bag of rice I had contributed. My colleague's elderly uncle,
a non-literate subsistence farmer, immediately moved to my side and
performed simultaneous translation into Kiriol, sustaining it for over half
an hour and enabling me to participate effectively in the discussion.

Unfortunately, the Guinean school system does not promote effective
L3 acquisition following successful L1 and L2 acquisition. All-Portuguese
submersion schooling leads to a more subtractive type of trilingualism,
where only Portuguese literacy skills are taught and valued. As a
colleague (Hovens, 2002) and I (Benson, 2002) have noted from experience in a number of developing countries, literacy in an official (second
or third) language can certainly feed back to L1 literacy, but the process
is inefficient at best, and is quite hard on student motivation and self-
esteem. Based on principles of bilingual education such as Cummins'
(1999) common underlying proficiency, we can assume that, in the

absence of mother tongue education, Guinean schools would build better Portuguese L3 skills by teaching beginning literacy in Kiriol, a familiar L2 with which students identify.

Linguistic Characteristics of the Languages Involved

Recent studies have discussed the possible role of linguistic distance between the three languages involved. The premise, as explained by Cenoz *et al*. (2001: 7), is that if the L3 is typologically closer to the L1 or L2 it may facilitate acquisition or, as discussed by Ytsma (2001: 15), promote strength of transfer. Linguistic distance can be analysed at different linguistic levels: phonological, syntactic, lexical and pragmatic (Cenoz *et al*., 2001: 7). While I will not attempt to do a comparative linguistic analysis of the languages involved, I will discuss the interrelatedness of the L1, L2 and L3 because this may influence the development of a bilingual or trilingual model. First, there are some generalisations that can be made about Kiriol as a creole or contact language.

The Kiriol of Guinea-Bissau, the Cape Verde islands and the Cassamance region of Senegal was recognised as early as 1455 by the Portuguese, who called it *lingual de preto* [language of blacks] or *falar Guiné* [Guinea speech] (Kihm, 1986). Until 1960 it was spoken principally in the political and economic centres of Guinea, but the war of independence from Portugal is commonly credited with promoting the widespread dissemination of Kiriol to the general population. It is very likely that the recent civil war has contributed in a similar way to Kiriol expansion, though data is scarce at this point.

Some Guineans and many Portuguese refer to Kiriol as *Português mau falado*, or poorly spoken Portuguese, failing to recognise the established nature of the language. It is true that Kiriol draws much of its lexicon from Portuguese. However, the Mandé and West Atlantic language groups of the continent constituted the substratum, or linguistic foundation, for the formation of Guinea-Bissau Kiriol, contributing many characteristics such as phonology, morphology and extended meanings (Kihm, 1986). Despite these origins, neither a speaker of Portuguese nor a speaker of an indigenous language can necessarily understand Kiriol, nor can a Kiriol speaker necessarily understand the others, without significant meaningful exposure to those languages. As discussed above, many Guineans gain such exposure to Kiriol even before they reach school age. Figure 8.3 provides a rough judgement of the linguistic proximity of Kiriol to the indigenous L1s and to the L3, Portuguese.

Linguistic level:	L1s	Kiriol	Portuguese
Phonological	◄─────────── K		
Syntactic	◄─────── K ──►		
Lexical		K ──────── ►	
Pragmatic	◄─────── K		

Figure 8.3 Relationship of Kiriol to indigenous languages and to
Portuguese

The following examples (a) and (b) compare sentence construction in
Kiriol and Portuguese. Both clearly follow an SVO formula, and Kiriol
demonstrates characteristics of a creole such as simplified verb construction. However, Kiriol demonstrates clear leanings toward the indigenous
languages in certain syntactic structures and phonological aspects, as the
examples show.

Message (a)	I	am going	to	school.
Portuguese	*(Eu)*	*vou*	*à*	*escola.*
	(I)	go	to the	school
	(optional)	(1st pers. present)	(prep. + def. article)	
Kiriol		*Nna bai*		*skola*
		I going go		school
		(1st pers. pronoun + future marker + verb)		

Message (b)	The cat	has	whiskers
Portuguese	*O gato*	*tem*	*bigodes*
	The cat	has	whiskers
		(3rd pers. present)	
Kiriol	*Gatu*	*tene*	*bigodi*
	cat	(to) have	whiskers
		(generic verb, no tense marker)	(generic noun, no plural marker)

Example (a) demonstrates one morpho-syntactic aspect that Kiriol has in common with the indigenous languages: use of the first-person pronoun 'n' as a prefix to the future marker. Examples (a) and (b) demonstrate phonological change of Portuguese lexicon, for example '*skola*' for '*escola*', '*tene*' for '*tem*', or '*bigodi*' for '*bigode*'.

There are also a number of cases that demonstrate the close semantic relationship between the L1s and Kiriol. It could be argued that Kiriol represents indigenous ways of thinking. For example, the basic Kiriol greeting is '*Kuma di kurpu?*' or, literally, 'How is the body?' not '*Cómo está?*' or 'How are you?' as one would say in Portuguese. The indigenous languages and Kiriol are also similar in the manner of categorising and symbolising the world. For example, the Kiriol term '*mamesiñu*' is apparently borrowed from the Portuguese '*mãezinha*', an affectionate term for mother, but used in reference to sisters of the mother, step-mothers, or other close female adult figures in one's life; this is consistent with the pan-African concept of such women as being 'other mothers', unlike the Portuguese specification of relations like '*tia*' (aunt), '*madrastra*' (step-mother), or even '*vizinha*' (female neighbour). Ervin-Tripp has said that, where there is a 'good cultural match' between the first and second language, second language acquisition is greatly enhanced (1981: 34). I propose that such a connection exists between the first language and Kiriol in Guinea-Bissau, and that Portuguese is culturally more distant.

Some critics of the Kiriol-Portuguese educational experiment questioned the usefulness of Kiriol on the basis that it is more of an oral language than a written one. Some also argued that use of Kiriol would interfere with acquisition of Portuguese. Regarding written forms, it may be acknowledged that Kiriol has more in common with pre-written languages than with written ones due to characteristics (Mühlhäusler, 1986) such as its focus on contextualised interaction of participants and its rhapsodical presentation of content. However, also according to Mühlhäusler's criteria, Kiriol appears to be in the process of establishing itself as a written language because it has social functions, because it is used by the news media and because there are published materials such as dictionaries, grammar guides, phonologies and so on (see bibliography in Benson, 1994).

The issue of Kiriol interference with Portuguese is more difficult to address, but has been taken up in another context which seems comparable. Siegel has analysed bilingual schooling in Tok Pisin and English in Papua New Guinea, where children speak a number of indigenous L1s and acquire Tok Pisin, an English-substrate creole, at an early age. He has found that even people who would otherwise be in favour of mother tongue schooling may oppose use of pidgin or creole languages because they are believed to interfere with acquisition of the 'standard' due to the 'apparently close relationship to their lexifier languages' (Siegel, 1997: 87). In his study, Siegel found that students schooled in Tok Pisin out-performed their peers on tests of English (the L3) and demonstrated significant advantages in terms of higher participation and lower dropout rates, cooperation and speed of learning. 'Preliminary formal instruction in a pidgin language is clearly better than none at all' (Siegel, 1997: 98). He attributes the success of the bilingual programme to the teaching of the two languages as separate entities in the classroom, a strategy that would be recommended for the bilingual or trilingual models presented in Figures 8.4 and 8.5 in the next section.

Experimental students in Guinea-Bissau demonstrated affective advantages that could not be mistaken. Although my aforementioned study did not find that experimental students performed significantly better than 'control' students on tests of Portuguese (L3) or mathematics, they did perform at comparable levels, despite the presence of a number of factors (such as rural–urban differences and use of Portuguese as the testing medium) that worked in favour of 'control' students. What was significantly different about the experimental programme was that, with more participative teaching methods and use of Kiriol, students demonstrated higher levels of participation and greater self-esteem. As teachers reported and our observations confirmed, Kiriol helped facilitate comprehension and learning, especially in the content areas; literacy skills were learned more easily; students expressed themselves freely and participated in class; students were more creative; and there was more dialogue between teachers and both students and parents. Parents began to demand bilingual schooling for all of their children, having seen graduates of the experiment go on to the complementary grades (5 and 6) and become academically successful.

Pedagogical Approaches to L3 Learning

The results of our study of the Kiriol–Portuguese bilingual experiment were quite encouraging and were a positive contrast to Portuguese submersion. It was unfortunate in terms of policy implications that the test results were not overwhelmingly demonstrative of the superiority of Kiriol-medium instruction, but there are identifiable reasons for this. I have already mentioned difficult school conditions and lack of exposure to the L3, as well as the existence of factors favouring 'control' students. However, the most important reason in my opinion is use of a 'weak' transitional model, what I call a short-cut model because it attempts to short-cut pedagogical principles and transition to the target language before the necessary prerequisites have been met. Figure 8.4 depicts both the primary bilingual model and its continuation through complementary schooling.

In the experimental model, which covered only the four years of primary schooling, oral Kiriol development preceded introduction of written skills in the early years, Portuguese was introduced quickly in grade 3 in both oral and written forms, and Kiriol was dropped in grade 4. The model reflects both political considerations, where it is felt that the high-status L3 must become part of the curriculum as soon as possible, and belief in the 'time on task' myth, where it is believed that the more time spent on the language, the better the language skills become. Post-colonial language policy considerations are beyond the scope of this paper. However, the 'time on task' myth has been effectively refuted by Cummins (1993, 1999) and longitudinal studies have demonstrated the pedagogical advantages of continuing to develop mother tongue literacy even after transition to the second language for most content area instruction (Ramirez *et al.*, 1991; Thomas & Collier, 1997; Williams, 1998; see also review in Dutcher, 1995).

The Guinean model failed to recognise the importance of the mother tongue. Based on what we know about the pedagogical principles of bilingual education, the L1 would probably have been the best language for beginning literacy, and conditions such as the linguistic homogeneity of many regions would make L1 schooling practicable. However, in the current absence of resources and/or political will for using the L1, I can

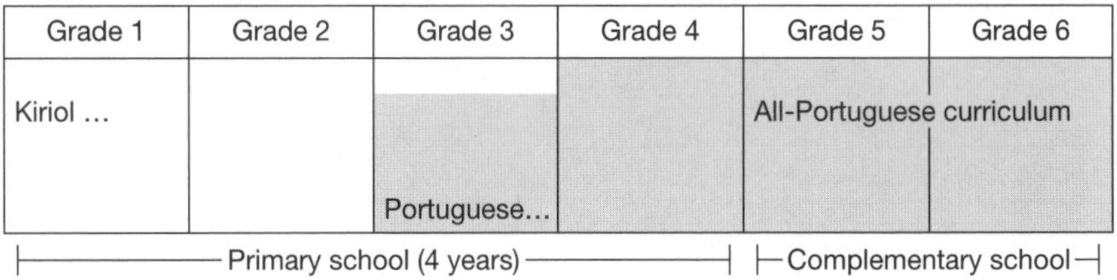

Grade 1	Grade 2	Grade 3	Grade 4	Grade 5	Grade 6
Kiriol ...				All-Portuguese curriculum	
		Portuguese...			

| — Primary school (4 years) — | | ⊢Complementary school⊣ |

Figure 8.4 Experimental primary bilingual model and continuation

only agree with Siegel that 'in many developing countries one crucial advantage of programs using widely known local languages, such as Tok Pisin, is merely their feasibility' (1997: 97). It appears indeed that Kiriol is a feasible school language, since our oral tests established that rural students either entered school with advanced Kiriol skills or acquired them by the time they finished grade 2. Therefore the bilingual innovation may be considered on its own pedagogical merits and as a step in the right direction toward improving primary schooling in Guinea-Bissau.

As already mentioned, the bilingual experiment was proposed as an alternative to a monolingual system in a trilingual social setting. Ytsma (2001) presents a three-part typology of trilingual education depending on its application to a trilingual, bilingual or monolingual area. The case of Guinea-Bissau, according to this typology, would superficially appear to be bilingual education in a trilingual area. Looking more deeply into the sort of triglossia that exists in the country, however, I would argue that Guinean society is actually bilingual in the indigenous languages and Kiriol, and that Portuguese is a third (foreign) language which is learned mainly through schooling. In this case, Cenoz and Genesee (1998) would recommend that the three languages be introduced in succession, so that L1 and then L2 skills are consolidated before students take on the more distant L3. Following these guidelines, a possible trilingual schooling model for Guinea-Bissau is depicted in Figure 8.5.

In this trilingual model, the L1 is used for beginning literacy and content area instruction, while Kiriol is developed orally and then

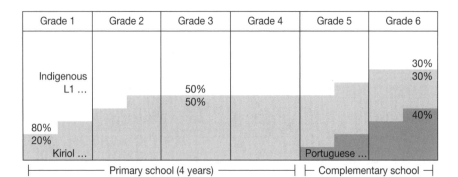

Figure 8.5 Possible primary trilingual model

gradually introduced in written form and for some instruction. Because so many Guinean children demonstrate high oral proficiency in Kiriol by grades 3 and 4, both the L1 and Kiriol can be used to an equal degree to consolidate bilingualism and biliteracy (Hornberger, 2002) by the end of grade 4. For students who meet the linguistic competence criteria established by the curriculum, Portuguese is introduced as an L3 in grade 5. Since Portuguese is presumably needed for secondary instruction, it can be used to an increasing degree for content area instruction; however, continued study of both the L1 and the L2 throughout secondary schooling is recommended (Thomas & Collier, 1997).

Cummins provides a number of recommendations for improving language learning that could be incorporated into a trilingual model. First, he notes that, as Krashen has established, 'sufficient comprehensible input is a necessary condition of acquisition of a second or third language' (Cummins, 2001: 61). In sociolinguistic and educational contexts where access to sufficient comprehensible input is limited, Cummins argues for instruction that develops a 'critical awareness of language' among students. This gives them a framework for 'harvesting' the target language to expand their 'cognitive, personal, and linguistic resources' (Cummins, 2001: 63). Cummins believes that students from historically subordinated groups can succeed academically by means of transformative pedagogy, which encourages students to challenge traditional power structures by participating actively in their own learning.

Small glimmers of potential for this transformation were detected by our research on the Kiriol–Portuguese experiment. Increased classroom participation, improved school attendance and happier students, teachers and parents were all small indicators that power shifted along with the language of instruction. The Kiriol–Portuguese model shown in Figure 8.4 could be improved, however, in at least three ways. First, inclusion of the L1 in the Guinean school system could arguably increase the potential benefits, both pedagogical and personal, of a power shift by increasing classroom interaction; a possible model for this is shown in Figure 8.5. Next, as Cenoz *et al.* (2001: 8) point out, the traditional strategy of 'one person-one language', where a parent or teacher uses only one language with the child, requires further research; in Guinea-Bissau, where there are limited resources for teacher education, this strategy might prove effective if teachers are allowed to specialise their teaching in either Kiriol or Portuguese. Finally, as mentioned by Ytsma (2001: 14), goals for L3 skills should be realistic; in the case of Guinea-Bissau, I believe this implies that there be less focus on native-like proficiency, that a more realistic time frame be applied to develop linguistic competence in all three languages, and that students receive more comprehensible input in the L3.

In conclusion, I would like to add a recommendation of my own for further consideration in assessing the success of trilingual education. Cummins refers to the need for teachers to think about their teaching and about whether students in bi- or trilingual programmes are 'being given opportunities for both knowledge generation and identity affirmation' (Cummins, 2001: 73). It seems that, if we focus too much on input, output, language proficiency and academic skills, we may forget what is truly important: that we want students who go through these programmes to have happy, healthy and productive lives in their multilingual societies. We as researchers need to continue exploring ways to assess the great potential benefits all three languages pose to students' futures, especially if we are to convince policymakers that trilingual education is the way to go.

Note

1. The MICEP study is regrettably dated; however, to my knowledge little research has been done in this area since then due to lack of resources and a recent civil war in the country.

References

Abdulaziz-Mkilifi, M. (1972) Triglossia and Swahili: English bilingualism in Tanzania. *Language in Society* 1 (2), 197–213.

Ahlenhed, B., Callewaert, G., Cissoko, M. and Daun, H. (1991) *School Career in Lower Primary Education in Guinea-Bissau: The Pupils and Their Socio-economic and Cultural Background.* Education Division Documents 54. Stockholm: Swedish International Development Authority.

Baker, C. (1996) *Foundations of Bilingual Education and Bilingualism.* Clevedon: Multilingual Matters.

Benson, C. (1994) Teaching beginning literacy in the 'mother tongue': A study of the experimental Kiriol/Portuguese primary project in Guinea-Bissau. PhD thesis, University of California, Los Angeles.

Benson, C. (2002) Real and potential benefits of bilingual programs in developing countries. *International Journal of Bilingual Education and Bilingualism* 5 (6), 303–17.

Brann, C. (1981) *Trilingualism in Language Planning for Education in Sub-Saharan Africa.* Paris: UNESCO.

Cenoz, J. and Genesee, F. (1998) *Beyond Bilingualism: Multilingualism and Multilingual Education.* Clevedon: Multilingual Matters.

Cenoz, J., Hufeisen, B. and Jessner, U. (2001) Towards trilingual education. *International Journal of Bilingual Education and Bilingualism* 4 (1), 1–10.

Cummins, J. (1993) Bilingualism and second language learning. *Annual Review of Applied Linguistics* 13, 51–70.

Cummins, J. (1999) Alternative paradigms in bilingual education research: Does theory have a place? *Educational Researcher* 28, 26–32.

Cummins, J. (2001) Instructional conditions for trilingual development. *International Journal of Bilingual Education and Bilingualism* 4 (1), 61–75.

Dutcher, N. (1995) *The Use of First and Second Languages in Education: A Review of International Experience.* Pacific Island Discussion Paper Series 1. Washington, DC: World Bank.

Ervin-Tripp, S. (1981) Social process in first- and second-language learning. In H. Winitz (ed.) *Native Language and Foreign Language Acquisition* (pp. 33–47). New York: New York Academy of Sciences.

Galli, R. and Jones, J. (1987) *Guinea-Bissau: Politics, Economics and Society.* London: Frances Pinter.

Hornberger, N. (2002) Multilingual language policies and the continua of biliteracy: An ecological approach. *Language Policy* 1 (1), 27–51.

Hovens, M. (2002) Bilingual education in West Africa: Does it work? *International Journal of Bilingual Education and Bilingualism* 5 (5), 249–66.

Kihm, A. (1986) Nasality in Kriol: The marked case? *Journal of Pidgin and Creole Languages* 1 (1), 81–107.

Krashen, S. (1982) *Principles and Practice in Second Language Acquisition.* New York: Pergamon Press.

MICEP/Ministério da Coordinação Económica e Plano (1981) *Recenseamento Geral da População e da Habitação, Resultados Provisórios 1979* [*General Census of Population and Habitation, 1979 Provisional Results*]. Bissau: MICEP.

MICEP/Ministério da Coordinação Económica e Plano (1993) *Recenseamento Geral da População e da Habitação, Resultados Provisórios 1991* [*General Census of Population and Habitation, 1991 Provisional Results*]. Bissau: MICEP.

Mühlhäusler, P. (1986) *Pidgin and Creole Linguistics.* Oxford: Basil Blackwell.

Ramirez, J., Yuen, S. and Ramey, D. (1991) *Final Report: Longitudinal Study of Structured English Immersion Strategy, Early-exit and Late-exit Transitional Bilingual Education Programs for Language-minority Children.* Washington, DC: United States Department of Education.

Rubagumya, C. (1991) *Language, Social Values and Inequality in Tanzania: Reinterpreting Triglossia.* Department of Linguistics and Modern English Language, Centre for Language in Social Life, Working Papers 26. Lancaster: Lancaster University.

Siegel, J. (1997) Using a pidgin language in formal education: Help or hindrance? *Applied Linguistics* 18 (1), 86–100.

Sridhar, K. (1996) Societal multilingualism. In S. McKay and N. Hornberger (eds) *Sociolinguistics and Language Teaching* (pp. 47–70). Cambridge: Cambridge University Press.

Thomas, W. and Collier, V. (1997) *School Effectiveness for Language Minority Students.* Washington, DC: National Clearinghouse for Bilingual Education.

UNDP (2001) *Human Development Report 2000.* New York: United Nations.

Williams, E. (1998) *Investigating Bilingual Literacy: Evidence from Malawi and Zambia.* Education Research 24. London: Department for International Development.

World Bank (2001) *World Development Indicators Database.* On WWW at http://www.worldbank.org/dataquery.html.
Ytsma, J. (2001) Toward a typology of trilingual primary education. *International Journal of Bilingual Education and Bilingualism* 4 (1), 11–37.

Chapter 9
Trilinguals at Four? Early Trilingual Education in the Basque Country

FELIX ETXEBERRÍA

Introduction

The population of the Basque Country is 2,100,000. According to a socio-linguistic survey carried out in this territory (Gobierno Vasco, 1996), only about 37% of people currently speak Basque (as well as Spanish), while 63% of inhabitants are Spanish monolingual. There are no monolingual Basque speakers.

With the Civil War and Franco's regime, there was no official acceptance of the regional languages for four decades (1939–79). After the Spanish Constitution of 1978 and the Statute of Autonomy in 1979, which set up an Autonomous Government, the Basque Parliament passed a Bilingual Decree (1983), establishing a bilingual education system based on the criterion that both Basque and Spanish should be compulsory subjects at all levels of education.

The Basque education system is bilingual with a dominant (Spanish) tongue and a minoritised (Basque) language. In order to respond to the different sociocultural situations, family motivations, sociolinguistic zones, the training of teachers and a series of other factors, bilingual education in the Basque Country presents four degrees of intensity, or four models (see Table 9.1), that vary from a minimum use of Basque to an instrumental use of this language in learning across the board (1983 Decree).

These four models were defined psychological-pedagogically and with the basic idea that the mother tongue is the one that must be used to begin any kind of learning, including the learning of other languages. In this way, model D is the most adequate for Basque-speaking children. Model B is the best for children with knowledge of both languages and the A model is aimed at children with low or zero knowledge of Basque. Finally, model X is the model for teaching pupils who are not going to study Basque at all, like short-term inhabitants and travellers.

The observed tendency in pre-school teaching in recent years has been that the truly bilingual models (B and D) have been the majority option in the Basque Autonomous Community. The same tendency can be observed in the primary and secondary sectors.

The fast rate of progress in Basque educational bilingualism is a fact recognised by experts worldwide as an efficacious experience for the recovery of a language at risk of disappearing (Cummins, 1993; Genesee, 2001; INCE, 1996; Killilea, 1994; Kuijpers, 1987; Nelde *et al.*, 1996; Siguán, 1994).

If we take into account the challenges of the 1980s we can see that the introduction of the linguistic models in all primary and secondary educational establishments in the Basque Country, the evolution of these models into more developed educational programmes, school results, teacher training and the production of teaching material in Basque have all achieved highly successful levels. The period 1983–2003 is the most productive that the Basque educational system has experienced to date.

Despite this, in other aspects the situation is either at an impasse or what was attempted or hoped for has not been achieved – or maybe was not even planned for at the time. I am thinking of vocational training, the university, the genuine use of Basque in the street, the literacy programmes for adults and other aspects, such as education with foreign pupils and Basque–Spanish–English plurilingual education.

Ten years ago (1991–2) a project to teach English to four-year-olds was introduced in a number of Basque schools and since then there has been

Table 9.1 Models of education

Linguistic model	*Main contents*
A	All learning is carried out in Spanish. Basque is a school subject.
B	Both languages are used as vehicles of learning, about 50% in each.
D	All learning in Basque. Spanish is a school subject.
X	All teaching in Spanish. No teaching in or of Basque.

a trend to introduce the early learning of English to the whole school population.

The importance of being conversant with English is commonly accepted in Basque society, where there is considerable unanimity about, and interest in, the learning of English at school. Having said this, it behoves us to analyse its teaching and to examine at depth the suitability of early trilingual education (Basque, Spanish and English) starting at the age of four, in our context.

We should ask ourselves what might be happening with progress in the learning of the Basque language in this diglossic situation (dominant Spanish with minoritised Basque) if a third language is introduced at such an early stage, and also about what real advances are made in the learning of English by pupils of such a young age.

In my discussion I rely on theoretical studies and research reports related to the topic. On this basis, I offer an analysis of an important aspect of the subject, which is the influence of fashion and the competition between the public and the private educational sectors in the Basque Country.

The Context of Trilingualism in Basque Schools

Unlike strong languages which have large numbers of speakers and a long historical and literary tradition, the Basque language, Euskara, can still be considered a minority language, despite the fact that it is the official tongue of the Basque Autonomous Community and despite its presence in the media and education, and notwithstanding the ever-growing number of speakers.

The theory of (subjective) ethnolinguistic vitality (Azurmendi, 1999; Bourhis & Leyens, 1996; Giles *et al.*, 1977) underlines the demographic and institutional dimension as well as the status of the language in question. In the case of Euskara we can state that this language is in an unfavourable situation when competing with other strong languages such as English and Spanish. If some authors (Baetens Beardsmore, 1994; Nelde, 1993; Siguán, 1993a) are already finding problems in certain trilingual educational programmes involving strong national languages, then putting into place plurilingual programmes which involve Basque is bound to be that much more difficult.

Fashion is also a factor in the social context, given that there exists a considerable amount of snobbery regarding the enthusiasm for trilingual education, particularly for the acquisition of English – 95% of all students study English as a foreign language while only 5% learn languages like

French, German and Italian. This derives from the belief that fluency in English is necessary if future generations are to find good jobs and succeed at university. Garagorri (2000) and Cenoz (2000b) have also pointed out the dangers of following this wave of enthusiasm if suitable measures for teaching in three languages are not taken.

Lastly, it also has to be said that schools have their minds concentrated on what they have on offer in the curriculum. The current educational market place is a reminder that there is strong competition among schools to conquer a market share at a time of falling school rolls. The Basque Country is the community in Europe which has the lowest birth rate (which creates keen competition between the public and private sector in attracting the enrolment of the small pupil population) and this is reflected in the multiplicity of curricular choice on offer when it comes to parents having to decide where to send their children. One only needs to browse through the publicity of the different educational centres for the period (since 1991 to date) to see that the offer of early learning trilingualism is one more choice on offer, alongside the school canteen, school transport, religion, sports facilities and so on.

When considering language issues in trilingual areas, an important aspect to bear in mind is the level of similarity between the languages in contact. We know (Hjelmslev, 1971) that the Indo-European languages in Europe belong to different families and that the Basque language, along with Turkish and Finnish among others, do not belong to the European family types. Thus, we have to take as a starting point that the situation of Basque trilingualism which we are considering here is made up of three languages which have no relation to each other (Spanish, English and Basque). This is a situation not found in other multilingual contexts such as in Friesland, Strasbourg, Catalonia, Andorra, Canada, Switzerland and other countries where the languages spoken are more akin to each other.

This is probably one of the factors which best explains the lower level of knowledge of the minority language in the Basque Country when compared to Galicia, Catalonia or the Balearic Islands (CIS, 1999). It would seem that, for a Spanish speaker, it is more difficult to learn Euskara than Catalan or Galician, and that this is to a large extent due to the greater linguistic proximity between any two Romance languages (e.g. Catalan–Spanish or Galician–Spanish) than between Euskara and Spanish. The Basque Country is at a disadvantage when trying to incorporate the early learning of a new foreign language.

On initiating a plurilingual programme, its suitability has to be examined, particularly in those cases when the acquisition of a third foreign language which has little general currency within our country, such as

English, takes place in the context where pupils in schools using the models (A and B), which are the least intensive in Euskara, are not guaranteed the acquisition of the Basque language.

There are also many other questions that need addressing, such as teacher education, the generalisation of early learning of English in all types of centres for all kinds of pupils, the production of suitable material, the move from teaching English as a subject to teaching through English (an objective in secondary education), the integration of the curriculum with the three languages, the turnover of teaching staff and many other issues that are far from being satisfactorily addressed.

The Foundations of Trilingualism in Basque Schools

In our analysis of early plurilingual programme planning we have looked at the texts of the various specialists and the papers and contributions presented at the four Seminars on International Plurilingual Education which have taken place in the Basque Country since 1992. In addition, interviews with a number of expert authors (Skutnabb-Kangas, Siguán, Genesee, Baetens Beardsmore) were carried out. In all the sources consulted, we found hardly anything, from a theoretical viewpoint, that could justify the setting up of plurilingual programmes for four-year-olds in the Basque Country. Surprisingly, in some cases, the authors participating in the various international seminars in the Basque Country do not mention trilingualism at all (Arnau, 1993; Cummins, 1993; Hamers, 2000; Vila, 1993) and present their contributions in the context of 'bilingual education'. One might imagine that their papers argue in favour of trilingual education, but the expression 'trilingual' or 'trilingual education' only appears once, in the title!

In other cases, the authors are openly against early trilingual education (Cenoz, 2000b; Genesee, 1994; Nelde, 1993: 77; Siguán, 1993a: 44). Only Artigal (1993: 69) boldly claims that plurilingual education at the age of four can be as accessible as bilingual education, although without providing any more information but simply expressing a belief in it 'if certain conditions are met'.

It is true that educational bilingualism is an issue that has been addressed in many countries as well as in Spain; and it is equally true that there have been successful programmes involving plurilingual programmes at primary and secondary levels. Similarly, experience has been acquired of programmes in which two or three languages are related to each other, such as in Catalonia or Friesland; and the same can be said of programmes in which majority languages with high prestige are involved. But what has not been demonstrated is the attainment of similar levels of success when such programmes are applied at a very early stage, or when three languages are involved and not just two, or when what is desired is the boosting of a minority language which has no relation to other linguistic families. Thus, an apologia for the early learning plurilingual programmes in the Basque Country has been mounted (by both public and private sectors), which consists of four parallelisms that, it seems, have no basis or justification.

From bilingualism to trilingualism

It has been demonstrated and accepted that, when well-organised, it is possible to establish bilingualism in the school context, and also that this bilingualism generates benefits for the pupils from the perspective of the learning of a second language, without detriment to the other language or to the rest of the curriculum (Genesee, 2001). The international scientific community supports this and the abundant research in the Basque Country on this subject gives credence to this type of programme. The research carried out by the INCE (National Institute for Quality Education) shows that early learning of English produces beneficial effects on results in that language. But that investigation was undertaken in bilingual contexts and there is no guarantee that the same would apply with trilingual programmes (INCE, 1999). Neither research nor the opinion of experts supports the idea that the good functioning of bilingual education means that the same will happen with trilingualism in the school (Cenoz, 2000a). This apparent leap of logic from bilingualism to trilingualism seems to have been made by Cummins (1993), Hamers (2000), Artigal (1993) and others.

From primary and secondary to pre-school education

We are aware of a number of research projects carried out at primary and secondary education levels (in the Basque Country), in general with good results. The level of acquisition of English has been assessed at both levels of our educational system and, in both cases, it has been shown that the achievement levels are not worse than in model D (bilingual education) schools; in other words, the learning of English at primary level is not detrimental to the learning of Basque or Spanish (Cenoz & Valencia, 1994; Lasagabaster, 2000). But there is neither theoretical nor experimental justification which leads us to believe that such primary stage plurilingual programmes can be applied to pre-school pupils.

From majority to minority languages

We know of trilingual programmes in which the languages employed are majority ones and where academic success has been the outcome, although in many cases the development was at the primary level. What we are unaware of is a similar situation involving a minority language such as Euskara.

From related to unrelated languages

Finally, there are some trilingual programmes that employ three languages where two or three are strongly linked linguistically, such as the 'Aula, escola europea' in Catalonia (Ribera, 1997), and others in Luxembourg, Strasbourg, Friesland, Andorra, Finland, etc. Apart from the fact that most of these programmes introduce the third language at the primary stage, they do not justify an automatic transference to similar programmes if in the latter a minority language without an assured future is involved and, in addition, this language bears no linguistic relation to the other two languages (Spanish and English).

The illustrative example of the bicycle, used by Cummins (1993: 45), suggests that children can progress with only one wheel (one language), but even better with two, when there is good organisation and balance. This defence of bilingualism does not constitute, within this metaphorical construction, a justification for trilingualism. What would happen if the bicycle had three instead of two wheels? It is clear that the child would not advance as fast as with the two-wheeled bike. And, more importantly, what happens when one of the wheels (Basque) is much smaller than the other two? The 'logic' of the wheels and bilingualism can lead us to quite opposite conclusions when applied to trilingualism.

Projects in Early Learning Trilingual Education

Although reports from projects on trilingual education in other countries are few and far between, particularly plurilingual programmes at pre-school level, we can point to some programmes that have been undertaken. The Project for Trilingual Education in Europe continues with the involvement of a number of experts from various parts of the European Union. Several trilingual projects, carried out in Friesland, the Basque Country and Finland, have been reported upon (Beetsma, 2002). An initial result of this research appears to be that there are fewer regions than originally thought which are using trilingual primary education. But neither in Friesland nor Finland is there any early trilingual education – that is, at four years. Only the example of the Basque Country remains.

The projects cited by Baetens Beardsmore (1994), regarding Luxembourg, Brussels or the European Schools (Baker & Jones, 1998), did not contemplate the teaching of three languages at pre-school age, but at primary and secondary levels. The same happened in Canada (Genesee, 1994), and Friesland in the Netherlands, where Ytsma (2000) analysed trilingual education, and in Finland (Björklund & Suni, 2000). It should be noted that, when initiating the learning at primary or secondary levels, some of the languages were interrelated linguistically.

Regarding trilingual education experiences in contexts closer to home, both Valencia (Perez, 2001) and Catalunya (Generalitat de Catalunya, 1999) have to be considered in order to see whether the third language was introduced at the primary or secondary levels, and in terms of the relatedness of the languages involved (Catalan and Spanish are closely related). The situation in Andorra (Doltz, 2001) can also be included. There, the third language is introduced at the primary stage and two of the languages in contact are Romance (French and Catalan).

Despite a lack of argumentation in favour of trilingualism and the linguistic distance between Euskara and English, it is in the Basque Country where we find that projects on early trilingual education are under way. There are basically two types of scheme in operation: that undertaken by the public sector schools and that developed by the Ikastolas (the Basque private sector schools). The latter (Cenoz, 2000b; Garagorri, 2000) was started in 1991–2 in eight Ikastolas and, by the 1998–9 academic year, took in 47 Basque schools, 450 classrooms and 8500 pupils in model D. In 2000–1, there were 58 Ikastolas involved, with 779 classes and approximately 15,000 pupils.

The general impression from the teachers, project coordinators and those with overall responsibility for the plurilingual programmes is a very positive one and, as such, has to be taken into account. However, the assessment of results to evaluate the success of the programme and to back up the positive impressions has not yet (2002) been made available. In any case, there are two important limitations to this experience: it is a programme limited to pupils in model D (Basque language immersion) and it cannot provide us with information regarding greater or less suitability for learning English at the age of six. What would be the results of those starting at six?

It is also significant that the international dimension of the European project with the Ikastolas (Garagorri, 2000) involves ten European countries, but the project concerns the 'teaching of second and foreign languages', so there is no reference to trilingual programmes.

Regarding the public sector centres, their trajectory has been similar. The scheme started in the 1996 academic year (Aliaga, 2002), following the study of new programmes for four-year-olds, 11-year-olds and ESO (compulsory secondary education), although the only centres that responded to the proposal for initiating the trilingual programmes were those that were involved in the project for the four-year-olds. There are currently 250 centres participating in the programme and the impression of the teachers and organisers is also positive, despite the lack of optimum conditions for its ongoing success (primarily lack of continuity among the teaching staff). We also lack in this case, once again, any data to back up the positive, and undoubtedly valuable, impressions of those involved or affected by the programme: parents, teachers and organisers.

There are other trilingual projects, both in the public sector schools and in the Ikastolas, in which the teaching of English as the third language at the primary stage (6–8 years) has been introduced (Arano *et al.*, 1994; Manrique de Lara, 2000; Martinez, 1997), but, again, we do not have any data or evaluation to guide us regarding results for the three languages involved.

Research in the Basque Country

Some research into the teaching of English in the Basque Country has been carried out. The most notable studies are Cenoz and Lindsay (1994), Lasagabaster (2000), the report on Ikastolas (Cenoz, 2000b), the projects coordinated by Aierbe and Etxeberria (in Etxeberria, 1999) and the one reported upon by Cenoz (2000c).

Cenoz and Valencia (1994) report on a study carried out in the Basque Country on 321 students of Curso de Orientación Universitaria (pre-university, or last year at school, 17–18-year-olds) from both public sector and non-public sector schools, and from both model A and model D centres. All the individuals studied English as a subject, although they differed in the number of years they had studied the language. The results showed that those who had received schooling through Basque (model D) had results in English that were superior to those obtained by pupils who studied through model A, when both groups had scored similar results in intelligence tests. Also, the greater the number of years spent with English as a subject, the better results obtained in the language.

Regarding the research carried out on the early learning plurilingual programme in the Ikastolas (Cenoz, 2000b), in the 1993–4 academic year, that is, four years after the start of the project, tests were carried out to measure the level of impact of early learning of English on the Spanish and Basque languages. According to this investigation, in which 76 students who started English at the early age of four formed the experimental group, the results confirmed that those who studied English from the age of four had not been held back in any way in Basque or Spanish three years later. Although the results in English will not be finally known until 2003, there have been positive impressions from parents and teachers. The main drawbacks of this study are:

(1) The sample is relatively small to obtain reliable results (76 pupils in the experimental group and 90 pupils in the control group).
(2) The pupils in the sample are from model D only and so we do not know what would happen in the case of models A and B pupils.
(3) The age difference, from four to seven, is small if we wish to talk about clear results regarding the development of children. We do not have the results for the assessment that was due in 1998–9.
(4) We do not know what the difference would be if the programme were to start at six instead of four years.

In the same text, Cenoz (2000b) reports on another piece of research where results are compared from three groups of pupils from within the same centre and where Basque is the language of instruction from the pre-school stage (model D). In this centre, the pupils from group 1 began learning English at four, those from group 2 started at eight years and the senior pupils (group 3) started the foreign language when they were eleven years old, as laid down by the previous legislation. The results for oral and written reproduction, for those children in their sixth year of English who had started at different ages (4, 8 and 11), show that it was pupils who started at eleven who had made the best progress in almost all of the parameters tested, followed by the intermediate age group. The four-year-old pupils had received fewer hours of English than the rest but the eight- and eleven-year-olds had received the same number of hours. Thus, it is the children who start English at an older age who progress more rapidly in the language.

Lasagabaster (2000) notes that the teaching of English did not start in the sixth grade (11–12 years) until 1993–4 but, since then, and owing largely to public demand, schools have introduced English in the third grade (8–9 years). Although a certain amount of confusion exists among some parents and teachers over the difficulties of certain pupils in their second language (Spanish or Basque) in immersion programmes, the fact is that the majority go for the early introduction of English and this is reflected in the education plans of the Basque Government.

Lasagabaster carried out his research on the level of competence in Euskara, Spanish and English in six schools covering the three different linguistic models (A, B and D) used in the Basque Autonomous Community, among pupils from the fifth and the eight grade. The principal working hypothesis was the expectation that those pupils in model D would score better results in English than those following models A and B. A total of 252 pupils were tested, taken equally from the fifth grade (10–11 years) and the eighth (13–14 years); that is, 42 pupils in each of the three linguistic models and from each of the two age groups. Equivalent groups of pupils from each model were compared for age, sex, socio-economic status, private English tuition and motivation. As previously mentioned, it was not until the 1993–4 academic year that English was introduced in the third grade, so that the tested fifth grade pupils had actually started in the fourth grade and the eighth grade students in the sixth (both groups at the end of their respective school cycles). The results showed the following comparative levels of competence:

Fifth grade
Euskara: model D pupils scored highest
Spanish: pupils from all three models achieved similar results
English: best scores in model D, no difference between B and A

Eighth grade
Euskara: model D pupils scored highest
Spanish: pupils from all three models achieved similar results
English: best scores in model D, no difference between B and A

In conclusion, it can be claimed that only those pupils who have balanced bilingualism (model D) are advantaged by the learning of English. Thus, according to the author of the study, the presence of three languages in the curriculum in model D is not so problematic as some parents, politicians and even some teachers believe but, on the contrary, would seem to have beneficial effects in terms of metalinguistic awareness.

Nevertheless, the sample is relatively small, comprising 252 pupils in total and 42 in each group, which makes it hard to draw reliable conclusions. And we do not know what the results would have been if the teaching of English had started at six or eight years of age.

Aierbe and Etxeberria (in Etxeberria, 1999), in their study with the largest number of pupils undertaken to date, examined more than 2000 pupils in 80 centres in the Basque Country who were doing the second year of the Bachillerato (16 years of age) in the 1995–6 academic year. They analysed the level of English of pupils being schooled in either linguistic model A or D (1000 pupils in each). The relationship of these models to the many school and socio-cultural variables was taken into account. The scoring in English involved both oral and written aspects. The main conclusions relevant to the topic we are considering were:

- The score differences in English between the pupils of the two models (A and D) were not significant. This fact is highly positive for bilingualism in the Basque Country as it shows that there is no deterioration, no 'holding back', in the achievement levels in the English language in either of the models, A or D. There was thus no evidence of a positive impact of bilingualism for pupils in model D when learning a third language (English).
- Those pupils who started learning English at pre-school and the first years of primary school scored better results than those who started in the second or third cycle of the primary stage or those who started at secondary school. But no differences showed up between those starting at pre-school and those starting in the first cycle of the primary stage.
- In this study it has to be remembered that a number of other variables reflected a much more significant direct relation to the English scores: the type of educational centre, the geopolitical area, the occupational profile of parents, the expectations of both parents and pupils, reading habits, self-image, working habits, intelligence, subject satisfaction, discipline, hours spent watching television, trips abroad and private English classes. On the other hand, neither the current linguistic model nor that through which English was taught (A, B or D), nor gender, appear to have had any significant influence on the results for English language. Neither did the intelligence tests throw up any significant differences.

The same authors (in Etxeberria, 1999) addressed the same problem in the sixth grade at primary school (12-year-olds), testing more than 2000 pupils going through models A, B and D. In this study, the best results were obtained by pupils following model A, followed by model B and, finally, model D. Thus, the positive influence of model D in English scores, as indicated in Lasagabaster (2000), is not borne out by the authors here either. On the contrary, it is the monolingual pupils who achieve the best results in English.

The contradiction between the data of the first and second pieces of research is remarkable given that, among sixth grade primary pupils, model A obtains the best results in English, whereas an analysis of the data from second year Bachillerato indicates insignificant differences.

Given that, in both cases, the research conditions were similar and the test sample was about 2000 in each case, I believe that there are still aspects of the teaching of English of which we are not sufficiently aware and that we therefore have to be prudent when drawing conclusions.

Although the next report to be considered was not carried out in a bilingual context, it is interesting to look at the research carried out in Spain by INCE (1999) on more than 10,000 pupils in the sixth grade of primary school who had started English in the third grade. The conclusion was that those pupils who had started learning English early obtained better results in that language. Nevertheless, this macro study did not take into account a number of factors regarding the population tested. For example, those who started in pre-school education were mainly those pupils who received schooling in private schools and who belong, in general, to upper class families, spend more than three hours a week in the study of the language and, in addition, spend more extra-mural time acquiring this language than other pupils. In essence, the improvement in the level of English at an early stage is not exclusively due to the age of commencement of the learning programme, as there are other factors closely linked to age, type of centre, socio-cultural factors and number of school hours and out-of-school hours in English. Is it the case that those who start English earlier obtain better results because they start earlier or because those who start earlier do so in better conditions?

Conclusions

I have considered the experiences of other countries as well as Spain and the Basque Country; I have compared the contributions of a number of experts on the topic of bilingual and trilingual education, and also various pieces of research undertaken in different contexts; I have looked into the writings on trilingual education both inside and outside the Basque Country as well as papers on the subjects on which the four International Seminars on Plurilingual Education (1992, 1994, 1997 and 2000) were focused; finally, I have attempted to draw out some conclusions. As a result of all this, I can state the following.

There is no solid basis for justifying the introduction of such programmes at the nursery stage. None of the studies examined provide the slightest theoretical justification that these kinds of programmes can be carried out with a minimum guarantee of efficacy or success. I believe that there has been a kind of unjustified logical jump in assuming that all that is valid for bilingual education must also hold good for trilingual learning.

There is little research available on the subject which can be usefully applied to decide on the suitability or otherwise of an early introduction of plurilingual education at the nursery stage in the Basque Country. We should not overlook the fact that, with bilingualism, we have more than 40 sets of research and some 25 years of research experience.

Little experience has been gained in the introduction of plurilingual programmes in schools but, in the majority of cases, the third language is started at the primary stage. Unfortunately, we do not have reports from other countries that might support the pre-school programmes in the Basque Country.

The 'obsession with English' has taken over families, educators and educational administrators and, although some do not believe in its efficacy, it appears that nobody wants to come off the bandwagon of market offers. Every day the publicity reminds us that a lack of knowledge of English is a handicap for our young people.

It is surprising that in the year 2003 early learning of English is being generalised in our classrooms, but still no one has demonstrated that such early trilingual education is beneficial for the learning of English.

My belief is that English should be started at the age of six, that is, at the beginning of the primary cycle. This would seem to be what is suggested by the experience of other countries and the research published to date. Other reasons supporting the proposal are: we ought to ensure that priority is given to a high level of acquisition of Basque and Spanish; and the fact that it is difficult to find both teachers of English in the region and the material required for carrying out such a programme throughout the whole of the educational system.

References

Aliaga, R. (2002) Introducción temprana de la lengua inglesa en las escuelas públicas del País Vasco. In F. Etxeberria and U. Ruiz Bikandi *¿Trilingües a los 4 años?* (pp. 85–104). San Sebastian: Editorial Ibaeta Pedagogia.

Arano, R.M., Berazadi, E. and Idiazabal, I. (1994) Enseñanza trilingüe y desarrollo discursivo. *II Jornadas Internacionales de Educación Plurilingüe*. Bilbao: Fundación Gaztelueta.

Arnau, J. (1993) La experiencia de la inmersión. *I Jornadas Internacionales de Educación Plurilingüe* (pp. 81–94). Bilbao: Fundación Gaztelueta.

Artigal, J.M. (1993) La enseñanza plurilingüe vista desde algunas experiencias en educación preescolar. *I Jornadas Internacionales de Educación Plurilingüe* (pp. 67–76). Bilbao: Fundación Gaztelueta.

Azurmendi, M.J. (1999) *Psicosociolingüística*. Bilbao: Servicio Editorial de la Universidad del País Vasco.

Baetens Beardsmore, H. (1994) Trilingual education progammes in Europe. *II Jornadas Internacionales de Educación Plurilingüe*. Bilbao: Fundación Gaztelueta.

Baker, C. and Jones, S.P. (1998) *Encyclopedia of Bilingualism and Bilingual Education.* Clevedon: Multilingual Matters.

Beetsma, D. (2002) *Trilingual Primary Education in Europe.* Ljouwert/Leeuwarden: Mercator-Education/Fryske Akademy.

Behle, E. (1993) Educación plurilingüe. *I Jornadas Internacionales de Educación Plurilingüe* (pp. 189–94). Bilbao: Fundación Gaztelueta.

Björklund, S. and Suni, I. (2000) The role of English as L3 in a Swedish immersion programme in Finland. In J. Cenoz and U. Jessner (eds) *English in Europe: The Acquisition of a Third Language* (pp. 198–221). Clevedon: Multilingual Matters.

Bourhis, R. and Leyens, J.P. (1996) *Estereotipos, discriminación y relaciones entre grupos.* Madrid: McGraw-Hill.

Cenoz, J. and Lindsay, D. (1994) Teaching English in primary school: A project to introduce a third language to eight year olds. *Language and Education* 8, 201–10.

Cenoz, J. and Valencia, J. (1994) Additive trilingualism: Evidence from the Basque Country. *Applied Psycholinguistics* 15, 195–207.

Cenoz, J. (2000a) Research on multilingual acquisition. In J. Cenoz and U. Jessner (eds) *English in Europe: The Acquisition of a Third Language* (pp. 39–53). Clevedon: Multilingual Matters.

Cenoz, J. (2000b) El aprendizaje de la tercera lengua. *I Jornadas Internacionales de Educación Plurilingüe* (pp. 121–38) Bilbao: Fundación Gaztelueta.

Cenoz, J. (2000c) Plurilingüismo temprano. In S. Oregi (ed.) *IV Jornadas Internacionales de Educación Plurilingüe. Nuevos caminos para la enseñanza plurilingüe* (pp. 185–92). Donostia: Eusko Ikaskuntza. Ikastaria Cuadernos de Educación 11.

CIS (1999) *Estudio sobre el bilingüismo en las Comunidades Autónomas.* Madrid: Centro de Investigaciones Sociológicas.

Cummins, J. (1993) Experiencias de diferentes países. *I Jornadas Internacionales de Educación Plurilingüe* (pp. 71–6). Bilbao: Fundación Gaztelueta.

Doltz, J. (2001) *La experiencia de Andorra en el contexto plurilingüe.* Ponencia presentada en el Congreso Internacional de Educación Plurilingüe, Getxo, Bizkaia.

Etxeberria, F. (1999) *Bilingüismo y educación en el País del Euskara.* Donostia: Editorial Erein.

Etxeberria, F. and Ruiz Bikandi, U. (2002) *¿Trilingües a los 4 años?* Donostia: Ibaeta Pedagogía.

Garagorri, X. (2000) Eleaniztasun goiztiarrari bai baina ez edonola. In S. Oregi (ed.) *Nuevos caminos para la enseñanza plurilingüe* (pp. 97–116). Donostia: Eusko Ikaskuntza. Ikastaria Cuadernos de Educación 11.

Generalitat de Catalunya (1999) *Les llengues estrangeres: Aspectes organizatius i didactics.* Barcelona: Generalitat de Catalunya, Departament d'Ensenyament.

Genesee, F. (1994) Double immersion programs in Canada. *II Jornadas Internacionales de Educación Plurilingüe* (pp. 1–22). Bilbao: Fundación Gaztelueta.

Genesee, F. (2001) *Second language education for all.* Ponencia presentada en el Congreso Internacional de Educación Plurilingüe, Getxo, Bizkaia.

Giles, H., Bourhis, R.Y. and Taylor, D.M. (1977) Towards a theory of language in ethnic group relations. In H. Giles (ed.) *Language, Ethnicity and Intergroup Relations* (pp. 183–221). New York: Academic Press.

Gobierno Vasco (1996) *Encuesta sociolingüística del País Vasco. La continuidad del Euskara II.* Vitoria-Gasteiz.

Hamers, J.F. (2000) The influence of plurilingual education on child development. In S. Oregi (ed.) *Nuevos caminos para la enseñanza plurilingüe* (pp. 225–48). Donostia: Eusko Ikaskuntza. Ikastaria. Cuadernos de Educación 11.

Hjelmslev, L. (1971) *Prolegómenos a una teoría del lenguaje*. Madrid: Editorial Gredos.

INCE (1996) *Evaluación del rendimiento escolar: Enseñanza Primaria*. Madrid: Instituto Nacional de Calidad y Evaluación, Ministerio de Educación y Cultura.

INCE (1999) *Evaluación de la enseñanza y el aprendizaje de la lengua inglesa. Educación Primaria*. Madrid: Instituto Nacional de Calidad y Evaluación, Ministerio de Educación y Cultura.

Killilea, M. (1994) *Informe de la Comisión de Cultura, Juventud, Educación y Medios de Comunicación sobre las minorías culturales y lingüísticas de la Comunidad Europea*. Parlamento Europeo.

Kuijpers, W. (1987) *Dictamen sobre las lenguas y culturas de las minorías regionales y étnicas en la Comunidad Europea*. Parlamento Europeo.

Lasagabaster, D. (2000) Three languages and three linguistic models in the Basque educational system. In J. Cenoz and U. Jessner (eds) *English in Europe: The Acquisition of a Third Language* (pp.179–97). Clevedon: Multilingual Matters.

Manrique de Lara, S. (2000) Introducción de una lengua extranjera L3 en la etapa infantil (4/5 años) y en el 1er ciclo de Primaria. In S. Oregi (ed.) *Nuevos caminos para la enseñanza plurilingüe* (pp. 49–63). Donostia: Eusko Ikaskuntza. Ikastaria Cuadernos de Educación 11.

Martinez, J. (1997) Factores organizativos y de interés para favorecer la educación trilingüe de los alumnos. In S. Oregi (ed.) *Planificación y organización de la escuela plurilingüe*. Eusko Ikaskuntza (pp. 131–51). Donostia: Eusko Ikaskuntza. Ikastaria Cuadernos de Educación 9.

Nelde, P. (1993) Conflictos lingüísticos en la Europa plurilingüe. *I Jornadas Internacionales de Educación Plurilingüe* (pp. 17–32). Bilbao: Fundación Gaztelueta.

Nelde, P., Strubell, M. and Williams, G. (1996) *Euromosaic: Producción y reproducción de los grupos lingüísticos minoritarios de la Unión Europea*. Luxembourg: European Commission.

Perez, A. (2001) *Los programas de educación multilingüe en el sistema educativo valenciano*. Ponencia presentada en el Congreso Internacional de Educación Plurilingüe, Getxo, Bizkaia.

Ribera, P. (1997) Un cuarto de siglo de experiencia de enseñanza plurilingüe: Aula, Escola Europea de Barcelona. In S. Oregi (ed.) *III Jornadas Internacionales de Educación Plurilingüe. Planificación y organización de la escuela plurilingüe* (pp. 123–29). Donostia: Eusko Ikaskuntza. Ikastaria Cuadernos de Educación 9.

Siguán, M. (1993a) Educación plurilingüe en el ámbito del estado español. *I Jornadas Internacionales de Educación Plurilingüe* (pp. 33–46). Bilbao: Fundación Gaztelueta.

Siguán, M. (1993b) Experiencia de otros países: Luxemburgo por ejemplo. *I Jornadas Internacionales de Educación Plurilingüe* (pp. 63–6). Bilbao: Fundación Gaztelueta.

Siguán, M. (1994) *Conocimiento y uso de las lenguas en España*. Madrid: Centro de Investigaciones Sociológicas.

Vila, I. (1993) *Aspectos didácticos de la educación plurilingüe*. Jornadas Internacionales de Educación Plurilingüe (pp. 159–74). Bilbao: Fundación Gaztelueta.

Ytsma, J. (2000) Trilingual primary education in Friesland. In J. Cenoz and U. Jessner (eds) *English in Europe: The Acquisition of a Third Language* (pp. 222–35). Clevedon: Multilingual Matters.

Chapter 10

Teaching English as a Third Language: The Effect of Attitudes and Motivation

JASONE CENOZ

Introduction

The interest in teaching foreign languages to young children is not new but it has undergone an important revival in Europe in the last two decades. This revival is related to several factors among which we could mention the political, social and cultural development of the European Union, the growing links between the European Union and Eastern European countries and the role of English as a language of intraEuropean and international communication (Cenoz & Jessner, 2000; Weiss, 1991). As Driscoll points out, European pupils 'need to be equipped with the competences, attitudes and skills to cope successfully with the social and economic changes which are transforming life in Europe' (1999: 9). Educational policy-makers in most European Union countries have opted for the early introduction of foreign languages in primary school and this policy stems from the conviction that students' communicative skills and intercultural competence will improve if foreign languages are introduced earlier in the curriculum (Cenoz & Lindsay, 1994; Driscoll & Frost, 1999; Kubanek-German, 1998; Rixon, 1992 etc.). The European Commission's White Paper *Teaching and Learning: Towards the Learning Society* (1995) considers that European citizens should be proficient in three community languages and recommends foreign language teaching at pre-school level in order to allow for second foreign languages in secondary school. Foreign language teaching in primary school or even at the pre-school level ensures an increase in the total amount of exposure to the foreign language, but research studies do not provide enough evidence to confirm the positive effect of the early introduction of the foreign language on the development of foreign language proficiency

(Blondin *et al.*, 1998; Burstall, 1975; Cenoz, 2003; Edelenbos & Johnston, 1996; Muñoz, 2000).

With the exception of English-speaking countries, English is generally the first foreign language and German and French tend to be the most popular second foreign languages in European countries (Ammon, 1996).The increasing role of English in Europe has developed a growing interest in learning English, which is reflected in demands for more English instruction and better quality English instruction in schools. As Hoffmann (2000) points out, there are important differences regarding the position of English in different European Union countries and the presence of English is much stronger in Scandinavia, Belgium and the Netherlands than in southern European countries. Weiss (1991: 29) explains that changes in attitudes towards the learning of foreign languages are also related to the size of the different countries and foreign languages have traditionally been more important in the educational curricula of smaller than larger countries.

Learning more than two languages in the school context is a common experience for many children in Europe. For example, several languages are used as languages of instruction in the European schools (Baetens Beardsmore, 1993; Baker & Jones, 1998; Hoffmann, 1998). Third and fourth language acquisition is also common in bilingual and multilingual communities such as Catalonia, the Basque Country, Friesland, Wales or Ireland. Third language acquisition in school contexts can also take place in multilingual classrooms in the case of children who speak a language at home which is different from the community language(s) and who learn the community language(s) and additional languages at school. This is a very common situation in many European countries where immigration has increased in the last years (Extra & Gorter, 2001). Third language acquisition in the school context is not a new phenomenon, but is becoming more widespread because of the trend to introduce a foreign language from an earlier age and a second foreign language at the end of primary school or in secondary school and because of the increasing use of minority languages in education.

Foreign Language Teaching, Attitudes and Motivation

Language attitudes are generally considered as one of the factors that influence language acquisition, and attitudes have been included in several theoretical models of second language acquisition (Cargile *et al.*, 1994; Gardner, 1985; Gardner & MacIntyre, 1993).

As Baker (1992: 10) points out, attitude is a hypothetical construct used to explain the direction and persistence of human behaviour. Ajzen defines attitude as 'a disposition to respond favourably or unfavourably to an object, person, institution or event' (1988: 4). Therefore, attitudes can be considered evaluative reactions towards an object and in the case of language learning they are evaluative reactions towards the activity of learning languages. According to this social psychological tradition, attitudes towards learning the second language are expected to be related to motivation and achievement. For example, in Gardner's model, motivation is a strong predictor of second language acquisition and is a construct resulting from three factors: the desire to learn the language, attitudes and the effort displayed towards learning the language (Gardner, 1985).

The social-psychological tradition has been criticised by several researchers working in the field of second language acquisition who propose a more education-centred approach to the study of motivation (Crookes & Schmidt, 1991; Dörnyei, 1994a, 1994b; Oxford & Shearing, 1994). Theories developed in motivational psychology, such as self-determination theory (Deci & Ryan, 1985), have also exerted a strong influence on the study of motivation (see Dörnyei, 1998, 2001 for a review).

There are not many studies on attitudes and motivation in child foreign language acquisition, and research on the effect of age in second language acquisition (see for example Harley & Wang, 1997; Singleton, 2001 for reviews) or the specific effect of primary foreign language teaching (Blondin *et al.*, 1998; Edelenbos & Johnston, 1996) has paid more attention to other areas such as general language proficiency. However, positive attitudes and motivation are often mentioned as necessary for language learning and even as one of the aims of pre-school and primary foreign language teaching (Cenoz & Lindsay, 1994; Driscoll, 1999; Halliwell, 1992; Kubanek-German, 1998; Moon, 2000). For example Kubanek-German says:

> Regional and national guidelines unanimously point out that the children's experience with a foreign language ought to be enjoyable and not put an extra burden on them. (1998: 94)

Specific research studies on attitudes and/or motivation in primary school have shown that children enjoy foreign languages classes (Blondin *et al.*, 1998; Burstall, 1975; Clyne *et al.*, 1995; Donato *et al.*, 2000; Hawkins, 1996; Johnstone, 1996; Nikolov, 1999; Satchwell, 1996).

In the case of English as a foreign language in monolingual settings, the study conducted by Nikolov (1999) is worth mentioning because it compares different age groups. Apart from interesting information about the reasons for learning English and the learners' general positive attitude towards learning English, it is reported that the number of students choosing English as their favourite school subject in primary school is higher (75%) in the case of the youngest group (years 1–2) than in the case of learners in years 3–4 (65%) or in years 5–6 (57%). These findings indicate that, at least in the case of the Hungarian students who participated in this study, positive attitudes and motivation towards learning English as a foreign language decrease with age. The study conducted by Nikolov also provides useful information about the way students evaluate different learning activities. She reports a positive attitude towards 'playful learning activities, intrinsically motivating tasks and materials, and a negative attitude towards tests' (1999: 51). Apart from enjoying active and interactional teaching methods, which are more commonly used in pre-school and primary school, younger learners could also be more motivated because of their general positive attitude towards learning as opposed to the rejection of the school system typically associated with older learners.

Other studies on the effect of age have been conducted in bilingual settings and have consistently found that attitudes towards the minority language become less favourable when age goes up (see Baker, 1992 for a review). For example, Baker (1992) found that attitudes towards Welsh became less favourable between 11 and 14 years of age and the most significant change took place between 13 and 14 years of age.

There are very few studies on attitudes and motivation in third language acquisition (see Cenoz, 2002; Sjöholm, 2002) and, in a recent study conducted in Barcelona (Spain) by Tragant and Muñoz (2000), the effect of age on attitudes has been found to be more relevant than the effect of the early introduction of English as a foreign language. When the attitudes presented by learners who had received the same amount of instruction but had started learning English at different ages (third and sixth year of primary) were compared no significant differences were found. The researchers also reported that the number of hours of instruction was associated with attitudes, so that learners who had received more instruction presented more positive attitudes.

Parents' attitudes towards primary foreign language teaching are also regarded as important (Donato *et al.*, 2000; Dörnyei, 2001; Gardner, 1985; Nikolov, 1999) and parents tend to demand the inclusion of a foreign language in primary school (Kubanek-German, 1998). The main reason to support primary foreign language teaching seems to be that they consider that children present advantages when learning foreign languages, as is reported in a study conducted by García, Torras and Tragant (1997).

Pre-school and Primary Foreign Language Teaching in the Basque Country

Traditionally, students in the Basque Autonomous Community achieved relatively low levels of proficiency in English at school and these poor results have been attributed to a number of factors, including large class sizes, the use of out-dated or traditional instructional approaches, the lack of well-trained teachers with adequate proficiency in English, the parents' limited knowledge of English and general limited exposure to English in the social context (Cenoz, 1998).

The Spanish Educational Reform that was implemented in 1993 pays specific attention to the role of foreign languages in the curriculum. In accordance with the Reform, foreign languages are introduced in the third year of primary school at the age of eight, three years earlier than previously. The Reform also considers changes regarding the methods and materials to be used, in an attempt to reflect more recent developments in language teaching and learning. The guidelines emphasise communicative competence, learner-centred syllabuses, cooperation and coordination among teachers, the development of positive attitudes plus new evaluation criteria (Eusko Jaurlaritza-Gobierno Vasco, 1992).

In the Basque Country, the national reforms for foreign languages pose an added challenge, since it is a bilingual community and English is a third language. Basque is a minority language and approximately 27% of the population in the Basque Autonomous Community are bilingual in Basque and Spanish, while the majority of the population are monolingual in Spanish. However, almost 80% of the children in pre-school and primary school are taught through the medium of Basque, 50.5% only have Basque as the language of instruction and 29.5% have both Basque and Spanish as languages of instruction (see Cenoz, 1998, 2001). The rest of the children learn Basque as a school subject. These figures indicate that many children receive intensive instruction in a second language (Basque) in pre-school and primary school when English is introduced as a third language.

A study conducted into primary foreign language teaching in the Basque Country indicates that parents and teachers supported the early introduction of English in the third year of primary, at the age of eight (Cenoz & Lindsay, 1994). In this study, parents, tutors and school directors filled in questionnaires, which included items on the perception of the possible linguistic and non-linguistic effects of the early introduction of English on the development of Basque, Spanish and other school subjects. A total of 500 families, 30 English teachers, 12 tutors and 25 school directors answered these questionnaires and evaluated the experience of primary foreign language teaching very positively. The observation and external assessment reports highlighted the children's positive attitudes and the teachers also perceived the children's attittudes as positive or very positive.

In 1991, a small project involving seven Basque-medium schools ('Ikastolak') went a step further and introduced English as a foreign language in the second year of pre-school, at the age of four. Children involved in this project have either Basque or Spanish (or both languages) as first languages but are also exposed to a second language at school and in the community and, therefore, English is their third language. This project became so popular that nowadays approximately 18,000 pupils from 62 schools participate in the original project. These schools also have Basque as the language of instruction and are public or private, but in all cases receive funding from the Basque Government. Moreover, as a result of pressure from parents and schools, the Basque Government Department of Education has decided to spread this project to most of the 606 pre-schools and primary schools in the Basque Autonomous Community. The popularity of the project could be due to the parents' positive attitudes towards English combined with the schools need to attract pupils in a community with a very low birth-rate.

Therefore, English is nowadays taught in most schools from the age of four, that is, four years earlier than the compulsory age stipulated by the Spanish Educational Reform. When English is introduced in pre-school, there are usually four or five 30-minute sessions per week. The teacher of English only uses English in the classroom and all the activities are oral. The methodology used is based on story-telling, songs and other oral activities and requires the children's active participation by means of collective dramatisation and playing.

Research Questions

The aim of this research study is to analyse the effect of the age of introduction of English as a third language on attitudes and motivation towards learning English in the specific Basque–Spanish bilingual school context. The research questions are the following:

(1) Do learners who have received the same amount of instruction but started learning English at different ages present similar attitudes and motivation?
(2) Do learners who are the same age but have received different amounts of instruction present similar attitudes and motivation?

The first research question tries to confirm the results of other studies, which report that younger children present more positive attitudes and/or are more motivated to learn the foreign languages than older children (see for example Burstall, 1975; Nikolov, 1999). The second research question looks at attitudes and motivation from the opposite perspective and aims at exploring whether the amount of instruction and the early introduction of English have a long-term influence on the development of attitudes and motivation. It explores whether the positive attitudes and motivation typically associated with young learners are maintained and are more positive than those of learners who have received less instruction in English as a foreign language.

Methodology

Participants

All the participants in this research study ($N = 171$) were primary and secondary school children from a single school in an industrial town in the Basque Country. This school has Basque as the language of instruction and it serves both as a total immersion programme for students whose first language is Spanish and a first language maintenance programme for students whose first language is Basque (Cenoz, 1998). Spanish and English are taught as school subjects but Basque is the main language of communication at school.

English is taught as a third language to all the students and, traditionally, the English language was introduced in the sixth year of primary school (11-years-olds). When the Spanish Educational Reform was implemented in 1993, the teaching of English was introduced in the third year of primary school when children were eight years old. The school took part in a specific project, which started in 1991, to introduce the teaching of English in the second year of pre-school at the age of four. Therefore, this school provides the opportunity of comparing groups of children who have started their English classes at three different ages within the same bilingual programme. The children in this research study have Basque or Spanish as their first language and come from the same geographical area and similar social backgrounds (middle class). The subjects included in this research study were selected on the condition that they did not receive any other form of instruction or were not exposed to English outside school (e.g. private classes, classes provided by language academies, summer courses, etc.). These conditions and the fact that three age groups can be compared within the same school provide an ideal setting to compare the effect of age of introduction on attitudes and motivation to learn English, because participants also share many other characteristics related to the general pedagogical approach adopted by this school. The complexity of the Basque educational system includes different models, different types of private and public schools, important differences in the use of Basque and Spanish in different areas and different approaches to the teaching of English. The combination of these factors make it difficult to generalise the results obtained in this study to the whole of the Basque Country.

The sample is divided into three cohorts (Table 10.1) according to the age at which English was introduced: second year of pre-school, third year of primary or sixth year of primary. The distribution of male and female subjects is quite balanced: 53.2% male and 46.8% female learners in cohort 1; 50.9% male and 49.1% female learners in cohort; 2 and 43.5% male and 56.5% female participants in cohort 3.

The data in Table 10.1 indicate that the mean age in the nine groups included in the three cohorts ranges from 9.1 to 17.4 years of age when the data were collected. The course in which the data were collected ranges from the fourth year of primary to the sixth year of secondary. The last column indicates the number of hours of instruction that the participants received when the data were collected (range 500–800). The data were collected in three consecutive years from 1998 to 2000.

Table 10.1 Characteristics of the sample

	Starting course and age	*Age (data collection)*	*Course (data collection)*	*Hours of English (data collection)*
Cohort 1 ($n = 64$)	2nd pre-school (4 years old)	9.1 10.1 11.1	4th primary 5th primary 6th primary	500 600 700
Cohort 2 ($n = 59$)	3rd primary (8 years old)	13.1 14.1 15.3	2nd secondary 3rd secondary 4th secondary	600 700 800
Cohort 3 ($n = 48$)	6th primary (11 years old)	15.1 16.3 17.4	4th secondary 5th secondary 6th secondary	500 600 700

Instruments and procedure

Apart from a background questionnaire, participants were asked to complete an attitude questionnaire based on Gardner's (1985) and Baker's (1992) questionnaires in order to measure their attitudes towards English. The questionnaire had an Osgood format and included eight adjectives (pleasant, important, interesting, appealing, useful etc.) and their opposites and students were asked to express their feelings towards learning English (Learning English is . . .). Each of the items had a score ranging from 1 to 7 and the total score ranged from 8 to 56 (higher = more positive).

Motivation towards learning the language was measured by a scale based on Gardner (1985), including a combination of the three components of motivation as proposed by Gardner: desire to learn the language (I wish to learn a lot of English; I am very interested in learning English . . .), effort (I try to learn as much as possible in my English classes, I make an effort to learn English . . .) and attitudes towards learning the language (I like my English classes, I like learning English . . .). The motivation questionnaire included 13 items and had a Likert format asking students to identify with one of the five positions ranging from 'I strongly agree' to 'I strongly disagree'. Each of the items had a score ranging from 1 to 5 and the total score ranged from 13 to 65 (higher = more positive).

Results

The first research question aimed at comparing the attitudes and motivation presented by learners who had received the same number of hours of instruction but started learning English at different ages. In order to answer the first research question we compared the means obtained in the attitudes and motivation questionnaires by different age groups who had received the same amount of instruction. Statistical analyses corresponding to 500, 600 and 700 hours of instruction were carried out in order to see if the differences between the groups were significant.

The mean scores and standard deviations corresponding to approximately 500 hours of instruction are presented in Table 10.2. The table includes the comparison between cohorts 1 and 3, that is, between students who had started learning English at the pre-school level and in the sixth year of primary school. Learners in cohort 1 had been studying English for six years and learners in cohort 3 for five years, but the amount of instruction was the same for both groups. There are no data available for cohort 2 after 500 hours of instruction.

Table 10.2 Attitudes and motivation after 500 hours of instruction

	Cohort 1 4th primary		Cohort 3 4th secondary			
	M	S.D.	M	S.D	T	S
Attitudes	44.1	9.9	39.4	9.6	1.81	0.07
Motivation	56.5	8.1	53.4	7.5	1.51	0.13

The results of the T-tests indicate that the differences between the means are marginally significant in attitudes (T = 1.81, S = 0.07). Learners in the fourth year of primary school obtained slightly higher scores in the attitude questionnaire than learners in the fourth year of secondary school. There were no differences between the two groups in the motivation scores (T = 1.51, S = 0.13).

The mean scores and standard deviations obtained in the attitudes and motivation questionnaires after 600 hours of instruction are presented in Table 10.3. Learners in cohort 1 had been studying English for seven years and learners in cohorts 2 and 3 for six years, but the amount of instruction was the same for the three groups.

The results of the ANOVA analyses indicate that the differences between the means are significant both for attitudes (F = 8.08, S = 0.00) and motivation (F = 5.19, S = 0.00). Learners in the fifth year of primary school obtained the highest scores both in attitudes and motivation. The Scheffe procedure indicates that there are significant differences in attitudes when the fifth year of primary is compared to the second year of secondary (S = 0.00) and also when the fifth year of primary is compared to the fifth year of secondary (S = 0.01). There are also significant differences in motivation when the fifth year of primary is compared to the second year of secondary (S = 0.00) but the differences in motivation between the fifth year of primary and the fifth year of secondary are only marginally significant (S = 0.09). The differences between the scores obtained in attitudes (S = 0.40) and motivation (S = 0.53) by the two secondary school groups are not significant.

The mean scores and standard deviations of the attitudes and motivation questionnaires after 700 hours of instruction are presented in Table 10.4. Learners in cohort 1 had been studying English for eight years and learners in cohorts 2 and 3 for seven years, but the amount of instruction was the same for the three groups.

Table 10.3 Attitudes and motivation after 600 hours of instruction

	Cohort 1 5th primary		Cohort 2 2nd secondary		Cohort 3 5th secondary			
	M	S.D.	M	S.D.	M	S.D.	F	S
Attitudes	42.8	10.2	32.8	10.4	35.6	9.3	8.08	0.00
Motivation	52.1	11.2	44.4	9.9	46.7	9.8	5.19	0.00

Table 10.4 Attitudes and motivation after 700 hours of instruction

	Cohort 1 6th primary		Cohort 2 3rd secondary		Cohort 3 6th secondary			
	M	S.D.	M	S.D.	M	S.D.	F	S
Attitudes	40	10.3	31.9	10.3	36.7	8.2	4.89	0.01
Motivation	48.7	9.6	45.7	8.7	47.6	8.6	0.79	0.45

The results of the ANOVA analyses indicate that the differences between the means are significant in attitudes (F = 4.9, S = 0.01). Learners in the sixth year of primary school obtained the highest scores in the attitudes questionnaire. The Scheffe procedure indicates that there are significant differences in attitudes when the sixth year of primary is compared to the third year of secondary (S = 0.01), but not when the sixth year of primary is compared to the sixth year of secondary (S = 0.39). The difference between the scores obtained in attitudes by the two secondary school groups is not significant (S = 0.19). The differences between the scores obtained in the motivation questionnaire by the three groups are not significant (F = 0.79, S = 0.45).

The second research question aims at examining the influence of the early introduction of English and the amount of instruction on the development of attitudes and motivation. In order to answer this question the means obtained by learners who were the same age (15.1 and 15.3) and were in the same course (fourth year of secondary), but who have received a different number of hours of instruction in English (800 hours vs. 500 hours), were compared. The data available corresponds to cohorts 2 and 3, that is, to learners who had started learning English in the third and the sixth years of primary school (see Table 10.5).

Table 10.5 Attitudes and motivation in the fourth year of secondary

	Cohort 2 800 hours		Cohort 3 500 hours			
	M	S.D.	M	S.D	T	S
Attitudes	35.4	9.6	39.4	9.6	1.21	0.23
Motivation	43.2	10.1	53.4	7.5	2.49	0.01

The results of the T-tests indicate that the differences between the means of the two groups are significant in motivation ($T = 2.5$, $S = 0.01$). Learners in cohort 3 (500 hours of instruction) presented significantly higher scores in the motivation questionnaire. The differences between the two groups in the attitudes questionnaire do not reach significance ($T = 1.2$; $S = 0.23$).

Discussion

In order to answer the first research question, the attitudes and motivation presented by learners who had received the same amount of instruction but started learning English at different ages were compared. The results of the statistical analyses indicate that younger learners tend to present significantly more positive attitudes than older learners after 500, 600 and 700 hours of instruction. The differences between the means are only marginally significant after 500 hours of instruction, but they go in the same direction, that is, learners in cohort 1 present more positive attitudes towards learning English than learners in cohorts 2 and 3. It is also interesting to see that there are no significant differences between cohorts 2 and 3, that is, between students who received instruction from the third and the sixth years of primary school. The scores of the motivation questionnaire go in the same direction, but only reach significance after 600 hours of instruction. Therefore, our results support the findings of other studies in which younger learners present more positive attitudes than older learners (see for example Baker, 1992; Burstall, 1975; Nikolov, 1999), but they are different from those reported by Tragant and Muñoz (2000) who found no differences in attitudes when they compared younger and older learners.

The more positive attitudes and motivation presented by primary school learners can be explained as being linked to psychological and educational factors. Psychological factors associated with age could explain a rejection of the school system and affect the attitudes and motivation scores obtained by secondary school subjects. In fact, learners in the second and third years of secondary school with a mean age of 13.1 and 14.1 (cohort 2) present the less positive attitudes and motivation and these results could be linked to psychological changes associated with adolescence.

An alternative explanation is related to educational factors and particularly to input and the teaching method used in secondary school as compared to primary school. Learners seem to enjoy their English classes when an oral-based approach and a very active methodology based on drama and storytelling are used. Their attitudes and motivation are less positive when more attention is devoted to grammar and vocabulary learning in secondary school. This explanation is compatible with the findings reported by Nikolov (1999) and Littlewood (2001). Nikolov (1999) reported that students enjoy playful learning activities but not tests. Similarly, in a recent survey conducted in eleven countries, most of the 2656 participants professed to enjoy active participation in the foreign language learning process and interaction with other students (Littlewood, 2001).

Our results also indicate that attitudes and motivation are dynamic and can change over time. For example, attitudes in cohort 1 suffer a decline between the fourth and the sixth years of primary school, but attitudes in cohort 3 experiment a slight increase between the fifth and the sixth year of secondary school.

The second research question aims at comparing the attitudes and motivation presented by learners who are in the same school year but who have received different amounts of instruction. In this case psychological factors associated with age that have been discussed as related to the first research question are controlled because the groups of learners compared were the same age. The results of the statistical analyses indicate that there are no differences in attitudes, but learners in cohort 3 (500 hours of instruction) present better scores in motivation than learners in cohort 2 (800 hours of instruction). A possible explanation is related to the type of input and methodology. Learners in cohort 2 started learning English in the third course of primary school at the age of eight and had an oral-based approach based on communicative materials in primary school. These learners experience a more grammar-based approach after they have moved to secondary school and this contrast between the two methodologies may affect their motivation. The results of this study contradict those reported by Tragant and Muñoz (2000), who also compared the effect of the amount of instruction in the case of learners who had received instruction from the third and the sixth year of primary school, and found that more hours of instruction were associated with more positive attitudes. It is difficult to find an explanation for these different findings, but one possibility is related to the dynamic character of attitudes and motivation in foreign language learning. Tragant and Muñoz (2000) measured attitudes when learners were in the first year of secondary school and our measurement corresponds to the fourth year of secondary school and to approximately 300 additional hours of instruction, so this important difference in exposure could be a possible explanation for our results. Another possible explanation could be related to the important presence of English in Barcelona as compared to the Basque town in which our study was carried out. Learners in Tragant and Muñoz's study might view English as more useful than learners in the Basque Country. They might even benefit from exposure at the community level, while learners in cohort 2 in our study are in their tenth year of instruction but are not normally exposed to English outside school.

Pre-school and primary foreign language teaching can exert a positive influence on learners' attitudes and motivation, but these positive attitudes and motivation are not necessarily maintained throughout primary school and into the first years of secondary school. Attitudes and motivation are dynamic and it is necessary for teachers to use strategies to motivate learners, particularly in the case of older ones. The commandments identified by Dörnyei (1994a) and Dörnyei and Csizér (1998) are useful steps in this direction. It is also important to conduct longitudinal studies in order to examine the linguistic and non-linguistic outcomes of the early introduction of English as a third language in bilingual communities in order to know the optimal age for third language acquisition in different formal contexts. However, due to the specific and complex educational and social factors involved in third language learning in bilingual contexts it is more likely that we would find several optimal ages for the introduction of a third language than a single one.

Acknowledgements

The work described in this chapter was supported by BFF 2000–0101 grants from the Spanish Ministry of Science and Technology and PI–1998–96 grant from the Basque Government.

References

Ajzen, I. (1988) *Attitudes, Personality and Behaviour*. Milton Keynes, Open University Press.
Ammon, U. (1996) The European Union: Status change of English during the last fifty years. In J.A. Fishman, A.W. Conrad and A. Rubal-Lopez (eds) *Post-Imperial English* (pp. 241–67). Berlin: Mouton de Gruyter.

Baetens Beardsmore, H. (ed.) (1993) *European Models of Bilingual Education.* Clevedon: Multilingual Matters.

Baker, C. (1992) *Attitudes and Language.* Clevedon: Multilingual Matters.

Baker, C. and Jones, S.P. (1998) *Encyclopedia of Bilingualism and Bilingual Education.* Clevedon: Multilingual Matters.

Blondin, C., Candelier, M., Edelenbos, P., Johnstone, R., Kubanek-German, A. and Taeschner, T. (1998) *Foreign Language in Primary and Pre-school Education.* London: CILT.

Burstall, C. (1975) French in the primary school: The British experiment. *The Canadian Modern Language Review* 31, 388–402.

Cargile, A., Giles, H., Ryan, E. and Bradac, J. (1994) Language attitudes as a social process: A conceptual model and new directions. *Language and Communication* 14, 211–36.

Cenoz, J. (1998) Multilingual education in the Basque Country. In J. Cenoz and F. Genesee (eds) *Beyond Bilingualism: Multilingualism and Multilingual Education* (pp. 175–91). Clevedon: Multilingual Matters.

Cenoz, J. (2001) Basque in Spain and France. In G. Extra and G. Gorter (eds) *The Other Languages of Europe* (pp. 45–57). Clevedon: Multilingual Matters.

Cenoz, J. (2002) Three languages in contact: Language attitudes in the Basque Country. In D. Lasagabaster and J. Sierra (eds) *Language Awareness in the Foreign Language Classroom* (pp. 37–60). Leioa: Universidad del País Vasco.

Cenoz, J. (2003) The influence of age on the acquisition of English: General proficiency, attitudes and code mixing. In M.P. García Mayo and M.L. García Lecumberri (eds) *Age and the Acquisition of English as a Foreign Language: Theoretical Issues and Field Work* (pp. 77–93). Clevedon: Multilingual Matters.

Cenoz, J. and Jessner, U. (2000) Introduction. In J. Cenoz and U. Jessner (eds) *English in Europe: The Acquisition of a Third Language* (pp. vii–xii). Clevedon: Multilingual Matters.

Cenoz, J. and Lindsay, D. (1994) Teaching English in primary school: A project to introduce a third language to eight year olds. *Language and Education* 8, 201–10.

Clyne, M., Jenkins, C., Chen, I.Y., Tsokalidou, R. and Wallner, T. (1995) *Developing Second Language from Primary School: Models and Outcomes.* Deakin: National Languages and Literacy Institute of Australia.

Crookes, G. and Schmidt, R. (1991) Motivation: Reopening the research agenda. *Language Learning* 41, 469–512.

Deci, E.L. and Ryan, R.M. (1985) *Intrinsic Motivation and Self-determination in Human Behaviour.* New York: Plenum.

Donato, R., Tucker, G.R., Wudthayagorn, J. and Igarashi, K. (2000) Converging evidence: Attitudes, achievements and instruction in the later years of FLES. *Foreign Language Annals* 33, 377–93.

Driscoll, P. (1999) Modern foreign languages in the primary school: A French start. In P. Driscoll and D. Frost (eds) *The Teaching of Modern Foreign Languages in the Primary School* (pp. 9–26). London: Routledge.

Driscoll, P. and Frost, D. (eds) (1999) *The Teaching of Modern Foreign Languages in the Primary School.* London: Routledge.

Dörnyei, Z. (1994a) Motivation and motivating in the foreign language classroom. *Modern Language Journal* 78, 273–84.

Dörnyei, Z. (1994b) Understanding L2 motivation: On with the challenge! *Modern Language Journal* 78, 515–23.

Dörnyei, Z. (1998) Motivation in second and foreign language learr
Teaching 31, 117–35.

Dörnyei, Z. (2001) *Teaching and Researching Motivation.* Ha
Education.

Dörnyei, Z. and Csizér, K. (1998) Ten commandments for motivating langua_ɓɛ
learners: Results of an empirical study. *Language Teaching Research* 2, 203–29.

Edelenbos, P. and Johnston, R. (1996) *Researching Languages at Primary School.*
London: CILT.

European Commission (1995) *Teaching and Learning: Towards the Learning Society.*
White Paper. Brussels: European Commission.

Eusko Jaurlaritza-Gobierno Vasco (1992) *Oinarrizko Curriculum Diseinua-Diseño
Curricular Básico.* Vitoria-Gasteiz.

Extra, G. and Gorter, D. (eds) (2001) *The Other Languages of Europe.* Clevedon:
Multilingual Matters.

Gardner, R. (1985) *Social Psychology and Second Language Learning.* London: Arnold.

Gardner, R. and MacIntyre, P. (1993) A student's contribution to second language
learning. Part II: Affective variables. *Language Teaching* 26, 1–11.

García, M.L., Torras, M.R. and Tragant, E. (1997) Croyances populaires sur
l'apprentissage précoce d'une langue étrangère. *AILE* 10, 127–58.

Halliwell, S. (1992) *Teaching English in the Primary School.* London: Longman.

Harley, B. and Wang, B. (1997) The critical period hypothesis: Where are we now?
In A.M.B. de Groot and J.F. Kroll (eds) *Tutorials in Bilingualism: Psycholinguistic
Perspectives* (pp. 19–51). Mahwah, NJ: Lawrence Erlbaum.

Hawkins, E. (ed.) (1996) *Thirty Years of Language Teaching.* London: CILT.

Hoffmann, C. (1998) Luxembourg and the European schools. In J. Cenoz and F.
Genesee (eds) *Beyond Bilingualism: Multilingualism and Multilingual Education*
(pp. 143–174). Clevedon: Multilingual Matters.

Hoffmann, C. (2000) The spread of English and the growth of multilingualism
with English in Europe. In J. Cenoz and U. Jessner (eds) *English in Europe: The
Acquisition of a Third Language* (pp. 1–21). Clevedon: Multilingual Matters.

Johnston, R. (1996) The Scottish initiatives. In E. Hawkins (ed.) *Thirty Years of
Language Teaching* (pp. 171–5). London: CILT.

Kubanek-German, A. (1998) Primary foreign language teaching in Europe: Trends
and issues. *Language Teaching* 31, 193–205.

Littlewood, W. (2001) Students' attitudes to classroom English learning: A cross-
cultural study. *Language Teaching Research* 5, 3–28.

Moon, J. (2000) *Children Learning English.* Oxford: Macmillan-Heinemann.

Muñoz, C. (2000) Bilingualism and trilingualism in school students in Catalonia.
In J. Cenoz and U. Jessner (eds) *English in Europe: The Acquisition of a Third
Language* (pp. 157–78). Clevedon: Multilingual Matters.

Nikolov, M. (1999) 'Why do you learn English?' 'Because the teacher is short.' A
study of Hungarian children's foreign language learning motivation. *Language
Teaching Research* 3, 33–56.

Oxford, R. and Shearing, J. (1994) Where are we regarding language learning motivation? *Modern Language Journal* 78, 512–14.

Rixon, S. (1992) English and other languages for younger children: Practice and
theory in a rapidly changing world. *Language Teaching* 25, 73–93.

Satchwell, P. (1996) The present position in England. In E. Hawkins (ed.) *Thirty
Years of Language Teaching* (pp. 171–5). London: CILT.

Singleton, D. (2001) Age and second language acquisition. *Annual Review of Applied Linguistics* 21, 77–89.

Sjöholm, K. (2002) English as a third language in bilingual Finland: Basic communication or academic language? Proceedings of the second International Conference on Third Language Acquisition and Trilingualism. Ljouwert: Fryske Akademy.

Tragant, E. and Muñoz, C. (2000) La motivación y su relación con la edad en un contexto escolar de aprendizaje de una lengua extranjera. In C. Muñoz (ed.) *Segundas Lenguas: Adquisición en el Aula* (pp. 81–105). Barcelona: Ariel.

Weiss, F. (1991) FLES in Europe: A revival. In G.L. Ervin (ed.) *International Perspectives on Foreign Language Teaching* (pp. 28–35). Lincolnwood, IL: NTC.

Chapter 11

English as a Third Language in Bilingual Finland: Basic Communication or Academic Language?

KAJ SJÖHOLM

Introduction

A common issue for policy-makers of national language programmes is whether the proficiency of each of the languages found in the national curriculum will develop adequately, if instruction is divided among three, or even four, languages. As the linguistic and cultural landscape, especially in Europe, has undergone radical changes during the latter half of the twentieth century, it has become even more difficult to assess the skills in the different languages. This is partly so because of the highly differing interaction and practice opportunities found between English, the major foreign language in Finnish schools, and other foreign languages taught in Finland (see Forsman, 2000; Sjöholm, 2001). Another problem pertaining to the assessment of languages has to do with whether language grades awarded in Finland share the meanings through common definitions with other community languages. In order to establish a common reference frame of language assessment, a series of common criterion statements defining a specified set of proficiency levels have been developed in relation to the multilingual and multicultural context typical of the countries in the European Union (see *Common European Framework of Reference for Languages*, 2001).

This study is focused on recent developments in bilingual Finland. According to Finnish legislation, Finnish and Swedish are official languages (or national languages) in Finland, and both languages seem today to enjoy relatively high social prestige within an integrated national state. The great majority belongs to the Finnish-speaking population

(94%), whereas a little more than 290,000 (5.7%) out of a total population of 5.2 million are registered as Swedish speakers (Swedish in Finland, 2000). Ethnically, Finland used to be a very homogeneous nation. During the last decade, however, there have been signs of an increasing linguistic and ethnic heterogeneity (Suomi Lukuina, 2002). Because of changing demographic structures and new school legislation, an increasing number of the Finnish–speaking majority, as well as the Swedish-speaking minority, are turning bilingual or trilingual. One reason for the growing number of Finnish-Swedish bilinguals in Finland is no doubt the rapid expansion of Swedish immersion programmes in Finnish-speaking schools (Björklund & Suni, 2000). A change in the Finnish educational legislation in the early 1990s granted the right of different school levels to decide freely on whether to use a language other than L1 when deemed appropriate (A 261/1991; A 262/1991). Because of the massive movement of Finns into some traditionally Swedish-speaking coastal areas (e.g. the Helsinki region) during the last 20 years or so, many formerly purely Swedish-speaking areas have got a Finnish majority, thus resulting in an increasing number of bilinguals (Tandefelt, 1999). In addition to being bilingual in the two national languages in Finland, an increasing number of Swedes and Finns estimate that their knowledge of a third language, English, is sufficiently good (even excellent) to take jobs or study abroad (cf. Väyrynen *et al.*, 1998). According to self-report data, a considerable amount of exposure to English input has been found to take place via mass media outside the school context, which has led to positive attitudes towards English (Forsman, 2000; Sjöholm, 2000).

It seems that popular youth culture, entertainment and mass media have led to an increased use of English for a variety of communicative functions by Finnish as well as Swedish adolescents outside the classroom. It has been argued that English, especially from a European perspective, has become the dominant language in a large number of domains, such as commerce, industry, sport, tourism, computer technology and especially the language of advertising for consumer goods, such as clothes, cosmetics, cigarettes and cars (Hoffmann, 2000: 10). It is assumed that the presence of English in these out-of-school activities will result in the incidental learning of this language to some extent, as well as to the development of positive linguistic attitudes. The desire to become a participant of these activities may provide the initial motivation to acquire English, or the spur to become more proficient in that language (see Hoffmann, 2000: 11). Many schoolchildren (especially Swedish-speaking) therefore feel they are trilingual rather than bilingual.

How does this corolate w/ Dutch ch.?

A crucial question is whether the incidental learning of English results in the same kind of proficiency as that resulting from formal learning of English in the classroom. According to Cummins (2000) we need to make a fundamental distinction between 'conversational' and 'academic' *—KEY POINT* aspects of language proficiency. Gibbons (1991) also clearly expresses the difference between the everyday language of face-to-face interaction, which she terms 'playground language', and the language of schooling, which she terms 'classroom language'. There seems to be some evidence that the incidental learning taking place outside the classroom is primarily beneficial to the development of conversational proficiency and especially to the development of receptive skills (see Takala, 1998). It has also been found that academic proficiency in English depends heavily on words of Graeco-Latin origin, whereas conversational skill relies more on a lexicon that is Anglo-Saxon in origin (Corson, 1993). In a later work, Corson (1997) pointed out that printed texts provided much more exposure to Graeco-Latin words than oral texts. It is assumed that the academic aspects of language are more visible at the advanced level. Because of the limited and unrepresentative classroom input advanced students are exposed to, learner English is believed to show certain features of bookishness.

Although we do not lack evidence in support of the relationship between quantity of input and language proficiency, it has convincingly been shown that the learner's output is not isomorphic with native speaker input, i.e. learners do not assimilate all the native speaker forms to which they are introduced (Larsen-Freeman, 1985: 442). In fact, the learners are clearly not passive recipients of target language input, but actively (though not necessarily consciously) choose what input to attend to. This is explained by Krashen (1982), who argues that an 'affective filter' prevents learners from using input that is available in the environment. According to Krashen, the learner's state of mind or disposition determines to what extent the filter limits what is noticed or acquired. When the learner is stressed, self-conscious, or unmotivated the filter will be 'up', whereas the filter will be 'down' when the learner is relaxed and motivated (see Lightbown & Spada, 1993: 28–9). The second language learning process is, however, also affected by various cross-linguistic factors, which may be exhibited as 'errors', but also as overuse, underuse or avoidance of certain linguistic features (see Sharwood Smith & Kellerman, 1986). In addition, second language learning may also be dependent on learner internal factors, such as general linguistic ability, verbal and lexical inferencing skills, metacognitive skills, ability to use communication and learning strategies etc.

The Finnish Scene

This study attempts to characterise the kind of linguistic attitudes and the kind of English proficiency that is being developed in Swedish secondary school learners in the multilingual and increasingly heterogeneous learning context typical of Finland. The process of acquisition may be described as a mixture of spontaneous language acquisition that has been termed incidental learning, and a more explicit classroom learning comprising consciously acquired language knowledge. Incidental learning, which is mainly a result of activities taking place outside school (e.g. through the mass media etc.), has been defined as 'the accidental learning of information without the intention of remembering that information' (Hulstijn *et al.*, 1996: 327). Television and film comprise good examples of mass media leading to incidental learning of English. As films and English programmes are not dubbed on Finnish television channels, and as subtitles are often provided in L1 (Finnish or Swedish), television exerts a very strong influence on the incidental learning of English.

It has repeatedly been argued that Finland has a relatively 'heavy language programme' in school (Takala, 2000: 49). In addition to the second national language (i.e. Finnish in Swedish-speaking schools), it is common that students in the lower- and upper-secondary school study two or three additional languages. The number of lessons reserved for L2 teaching per week in each language is, however, not very large in comparison to some European countries (two or three periods per week). The major languages in Swedish-speaking schools are Finnish and English. In Swedish-speaking schools, Finnish, the second national language, is usually chosen in Grade 3. In most Swedish schools, English starts in Grade 5 (in some urban areas, earlier). A third obligatory language (usually German or French) is chosen in Grade 8. In the upper-secondary school, an additional language is chosen. English is, however, by far the most popular first foreign language in Finland. In fact it was found that 86.3% had chosen English as first foreign language in Finnish comprehensive schools in 1996–7 (Björklund & Suni, 2000: 202). German was chosen by 3.9% and French by only 1.4%.

Although the new national curriculum of 1994 advocates communicative language teaching and a shift towards a more speech-oriented curriculum, most of the English lessons are, surprisingly enough, concentrated on written skills and grammar (Pietilä, 2001). In a study by Shepherd (2000), it was found that students at the upper-secondary level perceived the content of their English classes to be dominated by the teaching and learning of grammar/structure. Shepherd also found that written tasks had been prominent in the English classroom (Shepherd, 2000: 103). It was also found that the textbook was by far the most important instrument of teaching (Shepherd, 2000: 118).

Most students of English would probably opt for more speaking practice in the classroom, but schoolchildren in Finland are, in spite of this, highly motivated to learn English, and their attitudes towards using and learning the language are extremely positive (Sjöholm, 2000; Turunen, 2001). As a consequence of the popularity of English among Swedish-speaking learners (and Finnish-speaking ones as well), some school leaders, especially curriculum planners at the Finnish National Board of Education, have put forward arguments against the dominant position of this language. They argue that the usefulness of English as a European language tends to be overestimated, and leads to a diminished motivation to learn other foreign languages (see Björklund & Suni, 2000: 203).

In this study, the data are mainly collected from among Swedish-speaking learners of English in Finland. The Swedish population is spread over the coastal areas of Finland. On the rural western coast (Ostrobothnia), you still find a fair number of monolingual Swedes, whereas most of the Swedes in the southern regions are Swedish–Finnish bilinguals. Some complementary data have also been used from among comparable Finnish-speaking learners, and in addition some reference has been made to some recently published articles based on the International Corpus of Learner English (ICLE) database (see Granger, 1998).

The Aim of the Study

The general aim of the study is to try to point out some features typical of the conditions under which English is acquired inside school (formal learning) and outside school (incidental learning). The idea is that differing learning conditions will have consequences for the development of linguistic attitudes and ultimately for the kind of proficiency students will achieve. Basically, the study shows the development of language attitudes and proficiency among learners from lower-secondary (14-year-olds) to upper-secondary and advanced level (17–20-year-olds). The typical features in the learning situation, the linguistic attitudes as well as the resultant linguistic, especially lexical, achievement indicated by the data will also be related to what is advocated in the curriculum. The specific aims of the study are summarised as follows:

(1) To describe the conditions for informal (incidental) learning of English, development of linguistic attitudes and consequences for lexical achievement (proficiency) outside school.
(2) To describe the conditions for formal learning of English, development of linguistic attitudes and the resultant lexical achievement (proficiency) in a classroom setting.
(3) To discuss the classroom implications of the results of (1) and (2) in terms of the development of *conversational* and *academic* English (cf. BICS/CALP).

Ultimately, the goal is, of course, to obtain some insights in how learning situations may be organised in order for learners to derive maximum benefit from exposure to the L2 in teaching situations.

The impact of mass media at lower-secondary level

To start with, some data on the effects of the exposure of English input in informal situations will be presented. Anecdotal evidence tells us that English is increasingly present outside the classroom in Finland, mostly via mass media of different kinds. This, it is believed, will lead to a substantial amount of incidental learning of English. In fact, in a research project at the Department of Teacher Education at Åbo Akademi University it was found that English mass media do have an influence on the development of English as well as the attitudes towards English (see Sjöholm, 2000, 2001; Forsman, 2000). The data presented below will primarily be derived from the secondary level. Thus Forsman (2000) examines to what extent and how English mass media tend to influence the development of linguistic attitudes and lexical development among Swedish-speaking lower-secondary school children (14-year-olds). Her subjects ($n = 330$) turned out to be great consumers of activities where English was used, the most frequent ones being watching television/video and listening to music. Different activities with computers (e.g. e-mail, the Internet, computer games etc.) constituted a third important group of English leisure time activities in her data. In a study by myself (Sjöholm, 2000), it was found that Swedish-speaking upper-secondary school students (18-year-olds) were engaged in much the same English leisure time activities as the students in Forsman's study. Self-report data showed that my students were engaged in English leisure time activities for more than 20 hours a week, whereas Forsman's students were exposed to English input considerably more. In fact, Forsman's data indicated that the students in the western parts of Finland (Ostrobothnia) spent 36 hours a week on English activities, whereas those in the southern region of Finland reported 51 hours. These differences by region were statistically significant as also were the differences between rural and urban areas (see Figure 11.1).

The greatest differences between the upper- and lower-secondary school students were that the latter watched television and used computers (mostly computer games) more than twice as often as the students in upper-secondary schools.

Both Forsman's and my own studies indicated that the attitudes towards using and learning English are extremely positive among Swedish learners, even more positive than towards using and learning Finnish (Sjöholm, 2000). On the whole, the data seem to show that positive attitudes do not stem from classroom experiences, but rather from experiences outside the school context. Thus Forsman (2000) found a positive

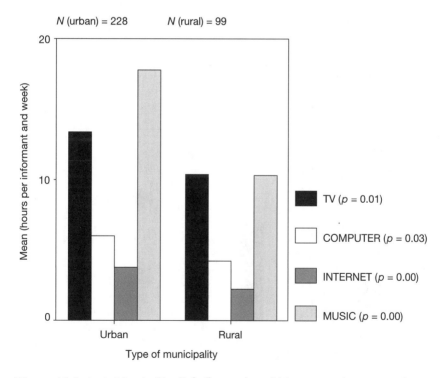

Figure 11.1 Activities in English (hours/week) by type of municipality
Source: Forsman (2000: 172)

correlation between the length of time spent on English leisure time activities and the preference for American vocabulary over British. In order to establish the learners' lexical competence, Forsman used a simple test format consisting of ten word pairs, one of which was American and the other British (e.g. *truck–lorry*) (see Figure 11.2).

Her results also indicated that the preference for American vocabulary was significantly stronger in the southern part of Finland where the students had spent most time on English leisure time activities. Forsman's test results also showed that the students in the southern parts of Finland were more knowledgeable of the meanings of the words than the students in the west. However, Forsman believes that her test results may well reflect the general positive attitudes learners of this age tend to have towards American English and American values. Because of the strong influence of American pop music and American television programmes

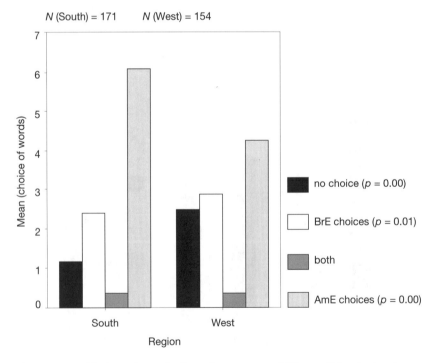

Figure 11.2 Choice of vocabulary (mean out of 10 possible choices)
Source: Forsman (2000: 173)

and films, British English may appear strange and old-fashioned to many students. This view may be strengthened by the fact that the great majority of the English teachers use British English in the classroom. Some excerpts of learner responses will illustrate this (Forsman, 2000: 175).

> *No, we learn British English and the pronunciation is impossible to understand.*
> *We learn British English. I don't like it. I use American English, I learn it from music and TV.*

By contrasting the kind of English students receive at school and the kind of language they actually wish to have, some interesting patterns emerged. The following excerpts in Forsman's data seem to indicate that many students prefer to acquire English for everyday use (Forsman, 2000: 178).

> *'Nice' English. Not useful. No slang.*
> *The way we learn English at school, nobody speaks that way for real in England or America.* relevant point
> *Sometimes our English is too English. When you're speaking normally to someone, you don't use nice words like 'Yes, indeed'.*

Forsman's data seem to suggest that Swedish lower-secondary school pupils tend to make a sharp distinction between two rather different language norms. One of the norms stems from the exposure to authentic everyday English speech which the learners basically have picked up on their own via television, music and computers. This norm, which was clearly favoured by the learners themselves, included colloquialisms and idioms slang expressions. This kind of English appeared to the students to be equated with American English. The other norm was classroom English, which to the learners sounded unnatural and bookish and which was associated with British English, partly because most teachers used this variety of English in the classroom. Another reason why some students expressed critical views about classroom English may stem from the fact that written material, which too often has a non-authentic ring about it, still tends to dominate practice in the language classroom.

To sum up, it is evident that Swedish-speaking lower-secondary school pupils are repeatedly exposed to a fair amount of English mass media input outside school. The greatest part of this input represents passive or receptive functions of language use, the most frequent one being watching television. It seems, however, that the strong influence of English mass media has created a linguistic demarcation between the language needs felt by the young generation of learners on the one hand and the views held by the somewhat older generation of teachers on the other. Because of the excessive use of non-standard forms and colloquialisms on television and in computer games, it is no wonder that students will eventually start questioning the language taught in the classroom. In order to bridge the gap between the linguistic expectations of teachers' and learners' actual language use, it is important that teachers from the very start give guidance to young learners on how to cope with different style registers, and be wary of not adding to the distance by expressing disapproval of, or by censuring, the students' language (see Forsman, 2000).

Classroom Learning at Upper-secondary Level

What is going on in the English classes? How do the activities in the classroom affect the learning outcomes? If you ask students what their English lessons consist of, they will tell you that the emphasis is on written skills and grammar. This is rather surprising, considering the great emphasis laid on communicative competence and oral proficiency in the new foreign language curriculum introduced in Finland in 1994.

In fact, Shepherd (2000) found that there is a considerable implementation gap between the curriculum envisaged by educational planners and the one actually experienced by learners or estimated by external classroom observation. Shepherd used triangulated data from three different perspectives of accounting for the teaching situation, i.e. those of the students, teachers and a participant observer. The subjects comprised Swedish- and Finnish-speaking upper-secondary school students and some first year undergraduate students (between 17 and 20 years old). The data were collected some years after the 1994 curriculum had been introduced. Shepherd's study indicated that explicit form-focused teaching was very dominant in the classroom of both language groups. Although the national curriculum recognises the significance of linguistic competence and grammatical knowledge as an essential prerequisite for developing communicative competence, as well as elucidating the major differences (and similarities) between L1 (Swedish or Finnish) and target language, it states that structures should mainly be practised in meaningful contexts (see Shepherd, 2000: 234).

Shepherd (2000: 103) checked to what extent the upper-secondary school classroom in Finland was dominated by grammar-based teaching, written tasks, errors and error corrections, as well as translations. It was found that Finnish- and Swedish-speaking first year undergraduates tended to agree rather strongly that form-focused teaching was a dominant feature in the upper-secondary school classroom. His data showed that form-focused teaching was more common in Finnish-L1 schools. A follow-up study three years later with upper-secondary school students indicated that many of the differences between Swedes and Finns had been evened out. Shepherd also asked the same students whether there was a lot of opportunity to use spoken English in class. The results indicated that the Finnish groups especially had very few opportunities to use spoken English in class, whereas Swedes used spoken English somewhat more (Shepherd, 2000: 107).

The classroom observations showed similar results as above, but the differences between Swedes and Finns were greater. The percentages of classroom activities referring to receptive and productive skills, and activities focusing explicitly on language structure, are illustrated in Table 11.1. Observations were made in eight lessons for each language group.

Table 11.1 Receptive vs. productive skill development according to classroom observation

Activities	Swedes (%)	Finns (%)
Receptive	40.8	42.4
Productive	43.7	25.0
Structure	15.5	29.3
Other	0.0	3.2

Source: Shepherd (2000: 149–50)

The table shows that activities referred to as receptive skill development constitute a major feature in the upper-secondary school classroom. The observational data also indicate that productive skills are practised more frequently in Swedish-speaking classrooms, whereas Finnish teachers devoted more time to explicit focusing on language structure. Teacher interviews suggested that the reason why Finnish EL teachers gave more prominence to the teaching of EL grammar was the perceived differences between Finnish and English. The interviews with the Swedish-speaking teachers revealed that the reason why they devoted less time and resources to the teaching of the grammatical system than Finnish-speaking teachers was the relative similarities between Swedish and English.

Conversational and Academic Learner English

This study also considers the relationship between the incidentally acquired English outside the classroom and the formally learnt classroom

English with reference to Cummins' distinction of *conversational* and *academic* language proficiency. These concepts were originally termed 'basic interpersonal communicative skills' (BICS) and 'cognitive academic language proficiency' (CALP)(Cummins, 1979). In a recent publication, Cummins (2000) elaborates the distinction further in the light of research evidence collected over the past 20 years and tries to respond to the criticisms that have been addressed to the distinction. Here, an attempt has been made to match my data collected from lower- and upper-secondary school students in Finland (mostly Swedish-speaking) with the more recent views of Cummins' concepts. As is well known, Cummins has elaborated the pedagogical implications of the distinction in a figure made up of two continua, one representing the range of contextual support, and the other representing the degree of cognitive involvement in the language task or activity (see Figure 11.3).

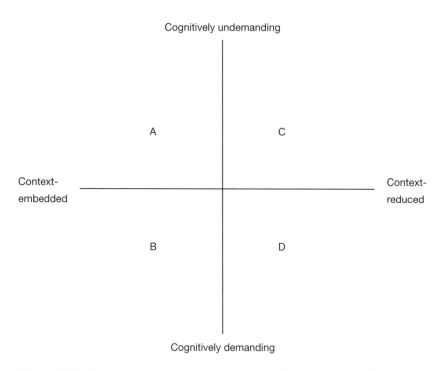

Figure 11.3 Range of contextual support and degree of cognitive involvement in language tasks and activities

Source: Cummins (2000: 58)

The upper part of the vertical continuum consists of two quadrants, A and C, in which conversational communication has become largely automatised and thus requires little cognitive involvement to become appropriately performed. At the lower end of the continuum the academic functions of language represent a high level of cognitive involvement which is either supported by a wide range of meaningful interpersonal and situational cues (quadrant B) or relies almost exclusively on linguistic cues to meaning (quadrant D).

By adopting Cummins' framework, my data can be explained in the following way. The mass media activities, for example, are no doubt cognitively undemanding, and the contextual support provided by English mass media input is artificial and restricted. In fact, this kind of contextual support could be characterised as one-way communication providing few opportunities for interaction and negotiation of meaning. Formal classroom learning, it is believed, results, especially at the advanced levels, in some kind of academic English. The proficiency of the advanced learners has, however, certain features that make it different from the language of native speakers.

Many researchers have pointed out that native speakers perceive advanced learner language as bookish, pedantic and non-idiomatic (De Cock *et al.*, 1998; Channell, 1994). This impression of bookishness among advanced learners (as well as teachers) may emanate from an overuse of rare, Graeco-Latin words. Many teachers (and advanced learners) tend to overemphasise the importance of these words of a higher register and see them as educational status symbols, but also as necessary tools for cognitive and academic development. Corson's (1995) observation that many teachers tend to see Graeco-Latinate (G-L) words as always 'better' or as always 'more correct', especially in academic and formal contexts, may at least partly account for this bookishness. Support for an overuse of Graeco-Latin words in the learner language was also found in my own studies (Sjöholm, 1995, 1998). In these studies, I found that advanced Finnish- and Swedish-speaking learners of English, in a choice situation, tended to prefer one-part verbs of Graeco-Latin origin to synonymous phrasal verbs of Anglo-Saxon origin (*explode*/*go off*). The instrument used in the study comprised a battery of multiple choice test items containing pairs of phrasal verbs and more or less synonymous one-part verbs. Both verbs were judged correct English, but the phrasal verbs were preferred by most native speakers (nearly 80%). The learners probably perceived the Graeco-Latin one-part verbs as representing a sample of familiar classroom expressions with a relatively high status and with a broad and general meaning. That learners preferred these verbs to synonymous phrasal verbs might well be due to what Hasselgren called 'the teddy bear principle', i.e. that learners tend to depend on what is familiar and stick to words they feel safe with (Hasselgren, 1994; cf. Hulstijn & Marchena, 1989).

It is obvious, however, that the avoidance of phrasal verbs is doubly determined. In my own studies on them (Sjöholm, 1995, 1998), it was found that the avoidance of phrasal verbs may also have been due to indirect L1 influence, since Finns avoided or underused them considerably more often than Swedes (cf. Laufer, 2000). The explanation of this could be that the phrasal verb structure is familiar to Swedes because more or less the same structure exists in their L1, whereas phrasal verbs do not exist in Finnish. In fact, they have also been alleged to be stylistically more informal and are believed to occur more frequently in the spoken than in the written language. One reason why phrasal verbs tend to be avoided by learners may thus be that most students have been exposed to such a bookish form of language at school more often than to phrasal verbs, so that they have not been acquired (Cornell, 1985: 277). In my study on the use of English phrasal verbs among Swedish and Finnish upper-secondary students referred to before, I found that the more these learners had been exposed to the target language culture, the more they tended to prefer idiomatic phrasal verbs (Sjöholm, 1995: 179).

The students at upper-secondary and advanced level were, however, more accustomed to the teachers' 'academic' classroom English than the lower-secondary school students. The academic learner language at more advanced levels of English differs from the native academic language in many respects. The impression of bookishness mentioned earlier may be traced back to various sources. De Cock *et al.* found that vagueness tags were underused by learners in informal interviews and this may go some way towards explaining this impression of bookishness (1998: 78). They refer to Crystal and Davy (1975: 111), who suggested that 'lack of precision is one of the most important features of the vocabulary of informal conversation'. A comparison between the frequency of vagueness tags such as *and stuff like that, or something* and *or whatever* in a native speaker (NS) and non-native speaker (NNS) corpus, indicated that NSs use almost four times as many vagueness tags as learners (De Cock *et al.*, 1998: 77).

Overuse of common, high-frequency verbs may also make advanced learner English sound strange and non-idiomatic. Thus core words with general meanings such as nouns like *time, way, people* and *things*, and verbs like *think* and *get*, tend to be overused by learners (see Ringbom, 1998: 50). In fact, overuse of common verbs illustrates, according to Ringbom (1998), one of the main shortcomings in advanced learner language, i.e.

lack of collocational competence 'in that a word is used in contexts where native speakers would normally choose some other word' (Ringbom, 1998: 44). Ringbom also demonstrates that learners with Swedish as their L1 show a predilection for the verb *think* and the phrase *I think*. In fact, Swedes and Finland-Swedes use this verb and phrase five times more often than native speakers (Ringbom, 1998: 43–4).

Concluding Remarks

The data presented in this study suggested that lower-secondary school students in Finland were more influenced by English language activities outside school than more advanced ones. It was also demonstrated that students at the lower-secondary level clearly preferred a spoken, 'conversational' variety of English which they had picked up on their own outside school. This type of English was sprinkled with colloquialisms and slang and tended to be associated with American English. Some students even questioned the appropriateness of the classroom English offered by the English teachers. Corson (1995) argues that discrepancies like these between the vocabulary that students bring from outside schools and the peculiar, decontextualised vocabulary demands that specialist meaning systems used in textbooks place upon them are very common. Corson's notion of the *lexical bar* may at least partly explain the conversational/academic language distinction. This means that the vocabulary of English falls into two different groups; first, the Anglo-Saxon vocabulary that native speakers of English acquire at an early age and use for everyday purposes, and second, the vocabulary acquired later during the adolescent years of education, through the school's special culture of literacy (Corson, 1995: 183). The difficulties in the latter group partly coincide with the frequent occurrence of words with Graeco-Latin origin in academic English, something that is unique to English.

The academic English provided by teachers was seen by many students as unnatural and rather bookish and was often associated with British English. In fact, the data drawn from lower-secondary school students indicated that the exposure to English mass media input exerted a strong influence on the learners' choice of vocabulary. Extensive out-of-school exposure to English could clearly be related to a marked preference for American vocabulary and positive attitudes towards American English. The dichotomy between the teachers' classroom English and the learners' incidentally acquired English arises because schools place higher status on an academic culture of literacy which is relatively removed from the English language youth culture of the learners. The data showed that the mass media influence was stronger in the southern parts of Finland and in urban areas at the lower-secondary level. This was clearly displayed in Forsman's data. She demonstrated that the students in the urban southern parts spent significantly more time on English leisure time activities than the students in the rural western parts. The reasons for this are still unknown, but it is assumed that these differences may fall back on differing cultural patterns among the adolescents in the south and the west. She also found that the students in the south scored better in a vocabulary test than the students in the west (Forsman, 2000). This may lead to regional differences in the students' skills in English in the future, and result in unequal opportunities for learning.

The gap between the students' and teachers' attitudes towards different varieties of English and their preferences for different style registers seemed to be extraordinarily large at the lower-secondary level. The lower-secondary students' preference for the 'conversational' aspects of English rather than the 'academic' aspects was probably caused by the great influence of the English input that students have received from mass media outside the school context (40–50 hours/week). In order to alleviate the effects of the lexical bar, Corson (1995) suggests that learners ought to participate in the discursive practices of the literate culture of the school, i.e. conversations in which Graeco-Latin vocabulary is included, but he also proposes that teachers should be taking measures in order to decrease the excessive use and valuation of Graeco-Latin words in cases when there is a choice between words of similar meanings. Corson (1995) argues that the differences between socio-cultural groups, especially concerning their active lexico-semantic range, may be very pronounced at 15 years of age with native speakers of English. It also seems that learners of English in the Finnish context who are above the age of 15 are less sensitive to the American mass media influence. In my own study on attitudes among 18-year-old upper-secondary students, it was found that Britons were ranked higher than Americans on a scale measuring stereotyped attitudes towards members of different ethnolinguistic groups (Sjöholm, 2000). Lintunen (2001) also found that older and more advanced students had a fairly positive attitude towards British English. His study with university students of English in Finland showed that they preferred the British accent over the American.

Some surveys about the situation in Finland have shown that what pupils need most is the ability to communicate orally (Pietilä, 2001: 101). However, the benefit of increased speaking practice in the classrooms will not be restricted to the development of the speaking skills. Conversation also provides an initial scaffold for more learning. This informal 'scaffolding' provided by the interlocutor's discourse is, according to Corson, 'the most basic kind of assistance that specialist vocabulary learning can get' (Corson, 1995: 192). The role of the teacher will therefore be to mediate in the construction of meaning by learners, i.e. helping them to construct the meaning from text. This is linked closely to Vygotsky's idea about the 'zone of proximal development', i.e. the difference between what people can do on their own, and what they can do in interaction with an older and more experienced language user (Vygotsky, 1962). Cummins (2000: 79) argues, however, that if academic language proficiency is accepted as a valid construct, extensive reading is also crucial for academic development, since academic English is primarily found in written texts. An ideal situation would then be to organise conversation as discursive practices of the literate culture of the classrooms, which, hopefully, would help students internalise and more fully comprehend the academic language they find in their extensive reading of texts (Cummins, 2000: 80). Cummins' ideas have, in fact, been implemented in Finland ever since 1991, when the new school legislation made it possible to set up bilingual programmes of different kinds. Learning academic (i.e. subject-specific) content through a foreign language has become an increasingly common exercise for today's learners at all educational levels (see Räsänen, 2001: 197). Especially in Swedish-medium schools, the great majority of the experiments with content-and-language-integrated learning and teaching (CLIL, a term favoured in Finland) involve content courses with English as the language of instruction (see Nikula & Marsh, 1996). Many of the Swedish students enrolled in English-based content classes could be classed as balanced Swedish-Finnish bilinguals with English as a third language. The International Baccalaureate section set up at the teacher training school at Åbo Akademi University (in Vaasa) for students between 16 and 19 years of age is a good example of where integration between academic and conversational English may be implemented. This programme, which has been operating since 1992, is an example of a kind of trilingual education in which half of the students have Swedish, and the other half Finnish as their mother tongue, but where the great majority of lessons are given in English jointly for both language groups (see Jungner, 1999).

References

Act no. 261/1991 Laki persukoulun muutoksesta [Supplement to Act of the Comprehensive School].
Act no. 262/1991 Laki lukiolain muutoksesta [Supplement to Act of the Upper Secondary School].

Björklund, S. and Suni, I. (2000) The role of English as L3 in Swedish immersion programmes in Finland: Impacts on language teaching and language relations. In J. Cenoz and U. Jessner (eds) *English in Europe: The Acquisition of a Third Language* (pp. 198–221). Clevedon: Multilingual Matters.

Channell, J. (1994) *Vague Language*. Oxford: Oxford University Press.

Common European Framework of Reference for Languages (2001) Learning, Teaching, Assessment. Council of Europe: Cambridge University Press.

Cornell, A. (1985) Realistic goals in teaching and learning phrasal verbs. *IRAL* 22 (4), 269–80.

Corson, D. (1993) *Language, Minority Education and Gender: Linking Social Justice and Power*. Clevedon: Multilingual Matters.

Corson, D. (1995) *Using English Words*. Dordrecht: Kluwer Academic Publishers.

Corson, D. (1997) The learning and use of academic English words. *Language Learning* 47, 671–718.

Crystal, D. and Davy, D. (1975) *Advanced Conversational English*. London: Longman.

Cummins, J. (1979) Cognitive/academic language proficiency, linguistic inter-dependence, the optimum age question and some other matters. *Working Papers on Bilingualism* 19, 121–9.

Cummins, J. (2000) Putting language proficiency in its place. In J. Cenoz and U. Jessner (eds) *English in Europe: The Acquisition of a Third Language* (pp. 54–83). Clevedon: Multilingual Matters.

De Cock, S., Granger, S., Leech, G. and McEnery, T. (1998) An automated approach to the phrasicon of EFL learners. In S. Granger (ed.) *Learner English on Computer* (pp. 67–79). London: Longman.

Forsman, L. (2000) Effects of media input on incidental learning of English and on linguistic attitudes among Finland-Swedish high-school students. In K. Sjöholm and A. Østern (eds) *Perspectives on Language and Communication in Multilingual Education* (pp. 167–81). Reports from the Faculty of Education 6. Vaasa: Åbo Akademi University.

Gibbons, P. (1991) *Learning to Learn in a Second Language*. Newtown, Australia: Primary English Teaching Association.

Granger, S. (ed.) (1998) *Learner English on Computer*. London: Longman.

Hasselgren, A. (1994) Lexical teddy bears and advanced learners: A study into the ways Norwegian students cope with English vocabulary. *International Journal of Applied Linguistics* 4, 237–58.

Hoffmann, C. (2000) The spread of English and the growth of multilingualism with English in Europe. In J. Cenoz and U. Jessner (eds) *English in Europe: The Acquisition of a Third Language* (pp. 1–21). Clevedon: Multilingual Matters.

Hulstijn, J., Hollander, M. and Greidanus, T. (1996) Incidental vocabulary learning by advanced foreign language students: The influence of marginal glosses, dictionary use, and reoccurrence of unknown words. *The Modern Language Journal* 80, 327–39.

Hulstijn, J. and Marchena, E. (1989) Avoidance: Grammatical or semantic causes? *Studies in Second Language Acquisition* 11, 241–55.

Jungner, S. (1999) The International Baccalaureate section at Vasa övningsskola. In Sjöholm, K. and Björklund, M. (eds) *Content and Language Integrated Learning: Teachers' and Teacher Educators' Experiences of English Medium Instruction* (pp. 62–9). Publications from the Faculty of Education 4. Vaasa, Finland: Åbo Akademi University.

Krashen, S. (1982) *Principles and Practice in Second Language Acquisition.* Oxford: Pergamon.

Larsen-Freeman, D. (1985) State of the art on input in second language acquisition. In S.M. Gass, and C.G. Madden (eds) *Input in Second Language Acquisition* (pp. 433–44). Rowley, MA: Newbury House Publishers.

Laufer, B. (2000) Avoidance of idioms in a second language: The effects of L1-L2 degree of similarity. *Studia Linguistica* 54, 186–96.

Lightbown, P.M. and Spada, N. (1993) *How Languages are Learned.* Oxford: Oxford University Press.

Lintunen, P. (2001) The relaxed RP and elegant GA: Does your accent reveal your true character? Paper presented at the Inaugural Conference of the Finnish Association for the Study of English (FISSE), Turku/Åbo, Finland, 28–30 September.

Nikula, T. and Marsh, D. (1996) *Language and Content Integrated Instruction in the Finnish Primary and Secondary Sectors: A National Survey.* Jyväskylä, Finland: University of Jyväskylä, Continuing Education Centre.

Pietilä, P. (2001) Speaking skills in a foreign language: Reflections on the teaching of conversational skills. In M. Gill, A. Johnson, L.M. Koski, R. Sell and B. Wårvik (eds) *Language, Learning, Literature: Studies Presented to Håkan Ringbom* (pp. 101–10). English Department Publications 4. Turku, Finland: Åbo Akademi University.

Räsänen, A. (2001) Integrating content and language in FL-medium instruction. In E. Kimonen (ed.) *Curriculum Approaches* (pp. 197–213). Jyväskylä, Finland: Department of Teacher Education/Institute of Educational Research, University of Jyväskylä.

Ringbom, H. (1998) Vocabulary frequencies in advanced learner English: A crosslinguistic approach. In S. Granger (ed.) *Learner English on Computer* (pp. 41–52). London: Longman.

Sharwood Smith, M. and Kellerman, E. (1986) Crosslinguistic influence in second language acquisition: An introduction. In E. Kellerman and M. Sharwood Smith (eds) *Crosslinguistic Influence in Second Language Acquisition* (pp. 1–9). Oxford: Pergamon Press.

Shepherd, J. (2000) Implementation gap: An investigation of the 1994 EL curriculum in Finnish upper-secondary classes using a multiple method perspective approach. Unpublished licentiate thesis, Department of English, University of Vaasa, Finland.

Sjöholm, K. (1995) *The Influence of Crosslinguistic, Semantic and Input Factors on the Acquisition of English Phrasal Verbs: A Comparison between Finnish and Swedish Learners at an Intermediate and Advanced Level.* Åbo, Finland: Åbo Akademi University Press.

Sjöholm, K. (1998) A reappraisal of the role of cross-linguistic and environmental factors in lexical L2 acquisition. In K. Haastrup and Å. Viberg (eds) *Perspectives on Lexical Acquisition in a Second Language* (pp. 209–36). Lund, Sweden: Lund University Press.

Sjöholm, K. (2000) Attitudes towards English and two national languages in Finland. In K. Sjöholm and A. Østern (eds) *Perspectives on Language and Communication in Multilingual Education* (pp. 121–43). Reports from the Faculty of Education 6. Vaasa, Finland: Åbo Akademi University.

Sjöholm, K. (2001) Incidental learning of English by Swedish learners in Finland. In M. Gill, A. Johnson, L.M. Koski, R. Sell and B. Wårvik (eds) *Language, Learning, Literature: Studies Presented to Håkan Ringbom* (pp. 77–89). English Department Publications 4. Turku, Finland: Åbo Akademi University.

Suomi Lukuina, Tilastokeskus (2002) On WWW at http://tilastokeskus.fi/tk/tp/tasku/taskus_vaesto.html.

Swedish in Finland (2000) On WWW at http://www.finland.org/finnswedes. html.

Takala, S. (1998) Englannin kielen taidon taso Suomessa – hyvää kehitystä. In S. Takala and K. Sajavvaara (eds) *Kielikoulutus Suomessa*. Jyväskylä, Finland: Soveltavan kielitutkimuksen keskus, Jyväskylän Yliopisto.

Takala, S. (2000) Some questions and issues on content-based language teaching. In K. Sjöholm and A. Østern (eds) *Perspectives on Language and Communication in Multilingual Education* (pp. 41–54). Reports from the Faculty of Education 6. Vaasa, Finland: Åbo Akademi University.

Tandefelt, M. (1999) Finlandsvenskan i tusen år – del två: Medborgare i republiken Finland. *Språkbruk* 4, 3–9.

Turunen, S.P. (2001) Aspects of attitudes to languages in Finland and Wales. PhD thesis, School of Education, University of Wales, Bangor.

Väyrynen, P., Räisänen, A., Geber, E., Koski, L. and Pernu, M.L. (1998) *Kieliäkö ammatissa? Ammatillisten oppilaitosten kielten opetuksen nykytila ja kehittämistarpeet.* Helsinki: Opetushallitus.

Vygotsky, L.S. (1962) *Thought and Language.* Cambridge, MA: MIT Press.

Index

239